THE PLAYBOOK OF TODD DAVISON

# HIS LAST SHIFT

## THROUGH HOCKEY, CANCER, AND THE JOURNEY BEYOND HIMSELF

## WADE DAVISON

HIS LAST SHIFT

The Playbook of Todd Davison

First Printing, 2022
Inner Lift Media

ISBN: 979-8-9858374-0-7

Cover and Interior Design by Transcendent Publishing

Printed in the United States of America.

## TO TODD

"The strongest metal goes thru the hottest fire."

*If you knew tomorrow was your last day, would you act any other way today?*
*If it were your time to go, what would you be proudest to show?*

*Have you really left more than you've taken,*
*Or did you refuse to give because you felt owed and forsaken?*

*Will you leave this world a better place for others,*
*Or did you play only for number one, not caring about your brothers?*

*If life is a school, what did you learn?*
*If life is a journey, what did you experience?*
*If life is a test, did you truly give it your best?*

*Are you excited to die because you have lived a righteous life?*
*Or, are you scared to die because you fear you will pay a heavy price?*
*Where is your heart right now?*
*It's not too late to start, somehow . . .*

*~ W. Davison*

# CONTENTS

# PRE-GAME

On December 2, 2006, shortly after 2:00 a.m., the body of Todd Jonathon Davison exhaled one final time and shut down forever. We had been kneeling at his feet since early afternoon of the day before; wiping tears from our eyes and holding our breath each time he stopped breathing, only to see his chest rise up again as the oxygen tubes brought air into his lungs. The real Todd – his consciousness and life force energy – seemed long gone by then, but his shell of a body, completely exhausted and damaged beyond repair after years of torment, fought to stay alive just a little longer. Finally, as the clock struck the second hour of that second day of December, Todd was released from the bondage of his physical form and called up to the big show behind the curtain. For the rest of us, the world became a darker place that night as the light from one of its brightest souls permanently faded from our reality. In the end, the game clock of Todd's life had run just twenty years, two months, and two days. But though it was short, much like he was in stature, it was nothing short of remarkable.

Two-and-a-half years earlier, only days after his high school graduation, Todd's life had changed in an instant. A phone call from the doctor revealed that his lingering shoulder pain – typically dismissed as a chronic hockey injury – was synovial sarcoma, a rare and aggressive type of cancer that attacks the soft tissues of the body. Our shock and disbelief at the news was so strong we felt it physically, as if the air was suddenly sucked out of the room. It just didn't seem possible that this could happen to a guy so young, athletic, and full of life.

Prior to that devastating phone call, Todd was known as an incredibly talented and dedicated Canadian hockey player with professional aspirations and a future as bright as his smile. Though he was typically the smallest player on the ice, Todd always found a way to play big. Despite the odds being heavily stacked against him, he was set on one day "making it big"; he was going to show the hockey world who he was and what he could do and nobody was going to stop him. After earning a roster spot with the Regina Pats of the Western Hockey League – one of the most elite junior hockey leagues in the world – at the tender age of sixteen, Todd was well on his way. Now, in the blink of an eye, he had gone from fighting to become a professional hockey player to fighting for his life.

After the initial shock of his cancer diagnosis faded, Todd became determined to heal his body and get back to living, which for him was all about playing hockey. He initially viewed this whole cancer thing as he did any other obstacle: a mere bump in the road (a couple small masses of cancerous cells weren't going to stop him!). He had big plans, and this was all just going to be part of his hero's journey. Even when he was shackled to a hospital bed with IV lines in his arms and chemicals being pumped into his body for days on end, Todd remained confident that he would fully recover. It helped that he was backed by a massive team of friends, family members, and medical professionals, all focused on supporting and loving him, and getting him back to full health and happiness.

After undergoing surgery, chemotherapy, and radiation treatments, his future was looking bright once again. But sometimes life doesn't happen the way we hope. Todd thought the worst news – that he would never play hockey again – had already come, but he was dead wrong. After battling hard and staying positive for nearly two years, doctors told him that there was nothing more they could do to help him, and that he should – this is a direct quote – "Go home and prepare to die."

Clearly, they did not know who they were speaking to – a person who attacked every challenge with a huge heart and an unwavering belief that the only way to lose is to give up. Like anyone, Todd was initially overwhelmed with the disbelief, sadness, and rage that accompanies a terminal prognosis; however, he quickly realized he had a choice to make: give up all hope and wait for his impending death, or live the best life he possibly could, right until the end – whenever that end might be. As he always did, Todd saw the light and chose the brighter option. He was not going to be "benched" by cancer, not when he still had life coursing through his body and breath in his lungs. He was still in the game. There was still time on the clock!

As his body and world slowly crumbled around him, Todd dug deep and found the strength to reframe his outlook on life. He now had a new mission: to make the world a better place with each day he was given. Instead of cowering in the face of physical pain and mental anguish, he shifted his focus to the opportunities, present in every moment, to authentically connect with others and be in a space of gratitude. Even in his darkest and weakest times, Todd was still courageous enough to get up early and face the day without complaint or self-pity, determined to shine his light into the world.

From diagnosis to death, Todd experienced a physical and emotional roller coaster ride – from intense pain, suffering, fear, and loneliness, to immense joy, peace, laughter, excitement and love. And while there were awful times of despair and dread, there were also amazing times filled with awe and wonder. Todd's story is not a tragedy, but one of beauty with sad and tragic parts. His legacy was far too great to die with his body, and there were far too many worthy moments to be limited to a seven-hundred-word obituary; no snippet in a newspaper could do his journey justice.

This book is not written to idolize Todd, but instead to document, encapsulate, and transmit various moments of his life – from toddler to teammate, teenager to teacher, and cancer patient to coach – for others to appreciate and learn from. From making teams as an age-advanced hockey player despite being the very smallest player on the ice, to facing off against Sidney Crosby and some of the world's best players, Todd was an extraordinarily talented player whose hockey career alone provides countless inspirational stories for any athlete or underdog in the world. However, this is not a hockey story, but a testament to the courage of the human spirit and triumph in the face of adversity. It is about cherishing and appreciating life, regardless of the obstacles and challenges that may be present; making it count, every single day; and contributing to the greater good through love and service to others. Ultimately, Todd's story is about living and playing with passion and purpose, and dying with no regrets!

As you read the following pages, ponder that your life is a temporary and fleeting experience – a mysterious state of being for an unknown amount of time. Though we don't understand its true meaning or purpose, we have all had those glimpses reminding us that, at its essence, life is something truly amazing and special. However, we're often so distracted by a noisy world and caught up in the day-to-day grind that we fail to appreciate it as such. Instead we treat our days as just something to get through, without awareness and gratitude for what we have, always thinking we need something different, or better. For some, it takes losing a loved one or facing our own mortality before we truly appreciate all the things we've already been blessed with.

As his brother, teammate, roommate, and friend, I felt a need to share the story of Todd's life, not only to honor him, but to provide you with hope in the face of life's toughest tests and painful challenges, illuminate your path to inner power and gratitude, and inspire you to live fully (as if you were dying) every single day you're on this Earth.

# THE SHOW

We didn't make it to the *Show*, Bro,
But we gave it a pretty good go, tho!
And tho the scouts looked at me and said,
"No…" — something about being too slow,
You just needed some time to grow,
Then they really could have seen you glow!

We made it past the 99th place,
And played against so many of the Greats!
What game you had, with a stick and skates.
You would set the pace, then win the race,
You were in a state that few can relate.
Where would you be now, if not for your fate?

When that dreaded news came that you could no longer play the game,
I can't imagine the depths of your pain
when your dreams were crushed in vain
as your arm went lame;
The challenge became just about trying to stay sane.

And tho you had to let it all go,
Do not discount what you brought to show!
Against the odds and doubting God,
Without hockey, who was Todd?

Like a man of great power, you did not cower,
You lived with all of your might, hour by hour.
You went deep inside and accepted the ride,
A noble example of setting aside one's pride.

As death drew near, you dispelled all fear,
You barely shed a single tear.
At the end of your years,
you were nothing short of a man to revere.

Brothers from the same mother,
Coached and pushed further by the same father;
We had a rare bond that was my true honor.
What a shame that it couldn't last longer . . .

Thinkin' back on all our moments,
I often tear up but don't like to show it.
And though I sometimes feel low,
I know this is just a temporary show.
I'll use your strength and light as fuel to flow;
I'll remember your courage until it's my time to go.

Like our inside jokes or your beaming smile,
I'll feel your joy again before a while.
So go on ahead to whatever awaits,
I'll see you on the other side when
I get called up to cross through those gates.
Bring the gear and an extra pair of skates,
We'll lace 'em up again, with all the Greats.

~W. Davison, March 2016

# 1<sup>ST</sup> PERIOD

# CHAPTER 1

# GAME TIME

## T-minus 20 Years, 2 Months, and 2 Days

Long before Todd's last breath tore a hole in our lives, his first, on September 30, 1986, brought a time of joy and gratitude to a family that had already been blessed with both. Though Todd was the baby (after Joel, born in 1983, and me, Wade, born in 1985) and the runt of the litter, he soon became the leader of our family pack in heart and mind.

As a baby Todd slept upwards of twenty hours a day – waking up only long enough to eat and be briefly admired before drifting off again. He figured out early that good sleep was key to good living. The schedules of others, including his busy parents, were of no concern. He was resting up for big things ahead and even in those earliest days set his own schedule and agenda.

When Todd finally found his footing as a toddler (his first steps were delayed because Joel and I carried him around everywhere), he basically skipped right to running and learned quickly that he had some serious speed. He saw that others had a hard time keeping up with him, and that was just fine with him. In addition to being extraordinarily fast, he was also feisty, fearless, and full of confidence. And though he was always the smallest kid around, he was fiercely independent and self-determined.

We grew up in a bungalow in North Kildonan – a quiet area in the northeastern part of Winnipeg. To clarify, this was not the North End of Winnipeg, which is one of the most dangerous areas in all of Canada, but a much tamer place, more conducive to street hockey fights than gang fights, and where stray pucks, not stray bullets, sometimes found their way into neighbors' vehicles.

Known to locals as "The 'Peg" and to outsiders as "Winterpeg," Winnipeg is Canada's "Gateway to the West." It is a diverse and culturally rich hub city located near the very center of North America, right where the Red and Assiniboine Rivers meet, just over a hundred kilometers north of the Canada-United States border. Though Winnipeg isn't quite as corporate or busy as Toronto or Vancouver, and isn't a destination point for tourists like so many of Canada's wondrous natural places, it is a lively little city with a charged vibe and great people that provide the foundation for so many great life moments. Teemu Selanne, also known as "The Finnish Flash" and Todd's all-time favorite Winnipeg Jet, once described it as "always a special place to come."

If you can get over the insanely cold winter temperatures (which casually dip under forty below), roads with enormous potholes, giant vicious mosquitos, and car break-ins, you too may come to really love the 'Peg. Or, like The Weakerthans, an indie rock band from the area, so eloquently put it in their song "One Great City," you may hate it. For me and my brothers, there was no better place in the world to be raised and spend our younger days, and though there were many reasons for this, it all really came down to one: hockey.

Even more than its richness in culture, food, and real human connection – most famously celebrated during *Folklorama* – Winnipeg is known as a hockey city, with the revered game playing a crucial role in connecting its various sub-communities. When you have hockey, you have entertaining action, drama, and excitement. On any given night you can expect to find bustling arenas filled with top-notch hockey talent showcasing world-class skill. The 'Peg breathes hockey, and, as far back as I can remember, so did we.

From the age of five or so, Todd and I spent pretty much every fall, winter, and spring evening at a hockey rink, either playing or watching the other play. By the time 1995 rolled around we were at the rink year-round, even when it was scorching-hot outside in the middle of summer. When on the ice, we worked as hard as we could and performed with intensity. If we were off the ice watching, you better believe we had sticks in our hands and a tennis ball or puck to shoot or stickhandle with wherever we could find space. We ignored every "No Shooting" sign around, pissing off a lot of rink maintenance guys and Zamboni drivers with our heated one-on-one showdowns in the corner of whatever arena Joel's team happened to be playing. Each arena had its own secret spots, and it was a constant battle to find new ones so we wouldn't get yelled at after the occasional bad-angle shot deflected off the crossbar or wall and onto the ice, interrupting the real game in action. When that happened, we'd sheepishly put our heads down, get our ball thrown back to us if we were lucky, then beetle out the back door of the rink to find our next spot. We were the ultimate rink rats – a lifestyle that brought us sheer joy and happiness.

## The ODR

In our childhood and teenage years we spent a ton of our time learning the game on outdoor rinks ("ODRs") at one of the many local community centers. Luckily for us, there was always an after-school shuttle (also known as Mom and Dad) rolling to and from the rink and, barring an extremely dangerous temperature or wind-chill warning, we'd be out there buzzing around whenever we could.

Experiences at the ODR range from meditative to downright chaotic. You might be the only player out there on a crisp, sunny winter afternoon or a late evening under the floodlights and sparkling night sky; at those times it's one of the most peaceful experiences on the planet – just you, the ice, your stick, and a single puck. Or, you could be amongst fifty other players of all ages and skill levels, just trying to get a touch on the game puck while avoiding taking a high stick in the beak during an intense game of "shinny."

Regardless of who was there with us, the ODR gave us the opportunity to improve our skills outside of a game or structured practice. Being there also taught us a lot of interesting life lessons, like don't mouth off to your elders, keep your head on a swivel, keep your stick on the ice, pass the puck, and protect your valuables, including your shoes and extra twigs from the bad kind of rink rats. You also had to learn how to stick up for yourself if things ever got out of hand; and, believe me, they did once in a while. The smaller youngsters had to be especially careful to stay out of the way of the bigger, stronger, older players, especially when they were shooting on net. Disobedience of this rule either led to getting shamed or ridiculed off the ice or severe pain from getting hit by a puck, and no one wanted the liability or hassle that came with that.

After the slap-shot and dangle warmup, an ODR "authority figure" would call the game. Usually they were dudes in their early to mid-twenties who rocked a hockey sock as a toque and an old knock-off NHL jersey and despite never playing high-level youth or junior hockey believed they were just a step away from the League themselves. They, like the rest of us, just needed their proper shot.

A single hockey stick, dropped at the center ice face-off dot, signaled that a game was about to fire up. Within seconds, all the sticks were piled up in the middle of the ice, then thrown into teams. Everyone scrambled to pick them up, and then – game-on! After distinguishing allies from opponents by the type of stick they had, you had to learn how to dodge the slashes and hacks from opponents while stick-handling through the snow piles and cracks on the ice. All of this served as excellent skill training and development, especially for Todd, who was only waist-high to most of the other players in those days. Surely if this tiny eight-year-old could survive and thrive in an intense shinny game, with dozens of other players of various skill chaotically flying around the ice, then he could do so in any league!

After skating for hours in the frigid air, Todd and I would finally and reluctantly take off our skates, bracing ourselves for the deep tingling burn of our frozen toes being exposed to warmer inside temperatures. These were incredibly painful moments, with us temporarily crippled and whining like babies as our extremities thawed. Imagine the jabbing agony of a brain freeze, only in your feet and hands and lasting for minutes instead of seconds. At times it was absolute torment, but it was nothing compared to the joy of playing or the anticipation of getting back on the ice the next day.

## Basement Battles

34 Ranch Road ("Ranch") was home as we knew it growing up, and it would be Todd's homebase for most of his life. Our setup was ideal in many ways: we had a beautiful yard and front street, with very little traffic to disrupt our daily street hockey games; a good-sized backyard, which backed onto a little forest perfect for exploration; and, most importantly, a large finished basement that served as the perfect spot for our indoor fun, including some of the most intense one-on-one mini-stick games ever played.

Sometimes we'd have friends or neighbors over for street hockey games, which would turn into big events. But most often it was just me and Todd out there playing. One of us – usually Todd first because he was younger and I made him – would strap on the "Street Warrior" goalie equipment and we'd play for hours on end. That goalie gear came to us on Christmas Day 1991 as we opened hockey-themed gifts while decked out in NHL pajamas. Years later, there was almost nothing left of those pads, and in their last days we were using sock tape to affix the broken straps and clips directly to our bare legs. In summer or winter, in bathing suits or snowsuits, we were out there dangling and sniping, or making sick saves. We were happy kids, our brotherly bond cemented by hockey, no matter if we were playing side-by-side or against each other.

When it got too late or cold to be outside, we'd head to the basement and start another best-of-seven series of mini-sticks. For those unfamiliar with the game, mini-sticks is essentially floor hockey played with smaller plastic sticks, typically on your knees in a contained area with carpeting, such as a basement, or – to the dismay of every non-hockey-obsessed guest – a hotel hallway. The point of the game is simple: keep the ball out of your makeshift mini-net and get the ball into your opponent's net. The beauty of mini-sticks is that it can be played one-on-one, and even during the days of Gameboys and basic cable TV this was where Todd and I found our real fun. With giant-curved plastic hockey sticks swinging around, rubber, foam, or tennis balls flying everywhere, and body checks being thrown into the couches or walls, no television screen, glass mug, or sheet of drywall was safe in our house. This would go on for hours until, finally, our sweaty, stinky bodies would collapse in exhaustion.

Though we always had a blast, it was certainly not all smiles. Sometimes things got intense, our basement turned into a mini-stick war zone with the backs of couches and walls serving as the boundaries. In his determination not to be beat or abused, Todd delivered nasty slashes to my feet, hands, and shins, and I returned the favor, which would spark a battle. A mini-stick slash square to an unpadded shin bone is especially brutal, but we were old school and that kind of pain only toughened us up. Still, I am not proud of the times our mini-stick games degraded into full-out slashing fights. Many tears were shed, and it was only by some miracle that no broken bones or severe injuries occurred – only nosebleeds, deep bruises, collisions with furniture, and rug-burns. Occasionally, the equivalent of a match penalty ended the game, sometimes even the night as well, and Todd and I would go to bed enemies, which was awkward because we shared a room! But no matter how furious we were as we climbed into our respective bunks, we would awake the next day with all animosity gone, ready to resume play.

When we needed an intermission break, we'd grab our Gatorades and watch Don Cherry's *Rock'em Sock'em* – a series of Canadian hockey highlight videos – on repeat. Todd received the new *Rock'em Sock'em* video cassette from Auntie Donna every Christmas, when the new season was finally released. We waited all year to see the NHL season's best plays or fights, plus Don rapping lyrics of players' names to background music, so much so that we'd watch it at least once on Christmas Eve after Ukrainian Catholic mass and gifts were exchanged – a tradition handed down from our mother's side of the family.

For many years, hardly a day passed by without us watching at least one *Rock'em Sock'em,* soaking in all the energy and learning all the moves of our favorite NHLers. When we were reinvigorated and inspired from all the highlight action, we'd grab our plastic sticks again, re-curve them to our liking, and get right back into another fierce one-on-one series with the *Rock'em Sock'em* video still blasting in the background.

Like any true Canadian hockey kid growing up in the '90s, our favorite time to play mini-sticks was during the CBC's *Hockey Night in Canada* – a classic Saturday night broadcast of NHL games that typically started around six or seven p.m. with a Toronto Maple Leafs or Montreal Canadiens game and concluded late into the night with a Vancouver Canucks game. Dad would often watch from a couch in the other section of the basement but also just close enough to keep tabs on us. He was our referee, always on-call to break up fights if they got out of hand or just yell loud enough to settle us down.

Whether it was organized hockey, the ODR, street hockey, Nintendo's *Blades of Steel,* or mini-sticks in the basement, we absolutely lived for the game. Most kids we knew played hockey, but to us it was all that really mattered in the world.

## The Real World

Dad's first career was as an accountant; however, after a six-year stint with Revenue Canada he finally came to his senses and realized that he wanted more out of his life and work. He became a full-time firefighter in 1986, right around when Todd was born. He also coached us kids in hockey and sat on the board of Gateway Recreation Center ("Gateway") – our local community center – and ran private hockey camps, supplementing his income with accounting work and labor jobs on the side. Most, if not all, discretionary funds went to me and my brothers, including our private school tuition and anything else we needed. Dad worked his ass off to give us education and opportunity and never, to my recollection, uttered one word of complaint.

Mom was more in charge of the home front and did a great job taking care of us on a daily basis. She'd be ready and waiting with after-school snacks or dinner, and would get us organized and out the door for evening practice or activities. For most of our younger years she also worked part-time jobs as an X-ray technologist and in other positions in the medical field, eventually becoming a full-time MRI technologist when that technology was implemented in the late 1990s. Mom also sacrificed herself and worked tirelessly for us kids, often taking on-call, overnight shifts in addition to her regular shifts at the hospital, which began before the crack of dawn. Each late-night shift or early morning call-in meant bonus money that went to us in some form.

Besides being wonderful, loving parents in general, Mom and Dad were especially great *hockey* parents. The equipment and registration fees were certainly not cheap, but we were never denied anything needed to play top-tier hockey, including spring/summer travel hockey and attendance at the best hockey schools around. Again, Mom and Dad sacrificed much for us to be able to play hockey at the highest levels, and to always have the best shot at developing and advancing, but they never made us feel bad about the costs involved.

And their support went far beyond finances. They were there to encourage us at every practice and game, and I cannot count the number of bitterly early wake-up calls and car rides on slick, snow-packed roads out to rural iceboxes in the dead of winter, or their attendance at outdoor youth hockey tournaments in sub-zero temperatures. Unless they were working, they were there, without exception and without complaint. Mom and Dad were the leaders of our hockey family, through and through, and viewed it as an honor to help us follow our dreams. I have heard it said that we all choose our parents before we incarnate onto the Earth. If that is so, my brothers and I knew exactly what we were doing.

The greatest thing Mom and Dad ever did, however, was instilling in us the strong work ethic, passed down from their own parents and grandparents, and holding us to it every time we hit the ice. Despite the fact that we were shoe-ins for virtually any team we tried out for (until age sixteen; then the only question was whether we'd be age advanced), we were never, ever allowed to take a shift off. If we did, we'd be hearing about it in the car on the way home. Sometimes threats of not letting us play were made. In other words, if we didn't work as hard as we could, we would forfeit the right to be on the ice. This work ethic – and the very real fear of missing a game of practice – created a drive to constantly push past our limitations and get to the next level.

Dad was our first real hockey coach, guiding us through various stages of development, starting when we were really young and playing for the Gateway Flyers. Rocking white Sorel winter boots that reached to just below his kneecaps and a thick, dark mustache, he commanded everyone's attention with a screechy, high-pitched voice when he yelled across the ice. Per the Winnipeg Minor Hockey Association rules, parents could not coach their kids beyond community club-level hockey during the winter season, which meant he could only coach us until we were ten years old. However, no such age restrictions applied to the spring/summer travel hockey season. Dad coached Joel for a few seasons; me during the winter between the ages of seven and ten years old; and then Todd with the Manitoba Mustangs during the spring/summer season, right up until he was thirteen years old. With Dad behind us on the bench, and Mom cheering us on from the crowd with hand signals and encouragement, we had extra boosts of support to be the best players we could be.

We were also fortunate to be surrounded by grandparents, aunts and uncles, and cousins. Jack and Mary Davison, our paternal grandparents, and Tony and Pearl Cherniak, our maternal grandparents, all lived in East Kildonan in northeast Winnipeg – fairly close to our home and the rinks where we often played. Other than Grandma Cherniak, who didn't really like leaving the house to go to cold hockey arenas, at least one of our grandparents would always be in the crowd to cheer us on.

Without a doubt, Grandpa Cherniak ("Pa") was our biggest fan. Whenever we played in or around Winnipeg we could count on seeing him in the crowd, decked out in a big fur hat and leather gloves, watching intently and smiling away. We could also always count on getting a little extra support in the form of a loonie or toonie after our games. He'd wait for us right by the gate where we exited and inconspicuously slip us a coin with a handshake. By our Midget AAA days, he upped the gift to five dollars in bill form, which he'd fold up and drop down from the spectator area above the dressing rooms at the Gateway blue rink. Pa would even make road trips on the bus with our Provincial Midget AAA Sharks team. Some of our funniest memories were seeing him walk out of the tiny bathroom at the back of the bus after he'd snuck a few puffs of "fresh air" in the form of a Players Light King Size cigarette, then proceed to casually sit back down as if he hadn't just stunk up the entire bus with smoke.

A retired superintendent of the vice division of the Winnipeg Police Service and Winnipeg's first narcotics officer, Pa had chain-smoked darts all day long as he solved crimes and beat guys in arm-wrestling matches around the police department. He was a bad-ass who did his own thing. Maybe that's where Todd got it from. Anyway, by the time he was making those bus trips with us, he had long lost his sense of smell and had no idea how bad it was, or how hilarious. The ol' boy sure could have used an e-cig back then.

With the grandparents always coming to watch our games, and our aunts, uncles, and cousins around to play with during Sunday dinners and holidays, we were surrounded by love and excitement. Hockey and family were what it was all about in those simpler times.

## Frozen Baptism

Considering how obsessed Todd became with hockey, it may be surprising to learn that he almost never played at all.

One of my earliest childhood memories is of our family going out-door skating at McIvor Park, also known as Bunn's Creek, on a sunny winter day. McIvor Park was a beautiful, expansive city park just down the avenue from our house on Ranch. During the winter months there was a decently-sized outdoor skating rink in the middle, surrounded by wooden benches, tall light posts, and hills covered with snow. The rectangular rink did not have boards or nets, but was merely a surface of ice bordered by mounds of snow on all sides. It was there that my brothers and I, decked out in our snowsuits, first attempted to skate altogether. For Todd, who was about three years old, it would also be his first time using real hockey skates instead of the "bob-skates," or flat platforms with two parallel blades that strap onto the bottom of one's shoes or boots.

After initially stepping around without issue, Todd took a hard and heavy fall. A flash of shock crossed his face as he felt, for the first time, the cold and unforgiving bite of the ice when he went down, then he burst out into tears. Our fun family skate temporarily erupted into chaos as Todd, with tears streaming down his cold, rosy-cheeked face, sobbingly declared that he would never skate again. In that moment, an innocent Canadian kid was baptized a true hockey player.

Despite his rough introduction to skating – and maybe because he wanted to follow in his older brothers' footsteps – Todd would change his mind drastically in the coming years. He was first exposed to hockey when Dad took him to the rink to watch me or Joel play with our respec-tive teams. Since Dad was the coach, he would bring Todd into the play-ers' box so could be around the boys. Todd couldn't see over the boards, so he would don a helmet, pick up his stick and spend the whole game shooting a puck, ball, or chunk of ice in the box. It wasn't long before he was chomping at the bit to play organized hockey himself.

Sometime between that harrowing experience on the ice at the ten-der age of three and his first official community club game for the Gate-way Flyers, Todd realized that not only could he skate without falling, he could do so better and faster than any of his peers.

Being around Dad, Joel and me was a huge help, giving Todd a jumpstart on hockey as a toddler. He began honing some serious skills very early on and fell deeply in love with the game. This combination of speed, natural talent, and pure joy and love for hockey created a powerful force within him, enabling Todd to dominate virtually all competition from a very young age. This was the beginning of something special.

*Todd in his early years, playing for the Gateway Flyers.*

*Todd (1986), Me (1985), and Joel (1983), with our dog Cola, in the front yard of the home on Ranch Road, in or around 1992.*

CHAPTER 2

# MVP, AND EVERYTHING ELSE

Todd's early hockey days were spent playing out of Gateway in North Kildonan, about a mile from our house. In the early 1990s, Gateway was basically an outdoor rink shelled with aluminum siding; there was gravel inside the arena and it usually seemed no warmer than it was outside. When Dad joined Gateway's Board of Directors he helped a group of inspired people transform Gateway into one of Winnipeg's best indoor hockey and recreation complexes at the time. Dad held many positions at Gateway, including that of president, and helped create a hockey utopia that served as a second home for us.

The best part about Dad's role with Gateway was that he held a set of keys, which meant that on special occasions Todd and I had a full rink of fresh ice all to ourselves – a sacred and special thing to any hockey player, especially in a nice indoor rink. It was incredible, and we got so pumped when Dad called the on-duty maintenance guy to check the ice-booking sheet for openings. The Gateway rink guys were beauties and always made sure we had a freshly flooded sheet to buzz around on. Over the years the cost of renting indoor ice has risen to astronomical rates, so most kids will never experience having an indoor ice sheet all to themselves. We were incredibly fortunate to have so many of those moments, and they remain among my most cherished memories of that time.

It was during those sacred indoor sessions and crazy ODR shinny games that Todd forged the foundation of his game. At all levels he played, he was an absolute stud on the ice. It's a shame that video recording wasn't more prevalent back in the 1990s, when we were playing youth hockey; if it was we'd surely have hundreds of highlight reel goals and plays to marvel over. Todd would have been that kid posted all over Instagram with ridiculous dangles and snipes. All I can tell you is that I, along with Todd's teammates, coaches, opponents, and spectators, witnessed some ridiculous highlights over the years.

Todd was a well-known player to fans and opponents alike, locally until age eight, then across Manitoba and western Canada. In Winnipeg, he was one of the few dominant players for his age group, demonstrating his speed and skill in every single game. Fans came to expect that he would light the lamp and set up his teammates from puck drop to final buzzer, and they were never disappointed. He was also one of those magnetic players who naturally drew their attention, not only with his performance but his presence as well.

His greatest strength as a player was his rarely matched quickness and deception as a skater, but that was only part of it. He also had incredible puck skills, vision, and a powerful and accurate wrist shot. Multiple-goal and point games were Todd's casual norm; it was never a question of whether he would put up points in any given game, just how many he would finish with. And these weren't "grinder goals" like I used to score, but often highlight reel, end-to-end rushes where he would blast past and deke his way through the whole other team to finish off with a nice move or shot. He would go coast-to-coast and score a goal with the humility of legend Bobby Orr. Like Orr, it was not uncommon for Todd to score so many of these types of goals that he would stop celebrating so as not to embarrass the other players.

I first realized how good Todd really was when I saw him compete at a Jets game intermission event with other players of multiple ages from around the province. There were upwards of ten thousand fans attending that game. After exploring the old Winnipeg Arena with early access, and seeing Teemu Selanee – his favorite player at the time – up close and personal during warmups, Todd was pumped. And, like other elite players performing on a big stage with so many fans watching, Todd rose to the occasion and took his game to a whole new level. He was easily one of the best players on the ice that day as he raced through an obstacle course and did other drills and competitions. While he had always excelled at the community club level, this is when he really started to thrive. What's more, with each new season and caliber of hockey, he would continue to level-up his game.

## Leveling Up

At eleven years old, Todd graduated from the Gateway Flyers to join the River East Marauders of the Winnipeg Atom AA league. During those years, the Atom AA league consisted of ten teams in the city and was the first advanced level beyond the community club level, where the stakes were significantly raised and competition tightened. Not only did Todd easily make the Marauders – made up of the top players from Gateway and eight other nearby community clubs – but he established himself as a leader and was named one of the captains.

It was at the Atom AA level that he really began to showcase his skill and work ethic throughout Winnipeg. That year at the All-Star game – the first significant league all-star game he was eligible to play in – Todd put on a show and was named MVP for the East team. Being named the team MVP of a citywide all-star game was no small feat, but on his road to success it would be just one of many similar accolades. After the All-Star game he continued to dominate and helped lead the Marauders to win the city championship.

Todd didn't just perform in big-time games, though. Every time he played, whether practice or game, he gave his all and left everything he had on the ice. It was rumored that Todd was never beaten in a skating drill, despite having some very worthy competitors and high-profile teammates, including Joe Barnes, who went second overall (behind Kyle Chipchura) in the 2001 Western Hockey League Bantam Draft, and sixty-fourth overall to the Carolina Hurricanes in the 2005 NHL draft. Joe, who was an incredibly powerful skater and player in his own right, especially in his mid-teen years, would openly display his frustrations at not being able to out-skate Todd in practice. The two of them had epic battles in those early days that helped them develop as players who wanted to make it big. Todd thrived on this internal competition, and when he was challenged he only stepped it up. Even when he was exhausted, he always found a way to flip the switch and find that *extra* gear, making it impossible for the other kids, no matter how hard they worked, to beat him. This attitude and work ethic laid the foundation for Todd's advancement and success as a player, and provided his teammates with an example of how to be great. It also led to Todd being named team captain or assistant of virtually every youth team he played for.

## Player Haters

Todd's success was not all roses, though: even before he hit puberty he had already attracted quite a few haters around Winnipeg – and not just opponents, but some parents as well. Even certain parents of Todd's own teammates would openly talk shit about him around the rink – this, out of jealousy that Todd outshined their kids.

While that was certainly not cool, some of the hate from opponents was justified and accepted as just part of the game. They dreaded playing against Todd for many reasons, including the fact that he was much faster and more skilled than they were, was chippy with his stick, and would outwork them every shift of every game. Though he had good sportsmanship, he was certainly *not* a pure gentleman on the ice, especially with his stick. Suffice it to say, if he ever made it to the NHL, he wouldn't have been a nominee for the Lady Byng Memorial Trophy. He also mouthed off to any opponent who tried to step up to him, and would basically laugh in their face or make a degrading comment about weaknesses in their game, simply to frustrate or anger them and establish mental dominance. Even Kyle Hampton ("Hammy") – who later became one of Todd's best friends – said that he absolutely hated Todd before they became teammates. In Hammy's words, Todd, starting at around the age of nine, was a "skilled shit-disturber."

Hammy said Todd "would do something dirty like give someone a little hack," causing the opposing team to go nuts. "Then he would score the game-winning goal and chirp you after he did." This style of play evolved and was refined as Todd grew older, and he became a major source of frustration to opposing teams as he flew around the ice with his long hair flowing out the back of his helmet and his jersey flowing in the air. Kipp Workman ("Worky") – a player from Brandon, Manitoba who later became one of my best friends – played against Todd during one season of Midget AAA, when Todd was fifteen years old. According to Worky, the entire Midget AAA Brandon Wheat Kings team hated both of us Davison brothers, "but especially Todd!" Of course, Todd and I loved the fact that we could leave such an impact on our opponents; in hockey, having someone hating to play against you is a badge of honor.

Worky said the hatred for Todd stemmed from the fact that "he would stick you, chirp you, but then score." Worky went on to say that "he was like a Theoren Fleury-type rat, but he was a good player too, just like Theo." The fact he was that good made opponents hate his chippiness even worse.

They also didn't appreciate Todd's confidence, security, and fearless attitude, both on and off the ice. He didn't give weight to the opinions of others, whether those opinions were about how he wore his equipment or styled his hair. He was his own authority and no one was going to tell him how he was going to look off the ice, or how he was going to play on it.

Dangling guys, slashing their calves, trash-talking, and sniping game-winning goals were all part of Todd's repertoire, but he always backed up his stick and mouth with his game. Being so small, he found his style effective to ensure that he was one of the top players on the ice at any given time. He would use others' frustration as fuel to amp up his own performance and put them on notice that they would have to contend with him if they hoped to win.

# CHAPTER 3

# TODD'S TROPHIES

In virtually any game he played where a "player of the game"; "most valuable player"; or "top forward" was awarded, Todd was always a top contender. Due to tournament rules designed for "fairness" to other participants, these awards would typically not be given to the same player in consecutive games. In Todd's case, however, this rule often went out the window due to his undeniably dominating performances, even when Todd himself did not think he deserved it.

In one particular tournament in Brandon, Manitoba, Todd was awarded "player of the game" in three consecutive games. According to Dad, after the third game, Todd crossed the dressing room and handed his award to a linemate he felt had earned it more. In Dad's words, "this spoke volumes of Todd's character." Acting with this type of independence, self-determination, and character not only allowed Todd to get stronger as a player, but as a person, with each passing day.

From a very young age, he realized that he was standing out and getting noticed on a regular basis. He didn't mind this; rather, he enjoyed and embraced it, seeing each higher-stakes game and larger venue a greater opportunity to improve and shine. He took responsibility for his abilities and focused on his strengths and his effort, holding himself to an elevated standard of performance.

## Mustang Days and Wild Ways

Chasing any dream comes with sacrifice. Chasing a hockey dream also comes with a lot of travel! Our family summer vacations were not to Disneyland or tropical beaches, but to random hockey arenas in the suburbs of Calgary, Vancouver, or elsewhere in western Canada, or down to Minneapolis to play other elite travel teams. We played, in our respective age groups, for the Manitoba Mustangs – a spring/summer hockey franchise known for hardworking, skilled players who weren't afraid to play an aggressive style of hockey... and for parents who feuded with the parents of players from the Winnipeg Junior Jets. I recall our father facing off against one of the main parent-coaches from the Junior Jets program – which was pretty hilarious considering Dad was five-foot-five and the other guy, a high-powered businessman, stood about six-foot-seven. As a result we never did get an invite to the program, and that was fine. Mustangs it was, and we were more than pumped about it.

Todd was lucky to have Dad as his Mustangs coach. They'd always had a special connection, but this player-coach relationship really forged their bond. Dad glowed with pride when he watched Todd roll into rinks across Western Canada and the United States. On the way to games he always wore his red and black Manitoba Mustangs golf shirt, which was untucked in a kind of sloppy way and matched his undercut, dyed red hair. As Dad and the rest of the family knew, Todd may have looked a bit dusty off the ice but he was about to put on an absolute light show for all of the new fans to see.

## Team North America

A major turning point early in Todd's career came in the summer of 1996, when he played in the Minnesota Hockey Festival. Along with the Edmonton Brick and Vancouver Can/Am Super Series, the Festival, which was held in the greater Minneapolis area, was one of the most well-known and competitive youth hockey tournaments in North America and consistently attracted excellent teams from Quebec to Los Angeles, Alaska, and beyond. The tournament was a pretty big deal for all the young participants, as it was a real international competition, and territorial pride was at stake.

As a 1986-born player with a September birthday, Todd played in the tournament as a ten-year-old. With Dad behind the bench and some of his best friends joining him on the ice, Todd elevated his game and clearly put himself in the top-player bracket. He turned heads in every game he played, leading the Mustangs in offensive performance and capturing the attention of spectators and tournament directors alike.

In addition to bringing together some of the world's best youth hockey talent, the Team Minnesota tournament organizers used this event for a secondary purpose: selecting the cream of the crop and inviting them to play on the North American Selects All-Star team. The North American Selects program typically took two teams overseas every two years. That year they were putting together teams bound for Denmark to play teams from that country and Sweden, Russia, and Czeck Republic. One team would be made up of 1985-born players, and the other of 1986s, which were my and Todd's respective age groups.

Todd was invited early on in the invite process for the 1986 team. The tournament directors told Mom and Dad that he was one of the top forwards and first picks. He was a sixth-grader at the time and became an even bigger deal around the school and community. Everyone knew these types of teams existed, and that the chances of getting selected to one were very slim. Most eleven-year-old hockey players would have done anything to have this type of opportunity; Todd just made it happen.

I was happy for my brother, but I'd be lying if I said I wasn't also envious, jealous, and disappointed that I wasn't invited to join the 1985-born team. I'd had a solid tournament, but apparently not solid enough for the North American Selects team organizers, or so I thought. Then one day, out of the blue, after another player declined his roster spot because his family couldn't afford the trip, I was invited. Though I felt sorry for the other boy, I was more than fired up for my chance to join Todd on that trip and play for that team.

The price was also a steep one for our family, especially now that two of us, along with a parental chaperone, were going. To offset some of the costs, a good old-fashioned Manitoba social, spearheaded by Mom's sisters, Auntie Donna and Auntie Judi, was held in the hall at Gateway. Friends and family came from all over to support us, and after a great night of fun we learned that several thousand dollars, in the form of beer and liquor sales, auction tickets and donations, had been raised. Our community's generosity was more evident than ever, and we were truly thankful. The Davison brothers were going to Denmark!

News of the trip spread in North Kildonan, to the point that we got some attention from our local newspaper, *The Herald*. I will never forget the day in early spring when Todd and I came home from school to find reporter Jim Timlick waiting to interview us. Todd and I could barely contain our excitement as we sat in the living room and answered his questions. We were about to embark on an extraordinary adventure, and, best of all, we were doing it together.

Though we tried to play it cool, Todd and I could barely wait the three weeks it took for our story to be published. Getting interviewed for a newspaper, especially one with a solid sports section like *The Herald*, would have been a big deal to an athlete, but especially to those who were in sixth and seventh grade. When the day finally arrived, school seemed to drag on forever; all we could think about was the moment we'd rush off the school bus and straight to our mailbox. Sure enough, there was a fresh copy of the newspaper waiting for us with a sports section article titled "N.K. brothers selected to represent North America" with a picture of me and Todd posing proudly in our Mustangs jerseys.

The trip to Denmark with the North American Selects proved to be one of the most cherished experiences of our lives. The journey started with an eight-hour drive down to Minneapolis, where we'd have a couple of days to learn our team systems and get comfortable with our new teammates before making the trans-Atlantic flight to Denmark. That leg of the trip was nearly twenty-five hours, and we arrived safe and sound but absolutely exhausted.

After overcoming jet lag Todd found his usual spark and speed and, within the first few games, established himself as his team's offensive leader.

In fact, after the first game, in which he scored four goals, parents of his team members came up to Dad and asked if it was true that Todd was ranked as the number one player in Winnipeg. Knowing that Winnipeg had some stellar 1986-born players like Cam Barker ("Barks") and Dustin Boyd ("Boyd") (who, along with others would later go on to make the NHL), Dad shrugged and humbly denied it, though he certainly knew inside that Todd was elite and was one of Winnipeg's top players for his age. Todd followed up that first performance by scoring hat tricks in his next two games, but then got back on pace with another four-goal game against an all-star team from Sweden. He only scored one goal in the fifth game, but followed up that relatively lackluster performance by putting away another four goals in the sixth game. In the seventh game, Todd scored the tying goal with two minutes left on the clock. And, finally, in the eighth game, he scored one goal and, according to Dad's daily journal, added a "beautiful assist."

Todd led the 1986 team in scoring by quite a substantial margin. To those European opponents, who were quite outmatched by the North American players' skill and speed, Todd appeared to be one of the next great Canadian talents to watch in the years to come.

24 -

## sports

THE HERALD - Wednesday, April 15, 1998

# N.K. brothers selected to represent North America

*Davisons anxious to take part in prestigious Danish tourney*

**By Jim Timlick**
*Sports Writer*

Todd and Wade Davison recently began to study about Europe at school.

The two brothers will soon get an opportunity to learn firsthand about European history and culture. They are two of just three Winnipeggers who have been chosen to play for the North American Selects hockey team at a tournament in Copenhagen, Denmark.

The nine-game exhibition series, which runs April 20 to May 2, will feature teams from Russia, Sweden, the Czech Republic and host Denmark in two age categories.

Needless to say, the two North Kildonan natives are a little more excited about the trip than flipping through some dusty history textbook.

**Excited**

"I was really excited when I found out. I knew it was a lot of money. When my parents told me I could go I was really, really happy. Not everybody has this chance," said 11-year-old Todd.

"It was kind of funny. I found out one of my friends from St. James (Derek Poplawski) was on the team," added Wade, 12. "I was happy for him but I wanted to go too. Then I found out I'd been invited too. I was really happy."

The two brothers, who both play summer hockey for the Manitoba Mustangs, were chosen to play for the North American team after participating with their respective teams at a tournament in Minneapolis last year.

They were chosen from a pool of more than 200 players aged 11 and 12.

"When we go over there we might get to see the next Russian Rocket (Pavel Bure). The size of the ice will be different," said Wade, who along with his brother attends St. Alphonsus School. "I'm going to be a little nervous. All the European players in the NHL have pretty good moves."

"I'm going to like playing with the people on my team. We all have the same qualities," said Todd. "I think that's why they

picked us."

The Davisons have been playing hockey since they were knee-high to Theoren Fleury. They both played AA hockey for the River East Marauders this past season — Todd with the atoms and Wade with the peewees.

**Dissimilar**

While they both play centre, that's where the similarities end, according to one of their coaches.

"They're both outgoing kids and they're very easy to talk to. But there's quite a bit of a difference on the ice," said Ken Cameron, who coaches Wade with the Mustangs and Todd with the Marauders.

"Todd has a little more scoring ability. Wade is more physical. You've got two good packages but they're both different."

Sending the two brothers to Denmark has been a real community effort. An aunt organized a social to help raise funds to pay for their trip.

"I don't think they realized how big a deal it is until they saw all the people at the social," said their mom, Barb Davison.

**Brothers Todd (left) and Wade Davison are looking forward to representing North America in Denmark.**

*Dad and Todd in Copenhagen, Denmark in 1998.*

# Popping Up to Peewee

A few months after the trip to Denmark, Todd was age-advanced to play Peewee AAA with my 1985-born Winnipeg Sharks team. In those days, Peewee hockey was typically strictly reserved for thirteen-year-old players, but a few of the standout twelve-year-olds from across the city popped up and made the jump to the older league. Being age-advanced was rare, and if you were being age-advanced in any AAA league in Winnipeg people knew who you were. On the ego side of things, it was perhaps the biggest swag move a kid could pull to assert themselves as a dominant player of their age group.

And speaking of ego, I was initially threatened when the idea of bringing my younger brother up to play on "my team" came up. Mom delicately breached the topic at the start of tryouts and asked my permission – even though it wasn't required – and it triggered insecurities and fears that I would be outshined by him. Of course, Todd would still have to make the team, but based on his tryout performance and his skill level he was all but guaranteed to get the offer. Somewhere during the discussion about getting along as brothers and future teammates, Mom agreed to buy us the Bush CD, *Sixteen Stone*, if we ended up playing on the same team. It's safe to say we won the negotiation; when Todd made the team, "Machine Head" was repeatedly blasted on the rides to practices or games.

As new members of the Winnipeg AAA Peewee Sharks, Todd and I proudly stood beside each other as teammates during the Canadian national anthem of our season opener, then went to work as linemates. When the puck dropped we instinctively went to the level that had been earned and crafted from countless hours of playing with and against each other. Early in the game, Todd got the puck and flew into the offensive zone on the far-right side; he then picked up speed, blew by the left defenseman, circled the net, and fed me in the slot for our team's first goal of the season. Our eyes met with beaming smiles, knowing we were on our way together. With that useful assist to my goal, I quickly realized that playing with my younger brother was going to be a good thing.

Although we didn't win the league championship that season, we teamed up for some highlight reel goals and plays, making some great memories along the way. "Winnipeg Sharks goal scored by #12 Todd Davison, assisted from #7 Wade Davison," or vice versa, was a commonly heard message over the loudspeakers at Maginot arena that season, and we absolutely loved it. We were brothers playing Peewee AAA hockey together, which was really rare and special. We even got to play in the league all-star game together. Not only did Todd get named to the All-Star game as an underage player – a feat in and of itself – he lived up to the hype by scoring a key goal in the form of a bardown snipe from the high slot. A *Winnipeg Free Press* reporter who covered the All-Star event wrote that Todd was one of the youngest and smallest players in the game, yet "showed exceptional skills and hit anyone in his way." That sounds about right.

That season turned out to be great for us on many levels and, though we didn't realize it at the time, set the foundation for and foreshadowed our futures in hockey. It would be the first of four seasons when our respective first initials would be put before "Davison" on our jerseys' name bars. It was also a great season for our family. In addition to seeing our on-ice chemistry, Mom and Dad loved the fact that we were playing together on the same team, which dramatically lessened their burden of chauffeuring us to and from separate games and practices. And our grandparents absolutely loved the fact that they could see both of us in action at the same time, playing together as teammates and brothers.

## MVP Underdog

The next season, Todd again played Peewee AAA, this time with his own 1986 age group. Though he'd thrived as an underager the prior season, he went back to dominating opponents when playing in his own age group. And to be clear, for young Canadian hockey players Peewee AAA is a big-time stage; to dominate is not a common feat. Todd was once again the leader of his team and the standout star in most games. Multi-goal and point games were not only expected, but came with ease. Todd won the "top skater" award at the mid-season All-Star game skills competition. He looked fast and strong in every game, and was certainly one of the best peewee hockey players in Canada at that time. There was no doubt that his name was known. This was confirmed when he was named the league's MVP that season over other future NHLers, including Barks.

Barks – who went on to be the third overall draft pick in the 2004 NHL Entry Draft (behind Alexander Ovechkin and Evgeni Malkin) – was a giant young player, standing damn near six feet tall when he was just eleven. At thirteen he could pretty much grow a full beard. He was an offensive defenseman who could smoothly dangle through his competitors like they were house league ankle-biters, then snipe with ease. Or, he would just walk the blueline and bomb bardown clappers. It was something to see! In his professional career, after playing several solid seasons in the NHL despite battling a nagging ankle injury, Barks jumped over to the Kontinental Hockey League (the "KHL") – the elite hockey league of Russia and much of eastern Europe and Asia – and went on to lead the league in defensemen scoring in 2016. Back in those Peewee days, Barks was a force to reckon with from Winnipeg's south end, and he and Todd had some epic battles.

After Barks and Todd got over their tensions for territory and status, they recognized and respected each other's talent and mindset, becoming great friends as well as competitors. Although Todd was not nearly as big or strong as Barks, he possessed similar puck skills, vision, and hockey smarts. They were both elite players, just in two completely different hockey packages. While Barks ended up taking home the league's Top Defenseman award that Peewee AAA year, Todd was the one standing in the center of the award recipients' photograph, holding the MVP award like a little boss. I recall the drive home from the awards banquet that night, knowing that Todd had once again entered a whole new level with his game.

This award was not to be taken lightly. In fact, just two seasons later, future NHL-legend Jonathan Toews would stand in the exact same place as Todd when he was named Peewee MVP. And though, due to his size,

Todd wasn't quite on the same pro-prospect level as Toews, Barks, or Colin Wilson – another Winnipeg player who was revered and recognized as being destined for the NHL from a very young age – he was certainly in the same league in terms of skill and ability. Simply put, Todd was amongst Winnipeg's very best players at that time, and had some serious potential for the future. He just needed a chance to grow and be seen.

*Todd accepting his Winnipeg AAA Peewee MVP award (presenter: Phil Cole [drafted 4th round, #125 overall, by the New Jersey Devils in the 2000 NHL Entry Draft]). Photo courtesy of Art Dutka.*

# CHAPTER 4

# DUB DREAMS

After being named Peewee MVP, Todd trained extra hard that off-season, knowing that the next season – his Western Hockey League ("WHL") Bantam draft season – would be a significant one in his envisioned path to professional hockey.

The WHL (also known as the "Western League" or "the Dub") is the top-tier junior hockey league in western Canada and the northwestern United States. The WHL is currently made up of twenty-two teams, from as far west as Victoria, British Columbia and Portland, Oregon and as far east as Winnipeg; with the Winnipeg Ice, formerly based in Kootenay, changing the league's makeup in the 2019-2020 season.

The Bantam Draft targets first-year bantam players – those having just played their "fourteen-year-old" season – from the Western Canadian provinces and territories, and every American state west of the Mississippi River. This draft is a major deal in the young minds of draft-eligible players, and no wonder, as there are a dozen or more WHL scouts scattered around the rink at any given bantam game across the region. We players all knew who the scouts were and what teams they represented, as they each had their respective team's logo brightly displayed on their jacket. It was an extra big game when you knew a scout of a team that you really wanted to play with was in the crowd.

The WHL is one of three leagues (the other two being the Ontario Hockey League and the Quebec Major Junior Hockey League) that make up the Canadian Hockey League ("CHL"). In total, fifty-two Canadian teams and eight American teams participate in one of the three smaller leagues under the CHL umbrella, making it the largest development hockey league in the world. The three leagues operate independently throughout the regular season and playoffs, but then converge for a season-ending tournament in which the three championship teams and a host-city team compete for one of the hockey world's most coveted, hardest-to-win trophies: the Memorial Cup.

The CHL is Canadian junior hockey at its finest. CHL hockey is typically referred to as "major junior," which is distinguished from "Junior A" – Tier II hockey. While the international hockey landscape is shifting, and leagues like the United States Hockey League are getting stronger and faster by the season, the CHL is still commonly accepted as the best junior hockey league in the world. But playing in it comes at a major cost: the loss of eligibility to play hockey in the National Collegiate Athletic Association ("NCAA"). In other words, a CHL player loses their ability to get a hockey scholarship to an NCAA program. To counter this loss, the CHL offers its players scholarships to Canadian universities – typically one year of school completely paid for per CHL season played. Though this fantastic program provides players with a solid Canadian university education after their junior career, the dilemma for the fourteen-year-old player deciding how to chart their future remains, and the choice has significant, real-life consequences.

## The Dub Dilemma

Choosing to play even one game in the CHL – even just one exhibition game at the age of fifteen or sixteen years old – would deem a player ineligible for the NCAA. The rationale behind this ridiculousness comes from the great rule-makers of the NCAA, who have deemed the CHL to be a "professional" league, even though it's only made up of sixteen- to twenty-year-olds getting paid biweekly, making barely enough money to afford tins of chewing tobacco and sub sandwiches for lunch.

Though most American hockey fans think playing NCAA college hockey is the only way to go, they have likely never felt the excitement of an intense CHL hockey game, especially through the eyes of a diehard Canadian teenager. On the other hand, most Canadian traditionalists have never felt the excitement and intensity of a Division 1 American college game, especially one played before fifteen thousand college students roaring allegiance to their team. The reality is that both NCAA and CHL hockey are awesome leagues, but having to choose just one of these routes would be brutal for anyone, let alone a teenager. It was, and continues to be, a major dilemma faced by so many talented players.

When Todd and I were old enough to understand the potential paths to the NHL – the main avenue then being through Canadian major junior, and the other through NCAA (American) college hockey – we focused our attention on the WHL. Back then, before the age of social media, we just didn't know much about what American college hockey was like. Though we would occasionally watch a college game on TV, the style and atmosphere of that hockey seemed so foreign to us, and we didn't really get excited about it. On the contrary, we would get very pumped to watch a broadcasted CHL game on Sportsnet-TV on Sunday evenings. We would get especially fired up to watch the annual CHL Top-Prospects game, which was loaded with NHL potentials, including some of our idols, and guest-coached by Don Cherry and Bobby Orr. Someday we wanted to have Cherry or Orr tap our shoulder for a shift in a game in front of every active NHL scout on the planet.

For us, and the vast majority of our Canadian friends, making the WHL was a really big deal, and it was all we focused on. We attended several WHL games at the Keystone Centre in Brandon, Manitoba, where the Wheat Kings played. We'd see the size and excitement of the crowd, the caliber of play, the NHL scouts in attendance, and how the players were treated like celebrities. We witnessed, first-hand, the sixteen-year-old knuckles of Jordin Tootoo bounce off his opponents' faces. We saw incredibly talented pro-prospects and draft picks playing for a team we could one day play for. We also saw how the teams were sponsored by the best hockey brands, and how players were given all brand new, top-of-the-line gear for free. While all these things may seem trivial now, in the eyes and hearts of Peewee and Bantam-aged players, they were what dreams were made of.

We were also obsessed with the annual World Junior Hockey Championships ("World Juniors"), which for Canadians is the biggest hockey event of the season – even bigger than the Stanley Cup finals. Watching Team Canada during those World Junior tournaments, we saw all the best Canadian NHL prospects in action, and saw them spotlighted as national heroes during the TSN broadcasts. Winnipeg hosted the World Juniors in 1999. I vividly recall how excited we were when Mom and Dad picked us up early from school to take us to the Team Canada semifinal game against Team Sweden. We eagerly changed out of our school uniforms and into Team Canada jerseys in the family minivan on the way to the Winnipeg Arena. The atmosphere of that game was absolutely electric. We wanted nothing more to be playing out there with that Team Canada logo on our chest someday! We thought the CHL was the only way to do that.

We also didn't really know anyone who had taken the college route. All of our local idols went to the WHL. This was before Toews decided to forego playing for Tri-Cities in the WHL and instead play for the University of North Dakota, thus paving a new avenue for generations of Winnipeg players to follow. Todd and I didn't dismiss the NCAA altogether, but it was definitely our second choice and, again at the time we didn't have anyone around to convince us otherwise.

Since then, after playing games against the University of North Dakota ("UND") as a member of the University of Manitoba Bisons after junior hockey, and subsequently attending law school at UND and attending countless electric UND hockey games, my views on this whole CHL versus NCAA debate have changed substantially. I have seen the incredible facilities NCAA students have in which they can flourish. I've skated on the ice at the glorious Ralph Englestad arena, one of the most beautiful hockey arenas in the world. I have come to learn that NCAA college hockey can be the right option for a player who wants to spend a few more years developing before trying to play professionally, which, really, should be most players.

But that just wasn't how we saw things back then. We didn't know how cool it would be to play for an American college team and walk around campus with all the boys, like a team of campus kings; and we certainly didn't know how cool the university parties would be. We only really knew what we saw right in front of us, and we wanted to be like our idols, playing in the Dub, for Team Canada, getting drafted to the NHL, and be playing pro by age twenty-one. And though Todd, based on his size, should have been destined to be a college hockey player, his hockey heart wanted to play in the Dub, and so did mine!

## The Draft

During my draft year, which was the 1999-2000 season, I had talked to many scouts of various WHL teams and was convinced that I would be drafted in the mid-to-late rounds. I had many great conversations with Gerry Hogue, the Prince Albert Raiders scout based in Winnipeg. Gerry even gave me a Raiders team hat before the draft, which to me, at fourteen years old, was a really big deal.

I was confident going into draft day, figuring that if no one picked me early on I would go to Prince Albert in the seventh round or so. Instead, it would be one of the most devastating days of my youth. I rushed home to scroll down through the draft results, only to see that my name was nowhere to be found. To say I was sad, mad, and ashamed would be completely inadequate. The best way I can describe it was "crushed," and even that doesn't quite cut it.

There was a bright side, however, to not getting drafted in the Bantam Draft: you become eligible to get invited to all the WHL teams' rookie or training camps. Teams started sending invites to non-drafted players about a month after the draft, so you better believe that I was running to check the mailbox every day when I got home from school. All players, drafted or not, would be on the same ice at training camp. Slowly but surely, my invite letters started to roll in. The first one, which was expected, came from the Brandon Wheat Kings, a team then managed and owned by Kelly McCrimmon, the General Manager of the Vegas Golden Knights. Many others soon started rolling in, including from the Prince George Cougars, Portland Winterhawks, Lethbridge Hurricanes, Kelowna Rockets, Calgary Hitmen, Spokane Chiefs, Seattle Thunderbirds, Moose Jaw Warriors, Saskatoon Blades, and, of course, the Prince Albert Raiders. In fact, within a couple of weeks, I was fortunate to receive invites to almost every single WHL team's rookie camp. Though it would sting for a while, not getting drafted would turn out to be a blessing in disguise, for it gave me the ability to choose which WHL team I wanted to try to be a part of.

## Rookie Camp

After carefully considering all the options on the table, I chose to attend the rookie camp of the Regina Pats (the "Pats"). The Pats are a legendary Canadian junior hockey franchise and the oldest major junior hockey team in the world. Another cool fact is that the Pats also served as a farm team to the Montreal Canadiens in the 1950s and '60s. When the time for training camp came in late August, Dad and I loaded up the minivan and made the six-hour drive straight west on the Trans-Canada Highway to Regina. Todd, who was more than curious to check out a WHL training camp, tagged along for the ride. Come to think of it, he didn't even ask if it was okay with us if he came; there was no way he would miss a chance to see top-level hockey being played and see for himself the caliber he was aspiring to move up to.

My performance at rookie camp drew attention from the Pats' scouts, coaches, and executives. I battled, scored, and even had my first-real hockey fight. After being passed over in the draft months earlier, the Pats now knew who I was. I vividly remember Lorne Molleken – the Pats' head coach and former head coach of the Chicago Blackhawks – skating over and giving me a tap on the shin pads after I drove the net on a cross-ice three-on-three game and tucked one in. At my evaluation meeting at the end of camp, I was told that I would not be listed at that time because their protected player list was maxed out, but I was on their radar and they would be watching me "like a hawk" back in Winnipeg. I left Regina encouraged and pumped up, knowing that I had at least made a name for myself.

Though he had spent that rookie camp watching from the stands, Todd left pumped up too! Feeling strong and confident coming off his award-winning season, he now knew what he needed to do to be noticed during his WHL bantam draft season, which was just weeks away.

# CHAPTER 5

# THE SIZE OF HIS HOCKEY HEART

In the early 2000s, hockey at the professional and junior levels in North America was a much different game than it is now. It was more systematically rigid, with more obstruction and stick work allowed, and more lenient body-contact rules that made it much more difficult for small players to survive without injury, let alone succeed. Open-ice shoulder-to-head hits were not only perfectly legal, they were encouraged by hard-core fans. If you need proof of this, recall that Scott Stevens didn't even receive a minor penalty for his blind-side shoulder-to-jaw hit on Paul Kariya during the 2003 Stanley Cup Finals, which sent Kariya into a different dimension. If you need further proof that hockey was a different beast back then, recall that Kariya was allowed to return to play in that game just minutes after sustaining that severe concussion! Granted, it was Game 6 of the Stanley Cup finals and he was "fine" enough to go on to score a rather miraculous all-time goal, but that hit caused a severe brain injury and left Kariya no memory of that goal, that game or Game 7, or even the days following the season.

The WHL was commonly considered the toughest junior hockey league in the world. Worky, a Brandon native who attended countless Wheat Kings' games as a kid and has since become one of the most knowledgeable and reliable armchair hockey analysts that Winnipeg's St. James area has ever seen, described the WHL in the early 2000s as "the peak of insanity." It had the roughness and violence of hockey in the '90s, but with increased speed and hard-capped equipment that made nearly every player capable of causing severe damage in the form of concussions and broken jaws, usually caused by shoulders or elbows to the head. Guys like Jordin Tootoo, who played for the Brandon Wheat Kings from 1999 until 2003, were absolute terrors. Tootoo would hop on the ice after his team just dumped it in for an offensive zone forecheck, and then he'd wind up to his team's blue line or beyond before torpedoing in towards the puck holder, looking to put them into outer space. Tootoo's hits resulted in many broken collarbones and concussions, perhaps even both at the same time. And if the shoulder-to-jaw concussion-inducing hits aren't enough to convince you, the league also allowed players to fist fight three times in one game before they got ejected! Those were definitely wild times.

Considering the state of play in those days, professional and junior hockey was seen as a big man's game, and smaller players were essentially denied the chance to showcase their talent at the highest levels. Scouts, coaches, and management often discriminated against players based on size without blinking; in fact, scouts often looked to the stature of the player before his skill, and automatically crossed off their potential draftees list any who fell below a certain height or size. To put this in perspective, when I was fourteen I was told by a WHL scout that I was a "small player," despite being close to five-ten and a hundred and seventy pounds. Players Todd's size typically wouldn't even get a sniff of playing.

This discrimination was most apparent in the case of Nigel Dawes, who, despite being one of the most talented players to ever come out of Winnipeg, dominating every season even when age-advanced, was not picked until the fifth round of the 2000 WHL Bantam Draft. Dawes should have undoubtedly been one of the very first picks, if not first overall, but the scouts and brass didn't think he was tall enough, and somehow let him slip to the mid-rounds.

Two seasons later, Dawes joined the Kootenay Ice as a sixteen-year-old, and had an incredible rookie season, helping the Ice win the 2002

Memorial Cup. The next season, at only seventeen years old, he had forty-seven goals and ninety-two points, and went on to snipe forty-seven more goals the season after that in only fifty-six games. He also made the Team Canada World Junior team twice, and even led the World Junior tournament in scoring in 2004. With his talent and those numbers, it is absolutely insane that seventy-two players were selected before him. Nigel would go on to play several solid seasons in the NHL before eventually becoming a superstar in the KHL, but it had been a tremendous, uphill battle. And, considering his story, it was unlikely that Todd would get picked at all. Nigel had several inches on Todd at that age, and was much better built. But there is one thing that scouts can't measure in inches: the size of a player's hockey heart.

Mark Romas ("Romeo") is a former Regina Pats' scout based out of Winnipeg. Romeo said that Todd's size was a "huge issue" while Romeo was vouching for the Pats to draft Todd, adding that he had to defensively address Todd's size whenever his name came up. He said other scouts thought Todd should, without question, be headed to play college hockey in the NCAA, instead of being fed to the wolves of the WHL. Romeo was Todd's biggest advocate, sticking to his guns even when he was borderline ridiculed for his beliefs. No matter what anyone said, he knew what he saw: a kid with a massive hockey heart and the skill to play at the highest levels. Romeo had witnessed Todd's skill for years, and knew there was something special about him as a player that wouldn't be limited by height or weight.

Todd proved himself all season long, both by leading his team in scoring and having great performances in the league all-star game and the Director's Cup, which was the Bantam Draft showcase event for Manitoba. Still, we were a bit surprised when, in the spring of 2001, Todd was drafted to the Regina Pats Organization as their eighth-round pick. Romeo's tactics had worked; he'd sold Todd as the Pats' next Matt Hubbauer ("Hubby") – a ridiculously talented Winnipegger who'd joined the team as a very small sixteen-year-old rookie and quickly developed into a phenomenal talent and fan favorite. Hubby's old-school white Nike skates were lofty boots to fill, but Romeo knew Todd could do it and had convinced the Pats to give him a chance.

While Todd would have been happy to be drafted by any team, he was especially excited and proud to join a franchise as storied and classy as the Pats – and to have a clearer view of his road to professional success. In late summer of 2001, Todd entered that Pats' rookie training camp with the intention of making it known that he belonged and could play and compete against anyone, and he did just that.

It's important to point out that aside from absolute phenoms like Connor McDavid or Sidney Crosby, fifteen-year-olds playing in the CHL are rarely granted "exceptional status." In fact, prior to 2020, when Connor Bedard was selected first overall by the Pats, the WHL had never before granted it to one so young. So it came as no surprise that Todd, who was actually just shy of his fifteenth birthday, was sent back to Winnipeg after rookie training camp to keep developing in AAA. He still left confident that he had made a solid impression on his new team.

Meanwhile, I, then sixteen years old, had a chance to stick around to make the team. I initially attended the Pats' training camp for that 2001-2002 season with the full intention of going back to Winnipeg and remaining NCAA-eligible for one more season. My heart wanted to stay in Regina and do anything I could to make the team, but my calculating mind was nervous, as usual, and leaning towards the "safe" choice. I knew my odds of actually making the roster at that age were not very high and I didn't want to make a premature decision to ruin my eligibility before officially securing a roster spot. It hurt to be walking away from camp without giving myself a true chance to make the team, but I had my plan. However, in a divinely orchestrated turn of events on the morning after the Pats Blue and White intersquad game, my plans changed. With training camp over, we were packing up the hotel room and began loading the van for the drive back to Winnipeg. Minutes before we were set to hit the road, Pa walked into our hotel room still

*Pa and Todd in Brandon, Manitoba at the Keystone Centre,
after Pats training camp in 2001.*

smelling faintly of his morning cigarette; he had the Sunday edition of the *Regina Leader-Post* in hand and a big grin on his face. He opened the paper to the sports section and, with eyes twinkling, flashed the front page in front of me. My own eyes widened when I saw the large photo of the moment I buckled Jeff Feniak – a six-foot-four Philadelphia Flyers draft pick – with a big body check behind the net. A wave of emotion came over me as I felt pulled right back into following my heart and my dream to play in the Dub.

Moments later, before I really had the chance to really dwell on the situation, Mom's cell phone rang. I felt a flutter of excitement as she handed it to me, saying it was Todd Ripplinger, head scout for the Pats. He was calling to report that I had officially been listed and the coaches wanted me to stay for the exhibition season, and that I actually had a decent shot at making the team. Though this was certainly excellent news, I told him I needed some time to analyze and feel out the situation. When we hung up, I discussed it with Mom and Pa, then with Dad by phone as he was back home in Winnipeg. They knew how badly I wanted to play in the WHL, much more so than the NCAA. A few minutes later, following my heart and excitement, I made a decision that changed the Davison brothers' paths forever.

## My First Sniff

My debut with the team was an exhibition game in Brandon against the Wheat Kings. The enormity of my emotions as I boarded the team bus that day is hard to describe; I couldn't wait to skate onto the ice proudly bearing the Pats logo on my chest in an official game jersey. My excitement, however, temporarily turned to embarrassment when, as the bus neared the Saskatchewan-Manitoba border and the stop for the pre-game meal, my teammates stood up and started changing into suits and ties. It had never occurred to me to pack dress clothes, so I had no choice but to sit there in my shorts, t-shirt, and flip-flops. I felt like an absolute dust-bag at that pre-game meal, and even more so when we were nearing the rink, but thankfully the bus driver took an underground ramp that led right next to the Keystone Centre's dressing room, thus saving me from feeling like a classless loser on the parade into the rink. Meanwhile, my dress clothes were being driven out to me from Winnipeg by one of the many family members coming out to watch me on this big-time occasion.

I still remember the smell of freshly made buttered popcorn radiating throughout the arena and the vibrations of the blaring music as I stepped on the Keystone Centre ice for my first warmup in an official WHL game. I thought back to all the Wheat Kings' games I'd watched, awestruck as a young kid, from those arena seats. To some, it was just an exhibition game, but to me it was the manifestation of a long-held dream.

As I lined up for an offensive zone faceoff during my first shift, I found myself standing across from Wheat Kings rookie and future NHLer, Eric Fehr, who I'd battled against during the previous Manitoba Midget AAA season. We gave each other discrete grins and slight nods, knowing we had risen to the next level. I was absolutely loving it.

Behind the scenes, the stars were just starting to align for the Davison brothers, things that never would have happened if I hadn't made that decision to play that first exhibition game with the Pats. If our lives had a blueprint, it was unfolding on a bigger level.

I played four exhibition season games — two against Tootoo's Brandon Wheat Kings and two against Jay Bouwmeester and Joffrey Lupul's Medicine Hat Tigers. During a game against the Tigers, as I battled on the right wall in the defensive zone, the puck got chipped out to the neutral zone and down to the Tigers' blue line. I eagerly chased down the puck in a footrace against Bouwmeester — a six-foot-four defenseman who would be selected third overall in the NHL entry draft to the Florida Panthers at the end of that season. Though I was skating as hard as I could, Bouwmeester seemed to casually take a few strides and beat me to the puck by a half-zone. It was a very, very humbling experience. My game needed work to compete against those fellas, especially my skating and my foot speed. Those boys were a small step away from the NHL at that point, while for me it was more like a massive leap. After that final game in Medicine Hat, as the exhibition season came to a close, I was sent back to Winnipeg to play Midget AAA for one more season. Though I had a great showing in training camp and exhibition season, it was decided that I would develop a lot more if I played as a first-line player in Midget AAA instead of being a fourth-liner or healthy scratch in the WHL. It was the right decision.

## Together As Sharks

By the time AAA tryouts started the following week, Todd and I were back on the ice together. He again quickly showed that his game was good enough to be age-advanced, jumping to the Manitoba Midget AAA league, where he would again wear a Shark on the front of his jersey and "T. Davison" on the back. Though I'd initially been reluctant for Todd to join my Peewee team all those years earlier, I now gladly welcomed him as an awesome addition to our team.

With each new level, Todd continued to prove his potential and show that his trajectory was sky-high. He established himself as an impactful underage player in the Midget AAA league. He was a key player on our Sharks' roster, pumping in goals on a consistent basis, and helping our team rise and stay at the top of the league all season. His game thrived as he became a selfless playmaker in a league filled with some truly elite talent.

Led by coach Kevin Benson, our team had a strong season that led us right to the league finals; this, despite losing our first game of the season ten to one to the Yellowhead Chiefs in what had to be the worst season-opening beat-down in team history. After that embarrassing and confusing loss, we bore ahead and became the top team in the league going into playoffs. After a wild ride there, which included beating the Chiefs ten to one in our first playoff game and knocking out Worky's Brandon Wheat Kings in double-OT of the quarter-final series, we suffered a heartbreaking loss in the best-of-seven-games provincial championship to the Eastman Selects. But hope was not lost; despite that defeat we were given a berth in the Western Canada Regional Championship because the Eastman Selects were hosting the regional event.

After playing our hearts out in that regional tournament and getting redemption against Eastman in the semi-finals, we ended up losing the championship game to the Tisdale Trojans, a powerhouse championship team from the Saskatchewan Midget AAA league. The Trojans went on to win the entire Air Canada Cup – the Canadian National Midget AAA Championship – with their defeat over Sidney Crosby's team, the Dartmouth Subways. Crosby was the scoring leader and named MVP of that event. In retrospect, our team was one win away from being able to give Sidney Crosby's team a run for the Canadian National Championship.

While our team had suffered a devastating loss in the finals of the Regional Championship, Todd was a scoring leader in the tournament and named "First Team All-Star" for his play. The following excerpt from a *Winnipeg Free Press* newspaper article, published April 7, 2002, came after we won the semi-final game:

"The diminutive forward, just 5-foot-6 and 157 lbs. went from goat to hero in a hurry. After taking an ill-advised high-sticking penalty resulting in the game-tying power-play goal for the [Eastman] Selects midway through the second, Davison scored just 32 seconds into the third to give his club a 4-3 advantage.

"Eastman quickly regained the lead as sensational forward Colin Lafreniere . . . netted a quick pair . . . for the hosts.

"But Davison tied the game 5-5 with a shorthanded goal . . .

"I knew when they scored with me in the box, I was in trouble," Davison said. "(Head coach) Kevin Benson talked to me just before the third period started, and he made it pretty clear I owed the team something. It felt good to get the first one, but that second one felt even better."

"Five minutes after Davison's second of the game, he added an assist, feathering a pass to Brent Kuik for another short-handed goal to [boost] his club to a 6-5 lead . . . ."

That short passage encapsulates the way Todd played hockey his entire life.

He was a stud playing age-advanced provincial Midget AAA hockey that season – typically a sign of good things to come in one's hockey future. With every season and opportunity he was given, Todd rose to new levels and claimed success. At that point he had no doubt in his mind that he was on the way up, and the next step was the WHL. It was just a matter of time.

After that AAA season together, Todd and I were called up by the Pats for their 2001-2002 playoff run against the Moose Jaw Warriors. I had been called up earlier in the season over New Years to play two games, but now Todd and I were making the trip together. Todd didn't dress, and I barely played a shift, but this Dub call-up during playoffs gave us a front and center look at the next level, and further showed us what we were working towards. Todd knew that in just a few months he would get the chance to make the jump of a lifetime, to a spot in that Pats dressing room. For Todd, it was a sacred space he knew he would have to earn.

# CHAPTER 6

# INNER VISION

## The Sacred Room

"Swear on the PDR?"

This was a phrase that stumped me for months! Todd and Jesse Deckert ("Decks") adopted it as their code phrase to replace "Swear on [insert "God", "family" or any other sacred meaningful thing here]"? For Todd and Decks, the "PDR" was sacred; to me, it was a frustrating mystery.

The first time I heard them say "PDR" I inquired about the meaning but got nothing but hostile stares and silence in return. It was the same with my subsequent requests, which were numerous. This was their sacred, insider-best-friend-phrase and they weren't cutting anybody in on it, not even a teammate or a brother. Knowing how much it bugged me was surely an added benefit as they repeatedly uttered the phrase throughout the Spring of 2001 and the 2001-2002 season with the Sharks.

One day, in a moment of illumination, I blurted out: "Pats Dressing Room!" Todd and Decks' jaws dropped as they stared at me in silence with wide eyes. Part of me wishes I hadn't done so, because it was something special between just them, but the larger part, I'll admit, was pumped that I had finally cracked their code. That room was sacred to me too.

Todd, Decks, and I shared a common goal: to play for the Pats the following season. We wanted to advance to the best level of hockey available to us, and to have a rightfully earned place in the dressing room. But before the team was picked we had some serious work to do!

## Itty Bitty

In the Spring of 2002, Todd, along with all other players on the Pats' protected-players list, were summoned to Regina to undergo team fitness testing. The other Winnipeggers on the Pats' list at that time were me, Decks, who was drafted along with Todd, as well as Hubby, David McDonald ("Mac"), and Kyle Ladobruk ("Lado"), who were already popular rostered players, and Scott Wagner, a brand-new draft pick.

As regional scouts also attended testing for meetings and player observation, Romeo was making the trip as well. He even offered to drive, and Hubby, Decks, Wagner, Todd, and I didn't have to think about it before jumping into the westward-bound minivan. Romeo was entertaining to be around and a great guy to chat with, so we knew it would be a fun trip together as a crew.

As Romeo drove, Hubby sat in the front passenger seat and the rest of us in the back two rows. As we turned west from the Perimeter Highway surrounding Winnipeg onto the Trans-Canada Highway, Romeo looked in the rearview mirror and sternly announced: "Alright, we aren't stopping until Moosomin!"

Moosomin, Saskatchewan is located near the Manitoba-Saskatchewan border, about three hundred and fifty-one kilometers – roughly a three-and-a-half-hour drive – from Winnipeg. It is also a popular pitstop for truckers and travelers from all over who hit up the Dairy Queen or the Red Barn restaurant on their way through the prairie provinces. Three and a half hours without a pee-break was too long for most passengers, especially a bunch of teenagers drinking liquids nonstop so as to stay hydrated for fitness testing. It was certainly doable, though, so we buckled up and mentally prepared ourselves and our bladders.

No more than forty minutes or so after making his declaration, and long before we reached Moosomin, Romeo shocked us with one of the more aggressive maneuvers I've ever witnessed as a passenger on the Trans-Canada Highway: a sharp right turn at a high rate of speed into a gas-station rest area. The other boys and I held on for dear life as the van screeched to a stop near the door and Romeo, without so much as a word, sprinted in. We correctly guessed that the call of nature, brought on by a McDonald's sausage and egg McMuffin and hash browns, was too strong for even him to ignore. A few minutes later we erupted into laughter as Romeo, with a sheepish smile on his face and a few beads of sweat dripping down his forehead, made the walk of shame back to the van. The situation had given us instant and endless ammo to chirp Romeo for that entire trip and beyond. Safe to say, the entertainment had started.

As we resumed our pilgrimage westward, Todd pulled out his binder of CDs and took on the role of DJ. He could always feel what the crowd might enjoy, and that day was no different. His binder, a prized possession, contained original discs and burnt mixes labeled by his tag-style: all-caps lettering in black permanent marker. After flipping through the plastic binder sleeves, Todd would carefully select a CD, pass it up to Hubby in the front seat, and then sit back and call out orders about what tracks to play.

Looking back, I believe Todd's taste in music revealed the many intricate layers of his personality. When he was really young, maybe around four or five years old, he was obsessed with New Kids on the Block. He would watch and mimic their dance moves as he belted out their lyrics. Before he ever wanted to be a professional hockey player, he wanted to be a boy band pop star. Those aspirations faded, however, after he and I got stage fright at a neighborhood dance party and were unable to perform Tom Cochrane's "Life Is a Highway" in front of the crowd. By 1995, Todd's music taste had shifted away from boy band pop to bands like The Smashing Pumpkins. Somewhere within the *Mellon Collie and the Infinite Sadness* album, Todd discovered rawness and meaning, and the type of music that can simultaneously remove rage and inspire greatness. From there he became obsessed with Metallica, which never failed to fire him up, then into more of a pop-punk-rock phase, starting with Blink 182. But, by the early 2000s, right around the ninth grade, rap became his music of choice, and, to Dad's dismay, was reverberating throughout the house on a regular basis. Later, when Todd finally got his license, we would hear the latest, bass-heavy beats bumpin' from his green Dodge Neon from blocks away. But his number one genre, especially as he grew older, was country music. There was something about country that just hit his heart the hardest. Knowing this, it came as no surprise that Todd popped a country mix into Romeo's CD player first; and as we cruised through the prairies on that bright and sunny morning it was more than fitting.

It was as we were listening to "Little Bitty," by one of country music's all-time best, Alan Jackson, that Romeo shouted:

"This is your theme song! You're Itty Bitty!"

Romeo, who was certainly not a country aficionado, thought Jackson was saying "Itty Bitty" instead of "Little Bitty." Upon arrival in Regina, Romeo successfully sold the adoption of the name, and it didn't take long to stick. From then on, Todd became known as "Itty Bitty" to most people within the Pats organization. And, within just a few months, Itty Bitty would have a chance to make the team he'd dreamed of playing for.

## Training Camp

Todd had a leather picture frame book with enough room for two eight-by-ten photos. On one side was a photo of the Stanley Cup sitting majestically on its table stand in the Hockey Hall of Fame. While most posters or pictures of the Stanley Cup involve a player triumphantly hoisting it above his head, Todd's rendering was more subtle: just the Cup, in all its power and glory, sitting upright on a draped table, as if it is waiting to be approached and picked up by the team's captain after the ultimate victory.

On the other side of the leather folder was a photo of former NHLer Darcy Tucker wearing his classic home-white Toronto Maple Leafs jersey. Todd had "borrowed" that photo from me, but I didn't put up much of a fight to get it back after I saw how much he cherished it. Todd looked up to Tucker in part because he was also a smaller-sized guy who had proven himself an effective force in the NHL. Todd would take the leather folder out of his bag on long bus rides and stare at the two separate photos inside. I recall watching him from across the bus aisle, wondering where he went in his mind during those daydreams. If I had to guess, I'd say he was envisioning where he would be playing in the next few years. That was Todd, always holding in his mind the next level and how he would get there.

While Tucker had been one of my favorite players for several years, Todd first started really appreciating his game when Jared Bousquet of Titan Sports Management, our agency at the time, told him a story about how Tucker broke into the WHL. At sixteen, Tucker had joined the Kamloops Blazers and ended up being a key player in a dynasty that included multiple Memorial Cup wins. Apparently, Tucker was a magician at face-offs, and could dominate at the dot when his team needed it most. Despite being a small rookie in the Dub, he was the player head coach Tom Renney counted on in big moments, which garnered Tucker some serious respect and pro recognition.

Todd faced a major uphill battle to make the Pats that season, and Tucker's story inspired him at a core level. If Tucker could do it, so could he! Throughout the entire training camp, Todd amped up his game in a serious way, which definitely showed on the ice. A fire had been sparked within him, and a deeper level of self-belief seemed to emerge. If you haven't yet realized, however, Todd was not like most other players. In his mind, he was going to do whatever it took to rise. He was going to battle and skate as hard as he could to stick around for one more day. He knew the odds were against him, but he didn't care. He'd been playing against the odds his entire life.

Todd and I were playing on different teams that camp. There were three or four separate teams of players, each composed of veterans, rookies, and hopefuls scattered equally amongst them. On the first day of scrimmages, Todd was playing on the ice time before mine, so he went to the rink a couple of hours earlier. Rather than waiting around, I headed out early, thinking I'd check out some of Todd's game as I taped my sticks.

I walked into the players' entrance of the Agridome and made my way downstairs to the dressing room – which was located at the ice level right near the entrance to the home and visiting teams' players' boxes – to grab my sticks. Tunnels led to the players' boxes and the ice, and as I glanced down one of them I saw Todd, huffing and puffing, hair all a mess. He was breathing hard, frantically trying to fix his helmet and rearrange his padding so he could get back on the ice.

"What's going on?" I asked.

"I just fought . . . " he replied, trying to sound casual in between gulps of air. His eyes remained fixed on his helmet straps.

"How'd you do?" I eagerly asked, wishing I had been there to see the fight.

"Good . . . I won . . ." he said casually, as he continued to look down at his helmet and straps as he hurriedly worked to get back into action.

Though he was way undersized and never should have been a fighter in hockey, he wasn't going to let questions about his toughness or his ability to handle himself keep him off the Pats roster. In his mind he was just as capable of defending himself as any bigger player, and he wanted that to be known. Aside from our odd living room "cage-rage" fights – when I would catch him with some pretty heavy punches to his face mask as Dad refereed – Todd had only had one previous hockey fight. It had occurred at the Winnipeg Saints spring rookie training camp several months earlier, when he dropped the gloves with Chris Benias ("Benny") – one of the other few shorter players on the ice that day. The two had actually been coaxed and corralled into a fight by the older, bigger players, who wanted to watch the little guys get after each other. Todd managed to catch Benny with a hard right cross to his nose, blowing it up pretty badly and leaving him dripping blood everywhere. For as small as he was, Todd could throw some pretty decent punches. Anyway, that fight with Benny managed to convince Todd that he was capable of handling himself in a scrap if need be. Apparently "if need be" in Todd's mind included at the Pats' main training camp, where he was fighting tooth-and-nail to prove himself. He wanted to make a bold statement, and he did.

Todd was feeling strong and proud after that display, but he seemed to go about it as if it were all business; like it was just something he had to get out of the way. He knew the fight had gotten him noticed even more, gaining him respect by anyone who witnessed or heard about it. The other players and coaches already respected him for his raw skill and determination, but that fight showed a side of a player willing to lay everything on the line. He obviously wasn't destined to be a fighter, but he brought fire to the ice and was willing to show the coaches that he was tough enough to play in the WHL. I was proud of his heart and willpower in that moment. Nothing was going to be stopping him now. Then he strapped his helmet back on and went right back to the bench to get back in the game and keep showing what he had.

Todd's training camp performance was not taken lightly. When camp came to a close, he did not ride back to Winnipeg in the car with Mom and Grandpa as previously expected, but on the Pats' team bus to play exhibition games on the roster with the big squad! When camp started, he was perhaps the only person who thought making the team was even a possibility, but he established himself more with each new shift, earning the right to finally pull that authentic Pats jersey over his head in a WHL exhibition game.

Todd's work ethic and performance paid off when he ultimately was signed to a contract with the Pats, thereby making the WHL at just sixteen years old. This was an incredible feat, but the best part of all was that Todd and I would be playing together again, this time in the best junior hockey league in the world, for a world-class franchise. This was big time!

Todd was an instant hit with the team and the greater Regina community as fans witnessed him work his heart out every shift on the ice. It didn't hurt that he was also seen as the ultimate WHL underdog that season. Fans cheered hard for Todd to succeed, and while he wasn't putting up points or highlight reel goals, they loved watching him buzz around the ice and compete against much bigger opponents. The "Itty Bitty" nickname spread to Rod Pedersen, the voice of the Pats, during live radio broadcasts, and before we knew it, was chanted by faithful Pats fans at every game. Rod also hosted pre-game and post-game radio programming, which included a call-in segment. One night, an elderly Pats fan who apparently didn't understand that the nickname was a term of endearment, called in to the radio station to demand, on-air, that Rod "stop calling Todd Davison Itty Bitty" because "it was mean to make fun of his size." Little did that sweet old lady know how much Todd liked being known by that name. On any given night, during the few shifts per period or game he had, Itty Bitty was witnessed buzzing around the ice giving everything he had. The fans loved him, and he loved them right back.

If Todd had listened to all of the doubters and haters telling him that he was too small or too weak, he would have led a common life; he certainly would not have accomplished all he did. Instead, he either ignored negative opinions and comments altogether or converted the hate and doubt into energy that fueled his fire. He controlled his visions, beliefs, and the effort he could expend towards making any dream a reality, or at least give it a fighting chance. For Todd, especially with regard to hockey, anything was possible, including making the toughest junior hockey league in the world as an undersized sixteen-year-old. Just like he envisioned it, there he was, sitting in his stall in the sacred room.

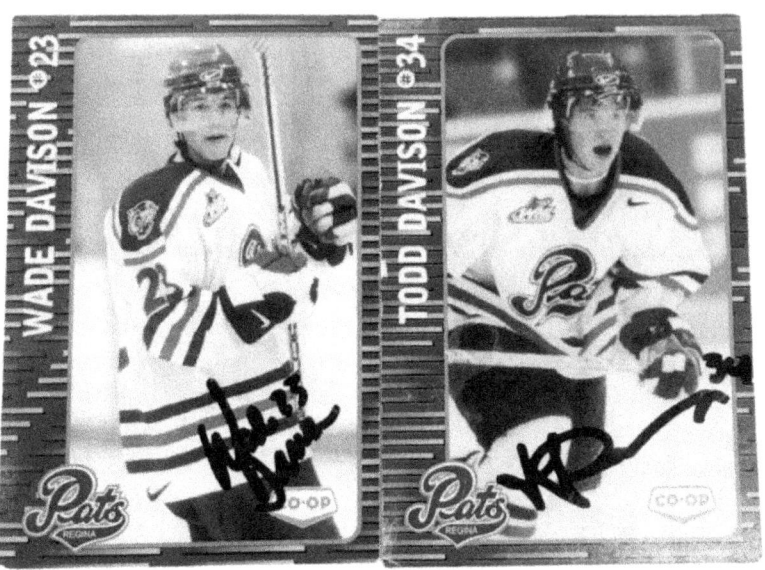

*Our official Regina Pats hockey cards for the 2002-2003 season.*

*Todd (left) and me (right). Photo accompanied the article titled*
*"Brothers Push Each Other to Success"*
*Photo by Greg Harder, courtesy of the Regina Leader-Post.*

# CHAPTER 7

# REGINA RITUALS

Hockey is a game of rituals. When hockey players put on their left skate first, or tape their stick in a specific way, they are performing rituals that mean something to them, as trivial as those acts may seem to an outsider. Performing rituals helps hockey players (and athletes in general) prepare for optimal performance by allowing the headspace to channel energy to focus on the challenge ahead. Rituals offer a sense of order and control to chaotic and uncontrollable game situations, and are part of the preparation process. Beyond individual rituals, there are team rituals; beyond team rituals, there are brotherly rituals.

The bond Todd and I shared extended far beyond hockey; we were side by side, not just on the rink, but during many major life events and tough situations, such as our parents' split. Yet our favorite battles came with skates on our feet and a stick in our hands, geared up with the armor and colors of our team. When we made the Pats together, our battles intensified. With that rise in intensity, new rituals emerged.

As with most teams Todd and I played on together, we had a team pre-game ritual while with Regina, which started with a dynamic warmup. Whenever the digital time clock in our dressing room ticked down to five minutes, a loud "time check" was yelled, intensifying the already high collective energy of the team as puck-drop drew near. Each player would begin making final adjustments to their equipment: jersey on and strapped-up; helmet feeling snug, with a crystal-clear visor; and, of course, gloves feeling good, with just the right amount of moisture in the leather palm. With the careful selection of his battle weapon from the stick rack, each man became locked, loaded, and ready to roll. We would then form a line to the dressing room door, our blood racing as we waited to get out onto the ice.

From the exhibition season onwards, our team's walkout line order was established, and very rarely was someone daring enough to deviate from it for the rest of the season. Although our stalls were not side-by-side, Todd and I came together in line, with him positioning himself directly in front of me, or maybe I positioned myself directly behind him. Either way, we had established our own brotherly ritual within the team's ritual. I loved seeing that "T. Davison" name-bar in front of me as we marched out of the dressing room, through the tunnel, and onwards to action.

The Agridome was a great junior hockey arena that held over six thousand fans. During the hockey season, Pats games were the big show in town, and that is how we liked it. While we didn't sell out every game, we had a very loyal fan base and always drew thousands of people. By the time we walked out of our dressing room door, most attending fans were already in their seats, and the entire arena was darkened, buzzing with excitement.

Our team entered the ice for the start of home games through a giant inflatable Pats-themed bulldog head that was positioned at the north end of the rink. Before storming the ice, we would wait in the Zamboni tunnel for the entrance lights, smoke show, and the music to get cued up just right. We usually had a minute or two to soak in the energy before *Sandstorm* by Darude – our intro theme song – would be blasted over the loudspeakers to kickoff the action.

Guys would be hollering one-liners, jumping around, or standing stoically still. I stood directly behind Todd, looking over him. I thought of myself as his protector of sorts; at least that's what I wanted to be. In reality, especially considering the WHL was such a tough league, we were lucky enough to have some real tough guys on our team, like future NHL heavyweight Colton Orr to protect us all. Symbolically, however, I had Todd's back, and he knew that.

Right before we hit the ice – as the announcer bellowed out over the loudspeakers, "Here come your Regina Pats!" – Todd would turn around and give me a few hard slashes across the shin-pads, and I would give him a few back. Those pre-game shin-pad slashes might have been my favorite thing about playing with Todd with the Pats. It was such a small act, but it was our ritual. In that moment, we would set aside all the other brotherly bullshit that may have been between us in the outer world; it no longer mattered. We would hit the ice as hard as we could and take some laps in our zone before making our way to the Pats bench. Then we'd stand beside each other as every voice in the place sang "O Canada."

## Teammate Bros.

As we waited for the "Davison" line to be called into action, we sat by or stood side-by-side with excitement and pride. How we ended up there together leads me to believe that some things are just destined to happen. The stars aligned for us to play together, and it was all part of some grander game plan. We weren't the kind of brothers who would have emotion-filled talks about our feelings and personal lives, but in those moments on the bench or on the ice, we were as close as brothers could be. In unspoken words – witnessed by the hockey gods and fans alike – that is where our true bond existed. We were hockey brothers, and game time was our favorite space to share.

We typically played together on the Pats' fourth line – Todd as centerman and I as the right-winger – and did our best every shift to contribute to the team's success. We weren't the type of line that was going to put up a lot of goals – we were there to defend the zone, put pressure on the other team, and generate energy and rest time for our team's top lines. We worked our asses off, and it didn't go unnoticed by the fans. Soon "T. Davison" and "W. Davison" jerseys were spotted in the crowd amongst the fans, including a particular pair of gals who habitually waited for us after home games. The girls were great fans and nice people, but they essentially stalked us.

One night, Todd and I were participating in a joint Pats-Western Pizza promotional event for which certain players delivered pizzas to customers. Imagine our surprise when we showed up for a delivery and found the two girls waiting for us, all smiles and flirty glances. Apparently they had called every Western Pizza in Regina until they found the location the Davison brothers were operating out of and specifically requested that we deliver their order. It was both flattering and awkward, and after a few moments of polite conversation we hightailed it out of that apartment looking at each other with raised eyebrows and a fair amount of relief that we had escaped unscathed. It was a strange experience, to say the least.

Todd and I were linemates pretty much our entire rookie season, right from the first exhibition game. One of those first exhibition games was against Barks' team, the Medicine Hat Tigers. We played well and ended up scoring two goals together. I scored both goals, but Todd created the rebound on the first one by driving wide and taking a good shot to the far side, which the goalie kicked out to the high slot right on my tape. If I'm not mistaken, Todd created some space for me to walk in, toe drag the Tiger defenseman, and go backhand bardown over the glove on the second one. We were named first and second stars of the game, and took our respective turns stepping onto the ice to give the fans a humble wave. That was the start of a special season together.

## Escaping the Boogeyman

As symbolized by our pre-game ritual, I had Todd's back and he had mine. We played beside each other, and we played for each other. And, despite all of our interpersonal tensions and brotherly baggage, we stood up for each other.

Later in the season in a game against the Tigers, I was hit from behind as I battled for the puck near the redline boards. My neck snapped back as the rest of my body thrust forward towards the ice. Before I could even get back to my feet I saw Todd swoop over, drop his gloves, and jump the guy who'd hit me. He had previously been tentative to jump into fights in the WHL – including one specific instance in Saskatoon when I got absolutely pumped in front of his eyes. (He actually caught shit from our equipment manager for not doing anything.) But his courage had grown over the course of the season, and now his short arms were throwing punches as hard as he could in retaliation to the dirty hit on his brother/linemate/teammate. Though I was instantly proud of him for taking action, I was not going to just stand back and let the fight play out. I regained my bearings and pushed myself to my knees, then dropped my gloves, grabbed the guy's other shoulder and started throwing punches. There we were, side by side once again, throwing punches in concert at the same guy's face as he attempted to turtle. In the words of Reid Peterson, the Pats' Assistant General Manager at the time, "The Davison brothers had *a* good fight!"

Two guys against one in a fight typically doesn't fly in junior hockey, and especially not in the Western League. Todd and I expected the chaos that ensued, however, there was one major problem we were completely unaware of: Derek Boogaard (also known as "The Boogeyman") just happened to be on the ice at the same time. While Todd was probably the smallest player to ever put on a Pats jersey, Boogaard (who is now deceased; and may he rest in peace) may have been the biggest of all time. With his skates on, Boogaard stood nearly seven feet tall and filled out his frame with nearly two hundred and sixty pounds. He looked like an absolute beast when he suited up in his hockey gear, and long before he became one of the toughest NHL enforcers in history, he was terrorizing young guys in the WHL by his presence alone. At the time of our brawl, he was sporting a Tigers' logo across his extra broad chest.

As gloves and gear flew around the ice and players paired off in a quasi-line brawl, the Boogeyman set his sights on me from across the neutral zone. At the time I was fixated on the Tiger who hit me and therefore oblivious to the fact that one of the toughest and most dangerous players in the hockey world was charging at me. Somehow, at the exact moment our fight was taken to the ice, the Boogeyman missed grabbing me and ended up tripping and falling over my back. Before he had a chance to turn around and come at me again, Jordan Clarke, one of our toughest veteran teammates, risked his own face and life by grabbing Boogaard, helping me avert the imminent destruction that was coming my way.

As the refs broke up the multiple tussles and settled things down, Todd and I were both sent to the dressing room – Todd for jumping the player who hit me, and me for being third man in, or something like that. We entered the empty "PDR" together and took to our individual stalls, both huffing and puffing as we heard thousands of fans cheering and yelling in glee from all of the carnage. Then, intuitively realizing it was a pretty rare and special moment, we looked at each other with slight smiles as we shared that sacred space without anyone else around.

The trainers soon came into the room to check on us and found we'd both escaped injury, albeit narrowly. When I undid my tie-down strap and peeled off my jersey, I was shocked to see a diagonal gash of about twelve inches across the "23" on my back. I held my jersey up to get a closer look and for Todd to see. Our jaws dropped and our eyebrows raised up as we realized that the gash was from one of Boogaard's size-fourteen or so skates – like a giant scar left behind from a shark that narrowly missed its meal. I'd gotten damn lucky during that one. Considering it was with a legend like Boogaard, that whole melee was one of the most legendary brotherly dust-ups of all time. Looking back at the highlight reel of life, that remains one of my favorite moments.

I recall our beauty-and-beast of a Pats teammate, former NHLer heavyweight and fellow Winnipegger Colton Orr ("Orrsy") telling me that he wished he could play on the same team as his younger brother, Jamison, who also played in the WHL. If brothers made the league they typically played on different teams and battled against each other. This was so with Orrsy, and also with Boogaard and his brother Aaron. Comments like that from Orrsy made me appreciate how special our situation was even more.

## One of the Boys

Todd was loved by all of the fellas on the team. You've heard of class clowns? Well, Todd was often the dressing room clown, or, depending on the day, the hotel clown. He found a way to have a deep connection with nearly all his teammates, which is no easy task in this world of delicate or hardened hockey personalities. And his connections with others typically resulted in their laughter, even if he made an ass of himself.

From a very young age he was a character amongst his teammates. One disturbing yet hilarious pre-teen performance that Todd used to put on was farting, then sucking the air back in, and then farting again . . . until he literally ran out of gas. He used to do the same thing on that bottom bunk, while I was dying laughing with the sheet over my face on the top bunk. Disgusting, I know; but this was real life, unfiltered. Sean Skene, one of Todd's teammates and a huge fan of the fart game, recalls a special performance for the Mustang boys in a Minneapolis hotel room. Todd – wearing only boxers and a t-shirt – was on all fours on the carpet, with a bunch of the boys around him counting with each push-out and suck-back in.

"He was at fart forty," Sean said, "and getting increasingly more excited by the numbers when suddenly he counts to 'forty-SHIT!' We all stopped, watching in silence, as he turned and picked up a popcorn sized turd-nugget off the carpet and ran giggling into the bathroom." He may not have broken the record that evening, but I think that was the end of the fart game for good. Thank God.

As Todd grew older he was still always down for some adventure and a little bit of mischief. In Regina, when the rookie party rolled around, Todd dove in head-first and went as hard as possible, slamming warm beers and shots with a giant grin on his face. He may have been a little too excited that night, and his alcohol intake resulted in him being taken home an hour after we arrived. Todd's eagerness to party at that event was not so much about trying to impress anyone, trying to fit in, or succumbing to peer pressure; it was more so about letting his teammates know that he was fully committed to the team, and was not holding back to save himself. He just wanted to have a good time with the boys.

Orrsy was one of a group of veterans who used to love having Todd around, and would sneak him out of our billet house past curfew for him to hang out with the vets and drive them around while they were having a few beers. On one particular occasion, Orrsy and some of the older vets snuck out to the casino and chose Todd to be their chauffeur. They knew he was loyal, and they knew he was down to get in on the fun – even if it meant just being their escort and waiting outside. I didn't find out that he was out with the boys until the next afternoon during our pre-practice meeting. Apparently the fellas were spotted enjoying themselves and heating up the tables at the casino a little too much, which resulted in an anonymous report being made to our coaches about Pats players putting on a scene in a place they weren't supposed to be. This whole dilemma resulted in an awful, punishing bag-skate led by Bob Lowes – one of the most intense coaches the WHL has ever seen, followed by a bus ride to Red Deer, and a 6-0 drumming by the Rebels. The point of the story is that Orrsy and the other vets weren't calling just anyone to drive them around and have fun when the stakes were high; they were calling Itty Bitty, and he loved every minute of it.

*From left to right: Me, Daniel Waschuk, Todd, Jesse Deckert ("Decks"), playing the Wheat Kings in Brandon at the Keystone Centre during the 2002-2003 season.*

*Me and Todd standing next to each other on the Pats bench during the 2002-2003 season.*

*Left to Right: Coach Bob Lowes, Todd, and me during the 2002-2003 season with the Pats.*

CHAPTER 8

# PLAYING THE BEST

## Tough Grinding

Though Todd was always an effective player on the ice, stirring up energy and creating momentum for the team, he struggled to rack up any points in his rookie season with the big boys in the WHL. The league was insanely good that year, and was composed of future NHL studs, including, to name a few, Duncan Keith, Shea Weber, Ryan Getzlaf, Dustin Byfuglien, Joffrey Lupul, Brent Seabrook, Dion Phaneuf, Johnny Boychuk, Devan Dubnyk, Brooks Laich, Boyd Gordon, Braydon Coburn, Nigel Dawes, Scottie Upshall, Kris Versteeg, Clarke MacArthur, Ryan Craig, Eric Fehr, and Jordin Tootoo.

At the end of the regular season Todd hadn't scored a single goal and had notched only two assists. In forty-eight regular season games, he typically got a few shifts per period, and virtually no special teams' play. The ice-time was allotted to the best and more effective players on the team, so talented nineteen- and twenty-year-old players rightfully got the lion's share, with us rookies basically giving the top line guys a longer rest and trying to keep the energy up for the team. But don't let those dismal statistics distract from Todd's talent and potential: the WHL was a tough league to put up numbers in general, but it is especially tough when you're an undersized, fourth-line centerman that gets minimal ice-time and no power-play time. Further adding to the difficulty was playing with me and a guy named Brit Dougherty – one of our team's fighters – who was the furthest thing from an offensive playmaker. Safe to say that Todd was not going to be racking up numbers as a fourth-liner in the Dub playing between us.

Despite Todd's ultra-low point totals, his game was developing well as he started to become more comfortable playing at such an elite level with giant men all around him. According to Worky, it was "all the more impressive that he was able to survive [in the WHL] . . . and I do mean survive." To do so Todd had to adapt his style and, like any young rookie playing at an advanced level, he knew he had a lot to learn about the game. Through hard work and determination his skills and abilities were consistently on the rise, especially relative to players his age. I knew he had the game, and so did most others. But with hockey, as in life, sometimes you just need the right chance to show what you've got. I always knew that Todd just needed his proper shot.

## Sid the Kid

The Canada Winter Games take place once every four years, and in late February of 2003, Todd left Regina for a two-week period to play for Team Manitoba. The event took place on the east coast of Canada that year, in Bathurst-Campbellton, New Brunswick. The hockey tournament was "U-16," meaning the players were no older than sixteen years old by birth year.

Team Manitoba was coached by our former Midget AAA coach, Kevin Benson. The team contained the very best players from the province, including Barks and Boyd. Barks was named captain of the team, and Todd was named as one of the assistant captains. Todd was also expected – based on his spring and summer Program of Excellence camp performances – to be one of the team's top performers in the competition. He was highly rated going into the tournament and figured to be a major asset in contributing to the scoresheet. The Hockey Manitoba brass evaluated closely and included the following comments on his official feedback report:

"Todd does so many things well and shows a great competitive spirit every time he steps on the ice; [his] greatest attribute is his speed and ability to read the plays and hit the 'holes' in full strides; [he] shows a great deal of offensive talent in combination with defensive zone awareness; and, [he] plays a gritty nature and doesn't allow his size to be a factor while playing." These were among several other comments praising his game and the attitude he brought to the rink.

Todd knew he would be getting way more ice time than he'd been getting as a fourth-liner or healthy scratch with the Pats, and he was going to be playing on a team with some of his best hockey buddies from home. As an added bonus, he would be getting a physical break from the much older, bigger, and tougher opponents he was facing in the Dub. The stage was set, and Todd couldn't wait to perform. He would be competing against the best sixteen-and-under hockey talent from across Canada, including Sidney Crosby, who captained Team Nova Scotia.

Crosby shouldn't need any introduction here, but to those who don't know, he is a 1987-born Canadian hockey phenom who will no doubt go down in history as one of the best players of all time. Crosby is the elite of the elite, and his professional career has been nothing short of spectacular thus far. By the time of the 2003 Canada Winter Games, Crosby had already been a well-known name in Canadian hockey rinks for nearly a decade. Every NHL team was watching and looking to draft him, as there was no doubt Crosby would have major success ahead. While most players and fans were also watching Crosby with awe, Todd was doing his best to size him up as an opponent and play him hard.

While I can't say it with certainty, Todd was likely focused on being as good as he could be in an effort to prove he was as capable as Crosby of impacting the game at hand. But an obstacle arose: several of the Team Manitoba players, including Todd, got really sick with a flu-like virus during the tournament. The sickness hit Todd especially hard during the game against Team Nova Scotia. Mom recalls watching him closely and seeing him throw up in between some of his shifts. During the first intermission, just before skating off the ice, Todd told Mom that he was very sick. Despite this, Todd, as he always did, played his heart out, every shift.

Todd scored the first goal of the game during the opening shift of the second period. Crosby answered to tie it up two minutes later. Then Todd assisted Boyd's goal to give Team Manitoba a 2-1 lead. Crosby again answered with an assist a few minutes later. In a fierce battle, Team Nova Scotia won 3-2 in overtime, with none other than Crosby scoring the winner. By all scouting reports, Todd's performance was very strong. He finished the game with one goal, one assist, and one minor penalty – a classic Todd game and his own spin on the ol' Gordy Howe hat trick. Crosby finished with two goals and one assist. But the coolest thing of all was that Todd got a chance to play against one of the very best in the world, and put up numbers on the game sheet right across from him. During the 2005-2006 season, three seasons after that game against Team Manitoba and Todd, Crosby went on to score more than a hundred points in the NHL, and was runner up to Alexander Ovechkin for the Calder Cup for NHL rookie of the year. Talk about playing the best. As he shined on ice and on the game sheet, Todd was getting closer to being recognized as a big-time player with the potential to play pro one day.

*Official Gamesheet of Team Nova Scotia versus Team Manitoba at the 2003 Canada Winter Games. Sidney Crosby (#9) scored two goals and got one assist; and Todd (#18) scored one goal and got one assist.*

*Cam Barker ("Barks") and Todd, playing for Team Manitoba in the 2003 Canada Winter Games in New Brunswick.*

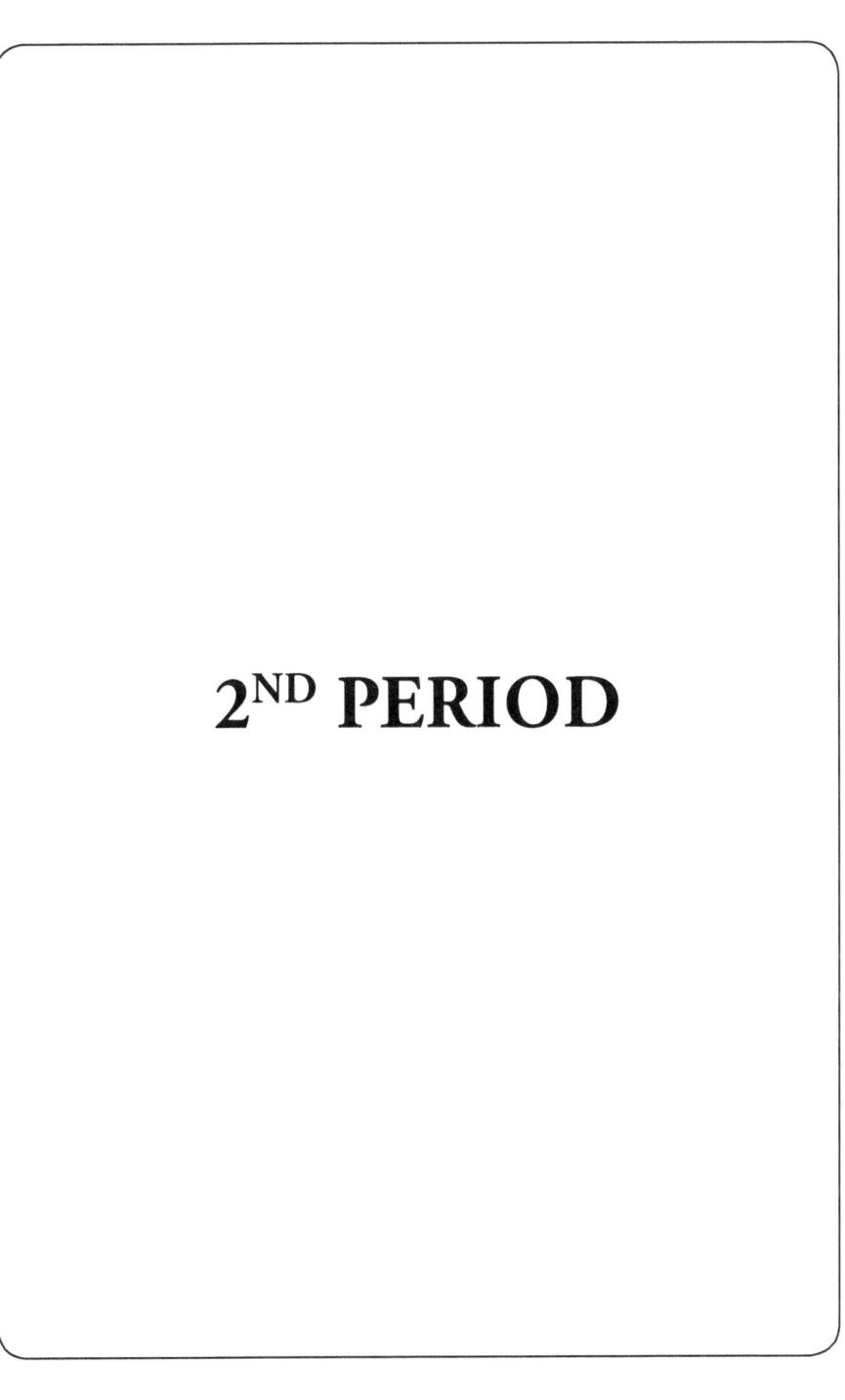

# 2<sup>ND</sup> PERIOD

# CHAPTER 9

# CRACKED ICE

Our sophomore season with the Pats got off to a seriously rocky start, and it took the form of a perfect storm brewing over the Saskatchewan prairies.

After driving six hours from Winnipeg to Regina, I had tight and heavy legs during my first pre-camp skate. Speed was never my forte to begin with, and the long drive certainly didn't help matters; plus, between supplementing with creatine over the summer and naturally gaining muscle I was ten pounds heavier than I'd been at the end of the previous season. That first sluggish skate was the first the coaches were seeing of my game in several months, and led to me being labeled as "out-of-shape" before training camp even began. Ironically, only one week earlier in Winnipeg, during an *Edge of Excellence* skating camp, I'd felt better than ever about my strength and skill. I had gotten a lot stronger and made significant progress in my game during the off-season. Apparently, others disagreed, something I learned when our team's equipment manager – who was probably a hundred pounds overweight himself – made a disparaging comment to me as I rode the stationary exercise bike in the weight room. It was something like, "You can't get into shape in one day."

I was incredibly rattled when I heard that statement, and though I didn't verbally respond I was thinking, *Fuck you, you fat fuck!*

To make matters worse, I took a very hard open-ice hit early in camp that jammed my wrist, weakening it to the point that I literally couldn't raise a puck off the ice. I would have had a hard time cracking a Junior B roster with the condition my wrist was in. I figured that I'd be out of the lineup for a few days letting it heal, but that didn't happen.

I told the athletic trainer about the complete lack of strength or mobility in my wrist, but he didn't take me seriously and basically dismissed it as no big deal. But it was a big deal, especially when I was fighting to keep my spot on the roster. When the coaches inquired about my wrist, the trainer told them it seemed fine and that I was likely exaggerating any pain or issue. That trainer was never my biggest fan, dating back to when he snapped on me for having my Sony headphones too loud when he was trying to sleep during a long, overnight bus trip home. Now he was passing biased and inaccurate messages to the coach, which didn't help my situation and put me in a less-than-stellar light in the eyes of the Pats' coaching staff and managers as we went into the new year.

Simultaneously, Todd was having his own, much more serious issues. He began to experience a lot more pain and sensitivity in his shoulder. The injury, which Todd first complained about the prior March at the Canada Games after taking a big hit, was not going away, but rather getting worse by the day. It flared up any time he gave or took a hit, or even made firm contact with another player. This pain – and his attempt to avoid triggering it – led to a hesitancy that dampened his typical feisty and fearless style of play. He was playing more guardedly and was avoiding the battle areas. Shoulder pads only do so much to dampen the blows, and they surely do not take the internal pain of impact away.

More importantly, Todd's shoulder pain was accompanied by a feeling that something wasn't quite right inside his body. His energy levels were down and his body was struggling to operate at full throttle. He fought through on a daily basis and continued to play as hard as he could every single shift, but the pain and tenderness in his shoulder would just not go away. He tried to ignore it, but the pain only worsened.

On the surface it simply looked like Todd's endurance was not very strong and that he was playing scared. He had worked his ass off all summer and should have been in great shape, but something was up. It appeared as if he was having a hard time taking in oxygen, and he was struggling more than I had ever witnessed in his entire life. My biggest moment of concern came when I noticed that the color in his face was off after hard-skating drills or after games. At one point after an early training camp skate, I noticed Todd's cheeks were a bluish color as he struggled to catch his breath. He was so uncharacteristically bagged and winded, as well as confused by what was happening. I was confused too, as I'm sure the coaches were. He didn't look strong and able; he looked compromised and vulnerable.

He went to the training staff, telling them he wasn't quite feeling like himself, and was really struggling. For a junior or pro hockey player to tell a trainer (or coach) that "something isn't right" without knowing what that "something" is, is a courageous yet risky act. When hearing something like that, so many coaches, especially at higher levels, have a tendency to quickly label the player as "weak," "soft," or an "exaggerator." Todd was none of those things, but he was getting desperate in trying to alert others that something was off inside of him. But no one had an answer for him, and he didn't know what to do. Time was ticking and his pain was getting worse, yet no answers were in sight.

Though I don't know exactly how the trainers and coaches responded to Todd's complaints, they at least heard him out and arranged a doctor's appointment, which led to blood work being done. The blood work results, reviewed in early September, revealed that he had low hemoglobin and hematocrit levels. According to the Mayo Clinic, "Hemoglobin (Hb or Hgb) is a protein in red blood cells that carries oxygen throughout the body . . . [and] can be associated with a disease or condition that causes your body to have too few red blood cells." Further, "[a] lower than normal hematocrit can indicate: an insufficient supply of healthy red blood cells (anemia), [or] [a] large number of white blood cells due to long-term illness, infection or a white blood cell disorder . . ." The tests had revealed that Todd was indeed sick, but with what remained a mystery.

Whoever had reviewed Todd's blood test results made the handwritten notation "viral effect?" on the page. Surely this was the smoking gun that explained Todd's low energy levels and change in health, right? It was probably something simple, like mononucleosis . . . at least that was on the radar as an option. But the mono test came back negative, and our confusion deepened. Though subtle, there were clear clues to the severity of Todd's situation, but thus far they had led nowhere. More testing would be necessary to get to the root cause of his low hemoglobin and hematocrit levels, and a follow-up appointment was called for.

One year after breaking into the Dub together with confidence and strength, there we were, in an utterly dismal state. Todd was playing through his shoulder pain and ultra-low energy levels, and I was without power to shoot or pass the puck because of my wrist injury. While we were both X-rayed, no MRIs or other testing was done. While I would never attempt to put my wrist injury in the same category as Todd's shoulder injury or disease, the injuries had one commonality: they both caused pain and weakness but could not be seen on X-rays. So, without "broken bones" we did what we always did: we showed up and played on as hard as we could.

## The Beatdown

Have you ever been punched in the face or head? Have you ever been punched in the face or head *really hard*, over and over again? Well, I have, and so has Todd, and when you are on the receiving end of a good ol' fashioned beatdown, there isn't much fun to be had.

As the 2003 Pats' training camp came to an end, exhibition games fired up in early September. As usual, exhibition games were played against the teams closest to us, which included games against the Moose Jaw Warriors, a team based forty-five minutes west of Regina and the Pats' biggest rival in the league. We made the short bus trip to the old "Crushed Can," one of the grimiest rinks in the league with some of the most ruthless fans, at least back in those days. Mom made the road trip

from Winnipeg to attend that game, and, more importantly, to introduce us to Molly – our beautiful six-week-old black lab cross puppy.

Late in the game, a full-out line brawl erupted. Every single player
on the sheet was paired up against an opponent. At that time, Todd had
not even yet turned seventeen years old and was still one of the smallest players in the league. He was also feeling weaker than ever. Now he
found himself tied up with a Moose Jaw player who towered over him
by at least six inches and probably had fifty pounds on him. Todd's odds
weren't looking so hot, and with the referees scattered all over the ice
and carnage happening everywhere, there was nowhere to escape and no
pause button to hit.

I was on the bench at the time, and from this vantage point I had
a clear view of Todd's fight, which started directly across the ice at our
team's third-period blue line. The Warrior struck first, catching Todd
with a few hard right-handed punches that sent blood spurting from his
nose and soon covered his face. He tried to tuck his head down to avoid
further punches but it didn't help. He fought back as hard as he could,
but the other player was too overpowering.

I helplessly watched as Todd got repeatedly pummeled; then, after
about a minute his opponent's arms weakened enough for Todd to tie
them up. Todd squeezed and pulled down hard, seemingly ending the
madness. They locked arms together and pulled in fairly close as they
glided around the neutral zone. Todd seemed to relax in that moment,
if only for a split second. Exhausted and beaten up by this point, he
turned and tucked his side into the Warrior logo on the chest of his
opponent's jersey, where he could rest for a few moments. His mouth
was gaped wide open gasping for air; I remember seeing his blue mouth
guard showing prominently. Things seemed to be calming down all over
the ice. The worst seemed to be over.

Then, something – I don't recall what – triggered the chaos to level-
up and resume. The Moose Jaw fans, wanting to see more blood and
mayhem, cheered louder. By this point, the refs had completely lost
control. When an on-ice situation such as a line brawl gets too insane,

refs will often just skate away and let players have at it until they tire themselves out and voluntarily lay down their swords. The experienced refs have seen these brawls go down before, and they know hockey players can only throw so many punches until their arms feel like they are going to fall off and there is literally no strength left to continue to fight. In the meantime, they'll have their notepads and pens out and jot down who did what and which players will be facing suspension or other disciplinary action.

Sure enough, Todd's fight seemed to wind down and I thought he and his opponent would just tie up with each other until the madness stopped. Suddenly, out of nowhere, his opponent dragged him down the ice and began to wail away again. I froze for a moment as I scanned the situation and quickly analyzed my options, which were: 1) watching my little brother get beaten up as Mom watched helplessly from the stands; or 2) jumping the bench and beating the shit out of Todd's opponent, or at least trying to. It was a no-brainer.

Pushing through my teammates, I jumped onto the ice, threw off my gloves and frantically skated as hard as I could. My vision narrowed as the adrenaline coursed through my body, and I tripped over some of the sticks or gloves that were scattered all over the ice as I skated towards my brother. As I regained my footing I caught the attention of the linesmen and referees, who started skating towards me from across the ice at full speed. By that point, Todd had gotten dragged to the goal crease at the far end of the ice in the Moose Jaw zone. I got within a few feet of Todd's fight before I was tackled by the linesmen. By the way, the WHL linesmen are not your typical scrawny teenage youths, but big strong men who had to be able to protect themselves in a league of beasts. I fought to resist and break free, but it was pointless as two of them tangled me up. Since striking an official is akin to hitting a law enforcement officer, I was pretty much helpless at that moment. At the signal of the referees, two arena security guards entered the ice and joined the crew in grabbing me. The two OBO security guards, in their big boots and orange security jackets, along with the two big linesmen, guided me off the ice through the Zamboni gate and pushed me in the direction of our team's dressing room.

Unfortunately for me, I didn't get a chance to dance with the piece of shit who beat up Todd. Considering my freshness and level of excitement, that one would have been fun, and I suspect the knuckles on my right hand would have a few extra scars today. On the bright side, Todd's fight had finally stopped, so at least he was saved from further beatdown.

After my early departure from the game, I showered in the dressing room and was one of the first of my team dressed and packed up. Todd was taken directly to the trainer's room. In visiting arenas, there is typically a designated spot where players can meet with their family members who attended the game. I went upstairs in the arena and found Mom waiting there, our puppy Molly by her side. Though she had tried to be strong in the moment, I could tell she had been crying … a lot. It wasn't the first time she'd witnessed a brawl, but to see her son beaten by a much larger player while blood-thirsty fans cheered on was something altogether different. Hockey moms learn to be tough, but they can't help but feel the pain they know their kids are feeling.

Eventually, Todd came up the stairs from the dressing room and joined us. His nose was split wide open right across the bridge and clearly broken. He had welts and scrapes all over his face, was spattered with fresh and dried blood, and had gauze in his nostrils. Half of the whites of his eyes were deep red from the broken blood vessels. The team trainer had tried to clean him up, but there wasn't much that could be done at that point. My brother was in rough shape.

When she saw him, the last bit of Mom's composure failed her and she began to cry again. She pulled Todd into an embrace while he played it cool in case anyone was watching.

Slowly, Todd pulled away and picked up Molly, holding her tightly but gently against his heart. Though beaten and bloody, Todd gave all his love and energy to an innocent puppy, that, in Todd's mind, needed protection and care far more than he did. In that moment, Molly became "Todd's dog," and would faithfully remain by his side.

## Everything Changes

I was given a five-game suspension for my actions. It was a heavy penalty, but I understood why it had to be enforced: jumping the bench is a cardinal sin in hockey and letting it go unpunished would lead to an already violent and volatile game turning into sheer mayhem. Our coach, Bob Lowes, told me that he was not upset with me, that he knew I'd just been trying to protect my brother. Though his words gave me some solace, they couldn't erase the disappointment I felt at being out of the lineup for the next several games, including the upcoming regular season home opener against the Saskatoon Blades.

With his face injuries still healing, Todd was scratched from that game as well. We watched together from the stands, not an easy thing for two boys who lived to play hockey. Between our respective physical states and the fact that I was suspended for four more games, things weren't looking great for the Davison brothers at the start of the 2003-2004 season. Little did we know these setbacks were just a hint of what was to come.

As the days dragged on, Todd's play became less tenacious as he continually attempted to avoid contact to his shoulder. He also still couldn't figure out why his typical strong and consistent energy was lacking. As usual, though, he showed up and did the work, playing through the pain and fatigue until he felt himself again. That's all he knew, and that's all he could do. But before he could return to health and get back to playing at a hundred percent, an absolute bomb was dropped on us.

## New Gear Day

On Tuesday, September 16, 2003, Todd and I arrived at the dressing room after school to discover that our team's new equipment had arrived. This was new gear day, which is like a junior hockey player's Christmas morning! As the name suggests, this is the day when the team's sponsoring equipment manufacturer finally delivers the custom-made, team-specific gloves, helmets, and hockey pants (also known as "breezers," for my American friends). No longer would the players have to wear last year's gear, which by that time had started to stink and fall apart. This was a day to get your fresh-for-your-palms brand new team gloves, and your new team helmet, shiny and clean as can be.

That season, new gear day was especially exciting: the entire CHL had cut ties with Nike and signed a new deal with CCM, meaning that no player would ever again be subjected to wear, in my opinion, one of the worst-looking hockey helmets ever designed – the Nike Quest. Anyone who played in the CHL around 2002-2003 knows exactly what I am talking about. Anyway, my new shiny blue Pats CCM helmet looked great, and my confidence was sky-high with a fresh visor locked in. My new blue, red and white gloves with "Pats" stitched directly on the glove were sweet too. I was loving the feel of them as I worked and massaged the gloves to loosen them up. After spending time getting my new gear dialed in to my liking, I sat down at my stall in an excited state, ready to start getting dressed for practice. Todd was doing the same. With that fresh gear, it was time for a fresh start to the season.

But just as I began to gear up for practice, the equipment manager, in an atypically solemn tone, said: "Davisons, head up to Brent's office . . ."

"Brent's office?" I thought, completely caught off guard.

Brent Parker was the Pats' General Manager, and though I knew he had an office in the rink I had never been up there. I didn't even know exactly where it was. Todd and I didn't say much, we just looked at each other with confusion then exited the dressing room and walked up the Agridome steps to the main concourse level. Our nervousness grew as we approached the executive offices of the arena, thinking that we were going to get traded. On the other hand, it might be about some promotional deal, or off-ice marketing function.

We were greeted by an administration lady, who politely pointed out the chairs we were to sit in while we waited. We took our seats and looked around at the unfamiliar place, which was decked out with all sorts of Pats memorabilia from decades past, trying to distract ourselves until we got called in.

After what seemed like forever, Bob Lowes opened an office door, peeked out his head, and said, "Wade, come on in." His tone didn't really reveal anything, but I found it odd that they were calling us in individually. I stood up and looked back at Todd, then walked into the office to see Brent, Lowes, and both assistant coaches, Chad Mercier and Drew Callander sitting solemnly.

*Oh boy . . . this doesn't look good.* I felt the blood drain from my face and my gut clench as I took the lone chair positioned across from them.

I was quickly told that I was being released. Apparently they had shopped around trade deals, but though some teams were interested in me nothing came about. They didn't go into a lot of detail, but thanked me for my service and wished me well. They tried to let me down easy, but it hurt like hell. Just like that – in the span of less than five minutes – I was snipped from the league of my dreams. They didn't say anything about Todd's status, but I had the feeling that wasn't going to be good news either.

I walked out of Brent's office and looked at Todd, who with wide eyes was eagerly awaiting an update.

"I got released . . . " I said in an ashamed and quiet tone.

"Are you fuckin' kidding me?!" Todd erupted, enraged by the news but trying not to lose it.

He didn't even have ten seconds to process things because he was instantly called in. I remember feeling that pit in my stomach again as I watched him get up and walk towards that office.

As I waited for him, my thoughts returned to my own devastating news. For so long I had been focused on my Dub dreams, and now that they had been crushed, I had no idea what I was going to do next. After what seemed like forever, Todd stormed out of the office with a scowl on his face and anger in his eyes. Sure enough, he had been released too. I was sad and contemplative, but he was furious.

Playing for the Pats, and being a part of that organization, had meant everything to him. He was so proud, so devoted, and so dedicated to that team, and he saw a big future with them… for good reason. Only weeks earlier when training camp began, he had been told he would be a key part of the team's future, so to say he was stunned by the news was an understatement.

We walked back down to the dressing room without many words exchanged. Our futures uncertain, we knew only that we no longer belonged there. We were now team-less outsiders, with no more right to be in the dressing room than any random fan.

We walked by the trainer's room and saw our game jerseys hanging separately from the rest of the team jerseys; soon the equipment manager would unstitch our "W. Davison" and "T. Davison" name-bars and throw them in the garbage. We arrived back at our stalls to see those new helmets and new gloves had already been taken away. They certainly hadn't wasted any time in removing evidence of us from the place.

## Garbage Bag Walkout

Being released is one of the worst things an athlete can experience. Being part of a team is a sacred thing, and players devote their hearts, minds, and bodies in service of it and to each other. When they are released, that relationship is instantly severed, leaving them feeling lost and alone. It is also a brutal blow to the ego, as implied in the release is that the player is valueless to the team, so much so that they were not even worth a trade. It is completely demoralizing and humiliating.

Getting released from a CHL team can be extra harsh, as these sixteen to twenty-year-olds have dedicated their entire lives to playing hockey at the highest levels, most with the hopes of making the NHL, only to be kicked off the ladder as they were climbing. They have also, as discussed earlier, forfeited their NCAA eligibility, meaning a hockey scholarship to an American university is no longer an option. In most cases, being released from a CHL team is essentially a good-bye kiss to the youngster's

NHL dreams, and leaves them with major regrets about choosing to play in the league in the first place.

Though I was hit hard by the news, my brother was even more so. He felt betrayed by the team he had given his hockey heart to so completely, and cheated out of the four more full seasons of junior hockey he'd thought were in front of him. He had risked his entire hockey future on a WHL career, which ended, at least temporarily, only one year after he was signed. I can only imagine how confusing and infuriating that was for him.

And we weren't the only ones shocked by the release. Many of our teammates were shaken by the news as well, and now worried about their own spots on the team. Some of the older veterans, however, didn't seem to care; they had seen countless releases and trades of teammates over the years and saw it as part of the game. Todd and I had previously been warned that junior hockey was a business, but something about how it all went down just felt so wrong.

One of the toughest things about being released – or traded, for that matter – is losing the tight friendships with your teammates. They end without warning, sometimes without even so much as a goodbye. In that sense, Todd and I were luckier than some, as we got to say goodbye to about half our teammates; the rest were already on the ice warming up for practice. We quickly said a few heartfelt words, and that was it. We never saw most of those guys again.

It was surreal. We had gone there that day pumped about getting our new gear; now, as our former team was practicing, we were in the dressing room with the equipment manager, who went through our gear and told us what we could and couldn't keep. We were stripped of our big, blue Pats official team hockey bag and were instead handed a black garbage bag. A fucking garbage bag. That was fitting, though, because we were feeling like garbage at that moment. We cleaned out our stalls quickly and in silence. Everything had changed.

We walked out of the Agridome with our garbage bags containing the few pieces of equipment we were allowed to keep: jock, shin pads, shoulder pads, elbow pads, and a few pieces of team underwear that contained the sweat equity of months of work and devotion. The whole experience was one of the worst of my life, and I'm sure Todd was feeling the exact same.

We remained silent during the ride home, each lost in our own internal storm of emotions as the black garbage bags flapped in the wind in the back of my red Mazda truck. As I tried to find the bright side of what just happened, I realized we at least got to keep a couple of nice one-piece sticks, but at that moment it was nothing compared to the pain, shock and confusion. For the first time, we were in uncharted territory, two Canadian hockey kids without a hockey team to call home.

We got back to our billet house on Broad Street and split into our separate rooms. We had been living with Tim and Shelley Kentz along with their two awesome kids, Parker and Carly, and their two dogs, Sparky and Oreo. They were like our second family, and Todd and I loved living there together. Now, in addition to leaving our teammates, the wonderful relationship with our billet family would also be severed, another casualty of the business of hockey. Anyway, there was no rush to pack up our stuff, because at the moment there was nowhere to go. We called to tell our parents, who were angry and frustrated by the news but far more concerned with our mental and emotional states. After a half-hearted attempt to let them know we were okay, we ended the call. Neither of us really felt like talking.

Before long the phone started ringing off the hook. First, it was Greg Harder, the Leader Post sportswriter for the Pats. Todd and I stood side-by-side in the basement with the cordless phone held up between our ears so we both could hear, then passed it back and forth as we individually answered the reporter's questions. Just a year earlier that same reporter had written a piece titled, "Brothers push each other to Success," about our joining the team together, which was featured on the front page. How quickly things can change. Unlike our excited responses to that first article, we now offered him short, succinct comments that expressed our shock and disappointment. Harder seemed surprised as well with the decision and said he didn't see it coming. This was a slight compliment that we graciously accepted and appreciated. After giving our comments we hung up the phone and went back to our rooms.

The article, which was printed the next day, began: "Last year at this time, brothers Wade and Todd Davison were a package deal for the WHL's Regina Pats. They'll be leaving the same way." Todd was incredibly hurt that things had come to this, but took the high road in how he left things with Regina and the city's fans, and rationalized the decision from a hockey business point of view: "I like Regina, I like the team, but it was a decision they made." He took responsibility for being released, pinning blame on his inability to perform. "I had my shot. It's my second year so I had more than enough time to show them."

Yet, implied within his words was that he felt shortchanged at not having the opportunity to show what he had in the pre-season: "I thought I had to show my offensive talent this year in the exhibition games. I only got to play two (games), but they made a decision." Recall that one of those games was the Moose Jaw line-brawl game, which was a disaster for our team and resulted in Todd getting his face pummeled. He'd only had one other game to display what he had, which, due to injury and illness, wasn't up to snuff for the coaching staff and managers.

As the news spread, so did the shock and disappointment of our former teammates, parents, billets and fans alike. One of the Pats' young water-boys, Jake, was so upset that he quit his position with the team in protest. For me and Todd, the only option now was to move on.

## Roster Change

I knew that I was a bubble player in the WHL and that nothing was guaranteed for me, but Todd never should have been in that position. He had way too much potential to be given up on that quickly, especially when he wasn't playing anywhere near one hundred percent. According to Todd, one of the reasons they gave him for being released was that "he wasn't the same player he had been in the past," and that "he wasn't playing with the energy or feistiness that he once had." This, despite more than one big red flag, including the blood test results that clearly indicated some illness was depleting his energy levels and strength. Now, in addition to not feeling well physically, my brother's spirit was crushed.

By no means do I write about this to speak disparagingly of any of the individuals who made that decision, but merely to provide context for what Todd was dealing with. I do not know to what extent any of the coaches, management, or trainers knew about Todd's medical situation at that time; in fact, there is a good chance they didn't know or understand the blood test results at all. They were all well-intentioned individuals who I truly like as people and appreciate on a human level. They were doing the best they could in that moment with what they were seeing and the information they had. And this should in no way be used against the Pats organization, which remains a world-class junior hockey franchise that has since undergone a complete change of ownership, management, and coaching staff. The situation is, however, a lesson we can all learn from as we move towards creating a better environment for all young athletes around the world.

# NEW ROADS & NEW COLORS

## The Trade Wire

When the news of our release from the Pats broke across the junior hockey trade wire our phones started buzzing from various Junior A teams across the western Canadian provinces. The wire is an internet portal that gives coaches, managers and scouts notice of who is eligible to be picked up as a free agent, or who is available to be traded. We heard pitches from various coaches and general managers about why we should sign with their team.

Todd and I were in different situations, though, based purely on age. Todd was under eighteen, which according to Hockey Canada rules at the time meant he was supposed to return home to Manitoba to play in the Manitoba Junior Hockey League ("MJHL"). Todd was vehemently against this, declaring with anger and passion in his voice, "I'm not going back to play in the fuckin' MJ!" That is not a shot at the MJHL by any means, which has since developed into a great league that produced many professional players, including NHLers; rather, it's to show that in Todd's mind, playing in the MJHL against players who couldn't make it out of Manitoba was not an option for him after he'd just spent a season competing against some of the best junior hockey players in the world.

In the meantime, calls continued to roll in from the Saskatchewan Junior Hockey League ("SJHL"), the Alberta Junior Hockey League

("AJHL"), and the British Columbia Hockey League ("BCHL"). The AJHL and BCHL were commonly known as the best Junior A leagues in Canada, so we focused our attention on those teams. Then a call came to me from the Lloydminster Blazers of the AJHL. The Blazers' coaches were very persuasive, and definitely captured my ear about their team's talent and potential for that season.

Lloydminster ("Lloyd") is a border city located on the Alberta and Saskatchewan provincial borders. I spoke to Lado, a former teammate who had been released from the Pats just a week or two earlier and signed by Lloyd. Lado passed along a beaming review of the Blazers' program. What Lado didn't tell me though, as he pumped up the program to me and Todd, was that the coaching staff was in the room the entire time monitoring the call.

In the end, I chose to go to Lloyd for several reasons, but largely because they were adamant about doing everything they could to get Todd on the team, despite the fact that he was bound by Hockey Canada's home-province rule. First, he would have to file a petition for a rule exception so that he could play in the AJHL instead of the MJHL. It was a sad moment when we parted ways, with me heading northwest from Regina up to Lloyd and Todd driving his little green Dodge Neon straight east on the TransCanada Highway back to Winnipeg alone, his future now in the hands of a few hearing his issue on appeal. Fortunately, within a week or so, Todd was granted the ability to leave Manitoba and come to Lloyd. Once again we would be playing hockey together, and beginning a whole new chapter of our lives that allowed for us to have some really great times together in a fun-loving hockey environment.

## Lloyd Days

When we initially joined the Blazers in mid-September of the 2003-2004 season, the team had a lot of highly-talented older players and the potential to make a run at the league championship. This was a big part of the attraction for me. Within the first couple of weeks of the season, however, two of the team's top forwards sustained serious injuries. Lado, a four-year WHL veteran who was set to be the team's offensive leader, messed up his knee pretty badly, and another stud player named Luke Hanna, one of the fastest players I'd ever seen, broke his femur after crashing full-speed into the end-boards. Lado was sidelined for months before requesting a trade to return home to Manitoba, and Hanna's injury was so severe that it ended his season. With those talents out of the lineup, the team fell back to being very average. We won games and we lost others just the same. Our championship hopes were lowered as we sunk down in the league standings.

Todd had much more space to play in the Junior A game and gained some confidence back. He scored some beautiful goals that season, including a memorable top-shelf snipe from the high slot after dangling several guys in an end-to-end rush. Yet he just couldn't seem to find his usual top gear. And it was more than just the shoulder pain, which he was still dealing with; something was not right in his game and body. He pushed through anyways, and still managed to be very effective. Looking back, it was absolutely remarkable that he was still playing so well in a league as good as the AJHL.

When we snuck into the playoffs as the seventh seed of the division, we pulled off a major first-round upset by eliminating the St. Albert Saints. That glory soon ended after we lost in the second round to the Grand Prairie Storm. Though our underdog AJHL championship hopes had ended, playing with the Blazers that season was about so much more than winning a championship. That season brought great times and left us with some fantastic memories and friendships. Lloyd was a transitional place where we were able to charge up; be a part of a great group of guys who made for awesome teammates and friends; and be a part of a terrific hockey community that supported us and gave us something to play for. We also recaptured our love of the game and were reminded that playing hockey was supposed to be fun. We had an absolute blast in Lloyd, on and off the ice. Still, at the end of that season we knew we wanted to return to the WHL, to play the game at the highest level.

*Me, Pa, and Todd, in St. Albert, Alberta in 2004.*

## The Golden Letter

In the spring of 2004, Todd and I returned home to Winnipeg for the summer to train and hang out with our friends and family. Todd had one thing on his mind: getting back to the WHL, and then on to the pros from there. Yes, he had fallen from where he was *supposed* to be at that point in his career, but his belief in himself remained strong. The journey back would be challenging, and he'd have to train harder than ever in the next few months. More importantly, though, he needed an invite to a WHL team's camp.

Within a few weeks the mailbox held two shiny and crisp letters to WHL training camps; one for each of us. Todd received his invite from the Brandon Wheat Kings, and I received mine from the Red Deer Rebels. This was big-time, and it was a major relief to know that Dub teams were still interested in us! After talking with the scouts of those respective teams, we were both told that our chances of making those teams were very good. Now we were getting somewhere! This was around May, and as we started envisioning where we'd be in just a few months the excitement really started to grow.

When training camp time hit in August, I would be headed off to Red Deer, Alberta, a city directly between Calgary and Edmonton, to join the Rebels, while Todd would be making the drive to Brandon, two hours west of Winnipeg, to become crowned as a Wheat King. It was a team that we, along with so many other Manitoba boys, had wanted to play for so badly when we were younger, and now Todd would finally have his chance to put on that golden jersey and play in front of home province fans. The letter from the Wheat Kings was not just a training camp invite; like a scene from *Willy Wonka*, the letter was Todd's golden ticket!

Though we would be separated after playing together for the previous three seasons, we knew our time had come to take our own paths. We were excited for one another. The vision was strong and the belief was there, we just needed to put in the effort over the off-season. I knew I had to improve my skating and get quicker, and Todd knew that if he were to have any chance of making it to where he wanted to be, he had to keep getting bigger and stronger.

## Like Marty

Despite the prejudice against them, and the repeated message that they were never going to make it big, some small players found a way to break through to the NHL. These players included guys like Martin St. Louis (5'8", 180 lbs.); Theoren Fleury (5'6", 180 lbs.); Paul Kariya (5'10", 180 lbs.); and Darcy Tucker (5'10", 180 lbs.). These guys all had tremendous skill, massive hearts, self-belief, and a hard outer layer that allowed them to succeed and thrive in competition against their much bigger foes. Many other little guys have made the NHL in recent years – including Nathan Gerbe, who stands five-foot-four and weighs a hundred and eighty pounds – but Fleury, St. Louis, Kariya and Tucker were the trailblazers when we were growing up, and a testament to the fact that a player's stature means nothing compared to the size of their heart. They also let the younger generations, including my brother, know that while the odds were stacked against them it was possible to make it big. Of all Todd's hockey idols throughout his life – and there were many – Martin St. Louis was his all-time favorite. Like so many other smaller guys, St. Louis had to deal with the naysayers who thought he would never ever make the NHL. After going undrafted, he climbed his way up through the minor leagues first. Through his relentless belief in himself – in his abilities and potential – St. Louis not only made the NHL but became a dominant player!

As a fully grown man, St. Louis was taller than Todd, but not by much. They were also both left-handed shooters with incredibly quick releases. Vision was a major strength in both of their games, and they used their quickness and dangles to make plays. They could wheel, snipe, pass, and defend. They even shared jersey numbers: St. Louis wore #26 in the NHL, as did Todd when he first cracked the Pats' roster at the start of the 2002-2003 season. He rocked that number in the WHL for several months, until a veteran twenty-year-old was traded back to the Pats and wanted his old number back. This is when Todd was first given #34.

Though Todd had never met or talked to him, he felt connected and drawn to St. Louis as a hockey player and as a person, and wanted to follow his lead to the top. In 2003-2004, while we were in Lloyd, Todd watched St. Louis closely and drew strength from him. That season, St. Louis had a career year, winning – in addition to the Stanley Cup with the Lightning – the Art Ross Trophy as the NHL's leading scorer; the Hart Memorial Trophy as League MVP; and the Lester B. Pearson Award as most outstanding player, as voted by his NHL peers. Not too bad for a player who was too small to ever make it big.

On June 7, 2004, after winning the Stanley Cup, St Louis said, "I just think everything is possible if you believe in it." You better believe Todd heard that statement and was fully prepared to make a big-time comeback. St. Louis had just lit the path for Todd to follow and reignited the spark in his hockey heart. With Wheat Kings training camp around the corner in a few months, Todd was mentally and emotionally raring to go. Now more than ever before, he believed he was going to do it, just like Marty!

## Pushing Pain

Todd's pathway to success would come through training and working harder than anyone else. It was the only thing he could control. He began the off-season training with Glenn Carnegie and Jeff Wood of Focus Fitness at their first gym, which consisted of old converted dressing rooms in the original Gateway building. It was a small, gritty space, but its character was perfectly fitting for the mission. Todd was training harder than ever with some top-notch hockey players and athletes who were pushing him to max-out. Todd was putting on muscle and looking stronger and faster by the day.

I specifically remember Ryan Bonni – a second-round, thirty-fourth overall draft pick to the Vancouver Canucks in 1997 – making a comment about how strong and jacked Todd was looking during those training sessions. But a major problem was hindering his progress: his shoulder, which was paining him more than ever.

The worst pain was triggered when he did certain simple arm, shoulder, and upper body movements. After doing a set of bench presses, I remember Todd rising up from the bench with a concerned look on his face, grimacing from the pain he had just pushed himself through for the umpteenth time. He talked to Jeff and Glenn about it, and they shared his concern; these guys knew Todd's character better than most, and knew he wouldn't dare exaggerate pain or make excuses. This, they realized, might be serious.

He also experienced severe pain whenever someone touched the top of his shoulder, such as when a buddy threw their arm around him. Any touch on top of his shoulder – even just light pressure – felt like an electrical shock. Considering he had a lot of buddies who wanted to throw their arms around him, and a harem of girls who wanted to hang off of him whenever he was around, this pain was happening a lot. The worst part, however, was not knowing the cause of it.

He had seen many practitioners over the course of the past fifteen months, but no one could figure out what was going on. Since by then he had been playing high-level junior hockey against much bigger and stronger opponents for two seasons, everyone who examined Todd's shoulder couldn't help but view that as the source of the injury and suggest it only needed rest and time to heal.

Todd couldn't help but be concerned that something deeper was happening. More than a year had passed without the pain subsiding. He intuitively knew that any hockey injury should have been long healed. Instead, the pain was only getting worse and the shoulder was more sensitive to the touch, so the "common hockey injury" diagnosis and treatment protocol was no longer giving Todd a sense of hope or peace. Mom had also become quite concerned by that point as well.

# CHAPTER 11

# A MOTHER'S INTUITION

While Canada's health care system attempts to provide first-class medicine to covered individuals without cost, the system is not without drawbacks. One of the worst of these drawbacks is the long waiting times for non-emergency medical procedures and tests, such as MRIs. As mentioned, X-rays of Todd's shoulder had already come back negative for any bone issues, but X-rays would not reveal any soft tissue issues. For that, one needed to get a CT scan or MRI, but since no physician believed Todd's condition was severe enough to warrant this sort of testing he was not even on the radar for it.

Mom – who worked as an MRI technologist at Health Sciences Centre (HSC), Winnipeg's busiest hospital – knew that something more needed to be done. She had previously been an X-ray technologist – a position she held for over twenty-five years before transitioning into the then-emerging field of MRI. This was far from an easy jump and took all of her courage and dedication to pursue. She had been selected as one of ten or so people from across Canada to get accepted into the first national training program. Five years later, that decision to become an MRI technologist paid off in an incredible and unforeseen way that went far beyond a paycheck.

A mother's intuition is a powerful thing, and isn't something that should be casually dismissed. As Todd's pain intensified, Mom just knew something more serious was happening beneath the surface.

On a quiet Saturday afternoon in mid-June 2004, while working the weekend shift alone, she saw that the MRI scanner schedule had some gaps due to last-minute cancellations. Seizing this rare opportunity, Mom worked up the courage to explain Todd's situation to her department supervisor and requested permission to perform a quick "scout scan" of his shoulder instead of taking her lunch break that day. The supervisor agreed.

A scout scan, which is just seven minutes, creates a rougher image that lacks the precision of a full diagnostic exam. Still, it was better than nothing, and Mom eagerly called Todd and told him to get down to the hospital. He arrived just before noon and met her in the MRI department.

Todd grimaced in pain as Mom placed the MRI coil on his body, which cupped the top of his shoulder – the most sensitive area – and caused the "electrical shocks" he had described. The pressure immediately caused him great pain and distress, and it only got worse as she slid him into the scanner. Todd was always way more fidgety than most, and the tight confines of the MRI tube, coupled with his pain and anxiety, made him even more so in that nerve-wracking moment. He'd always hated confinement – be it in the form of a snug button-up dress shirt with a tie or a too-tight chin guard on his hockey helmet. He also hated sitting still.

Todd's abrupt movements caused the initial images to be distorted, yet Mom saw something within the first ten seconds that raised her eyebrows and made her heart race.

*What the heck?* she thought, as she strained her eyes to look closer at the scan.

The screen in front of her lit up with bright spots that indicated danger. Starting to panic and needing more high-resolution images, she desperately pleaded through the scanner microphone, "Todd, you gotta hold still!"

I wonder if Todd could hear any fear and panic in Mom's voice through those MRI speakers.

As the scan continued, a series of worst-case scenarios flooded Mom's mind. Though she was not trained as a radiologist or physician, she was certainly experienced enough to know that what she saw was "something really bad!"

I can't imagine the sickening fear and worry that she felt in what was surely one of the most shocking and traumatic moments of her life. Prior to that moment, she recalls thinking, *These poor parents,* when she saw tumors in their kids light up on the monitor in front of her. Now, she was experiencing the same pain first-hand.

## That Sinking, Suffocating Feeling

Over the course of those seven minutes, Mom first glimpsed the images that would change our lives forever. The MRI revealed two distinct sizable masses in Todd's shoulder area. These masses were completely different – one was like a "capsule," and the other like a "bag of grapes." Mom knew that capsule-type tumors are typically benign, but the grape-like formation caused a lot of concern. This wasn't good.

As she got Todd out of the tube, Mom was careful to compose herself so as not to pass that worry or fear on to Todd. She knew that a radiologist needed to look at it and there was no use in jumping to conclusions just yet, but inside she was terrified. She calmly told Todd that something didn't look quite right and that more investigation was needed. She saw and felt Todd's confusion start to brew. On one hand he may have been relieved that there was a possible explanation for his pain, but any sort of relief was overshadowed by worry about what that explanation was.

## Monday

When Mom finished her Saturday shift at the hospital she left Todd's images in the MRI department, along with a note to the radiologist asking him to look at the images as soon as possible. The following Monday he reached out to Mom to let her know that he too was concerned and, given the unusual appearance of the tumors, was recommending that Todd see an orthopedic radiologist at St. Boniface Hospital as soon as possible. Mom got an appointment for the next day.

Todd returned to the hospital on Tuesday morning for the follow-up scan with much more hesitance and emotional heaviness than he had three days earlier. He knew the urgent request from the radiologist meant that things were getting more serious.

The previous seven-minute scan was bad enough to endure, but now he had to undergo thirty minutes of pain, discomfort, stress and worry. The other MRI tech on duty performed the scan as Mom stayed in the room with Todd to try to comfort him. That half-hour must have seemed like an eternity. Within seconds of that scan the tumors again lit up the screen. One tumor – the "capsule" type – was in the postural back muscle, while the bag of grapes was in the nerve sheath.

Upon completion of the scan, tensions were incredibly high. Two radiologists viewed the images and, from the way they were speaking quietly to each other, were clearly confused and concerned by what they were seeing.

After telling Todd it was very unusual to see both tumors together like that, they simply said, "We'll get back to you . . . " In the meantime, he should immediately see Dr. Caners, our family doctor, so his case could be referred to an orthopedic specialist.

Todd was silent when he left the hospital. He knew just enough to know that things were more serious than he'd anticipated. Worst fears and reality shook hands at this point, but there was still hope that this was all just doctors taking extreme precautions.


## Universal DJ

Childhood appointments with Dr. Caners were most often obligatory annual physicals, and, considering Todd was typically a very healthy child and teenager, quickly moved beyond any health concerns and shifted to the topic of hockey, of which the doctor was a big fan. That Wednesday in June 2004, however, was going to be much different.

Although nothing was known about Todd's condition, the intensity of his situation was increasing with each passing moment. With fear and anxiety swirling inside, Todd sat in the passenger seat of Mom's Chrysler Intrepid as they drove to the doctor's office. QX104 FM, Winnipeg's best country music station at the time, played through the speakers, helping to distract both of them from the frightening mind chatter. Only a block from Mom's house, as the car turned onto McIvor Avenue, a song started playing, as impeccably timed as if it were cued up by the Universal DJ.

"Live Like You Were Dying" by Tim McGraw is a song about a man in his early forties getting diagnosed with cancer. The diagnosis forced the man to reevaluate his priorities in life, and triggered a change in attitude and perception of what this life was all about. As the title suggests, the man begins to live like he was dying – doing things such as skydiving, mountain- climbing, bull-riding, and being the best husband, father, son, and friend he could be on a daily basis. The man ultimately realized the preciousness and fleeting nature of this life and began to live, *fully*, with his death in mind. If you have not heard the song, cue it up and be prepared to feel something powerful.

That morning was the first time Todd had ever heard it, and when the opening lyrics began he was floored. Mom, who had also never heard it before, said his eyes grew big as he sat stunned in silence and stillness, while she white-knuckled the wheel to stay composed. Though Todd had not yet been diagnosed with cancer, that song, in that moment, shifted everything for him.

It was, during the most chaotic time of his life, a beautiful gift that gave Todd strength and courage when he needed it most. Though there were all kinds of bangers and ballads that fit his life throughout his years, "Live Like You Were Dying" would become the most played song on the soundtrack of Todd's life. From that first car ride to the doctor's office until the last days of his life, it framed his reality and added intensity, realness, and power to any situation he was in.

# CHAPTER 12

# THE DANCE

At the appointment with Dr. Caners, Todd learned that his case would be referred to one Dr. MacDonald, an orthopedic surgeon specializing in, among other things, shoulders. A biopsy would be scheduled within the next two weeks. In the meantime, all Todd could do was wait. Those were some anxious days.

On the drive home from Dr. Caners' office, Todd curiously asked, "How do you spell MacDonald?" He was trying to confirm that it was "Mac" instead of "Mc" before "Donald." He knew this was a fairly common last name, but was trying to determine whether this Dr. MacDonald was the father of Lindsey MacDonald ("Lindsey"), Todd's dear friend and grad date to the St. Paul's High School Grad, which just so happened to be on the calendar for the following Monday, five days away. As the Universe would have it, Todd's specialist to-be was indeed Lindsey's father.

Dr. Peter MacDonald is highly regarded as one of the top orthopedic surgeons in North America. Pete is the Chief Research and Innovation Officer at PanAm Clinic, Winnipeg's top orthopedic clinic. In addition to PanAm, Pete has recently held the position of president of the Canadian Orthopaedic Association, and, at the time of this writing, is the head physician of both the Winnipeg Jets of the NHL and the Winnipeg Blue Bombers of the Canadian Football League. Quite simply, he's world-class, and the guy you want to be working on your body-vehicle when a repair is needed.

Upon hearing that he would be receiving Todd's case Pete immediately went to work, remotely accessing the MRI images on the Winnipeg Regional Health Authority database. Despite his decades of experience, he had never before seen the type of growths that Todd's MRI images revealed. The formations were that rare. Not wanting to get drawn into a panic, Pete worked methodically and started with the premise that the tumors were lipomas, or benign tumors of fatty tissue. He knew a biopsy would be the only way to gain certainty, and there was no use in wasting energy on possible negative results in the meantime.

It's funny how even under the most stressful and strenuous circumstances of life, the world just keeps on spinning. In Todd's case, the most relevant of these life events was Todd's high school graduation dinner and dance – "Grad."

Separate and distinct from a formal graduation convocation, Grad is similar to an American high school senior prom, except it also includes a formal celebration dinner that parents also attend. After the dinner portion of the event, the parents get sent home while the graduates and their dates are transported to an off-site location for a "Safe-Grad"– which is typically code for a big-time dance party chaperoned by some of the chiller parents and faculty who want to share the vibes with the graduating class.

The evening of the Grad, Todd met Lindsey at her house in Winnipeg's Tuxedo area. He was picking her up to attend a "pre-game" party at the home of Todd's great friend Brendon Corbett. Here, their close-knit group of St. Paul's and St. Mary's High School friends would be having a few cocktails as they fired their party up and awaited the limousines that would take them to the festivities at the Winnipeg Convention Center. And so, Todd found himself standing in his new specialist's home, about to take his eldest daughter out for the night.

Todd stood before Pete near the front door, looking sharp and handsome in his tuxedo. Though his appointment wasn't scheduled until the following week, Pete knew that Todd played high-level hockey; he could also see the uncertainty and nervousness in Todd's eyes as he looked up to Pete for his expert opinion in such tumultuous times. While an on-the-spot diagnosis was obviously out of the question at that time, Pete offered to give Todd a brief physical examination of his shoulder to get a head start on what he would be looking at the following week at the clinic. Todd took off his tuxedo jacket, dress shirt, and bowtie and underwent the brief examination, no doubt desperately hoping for such an experienced surgeon to tell him the pain was being caused by a common and simple issue and that he didn't have to worry.

But those words would not come. What did come, though, was a sense that his new specialist truly cared about him. From that first meeting onwards, Todd could feel that Pete was deeply invested in his case and his well-being. Little did Todd know at that time, Pete would become far more than just his physician; he would become a rock of strength, wisdom, and comfort; a true friend.

After completing that initial informal examination, Pete said he would be in touch soon. The biopsy, which Pete would personally be performing, was only days away on the calendar. As Lindsey and Todd went on their way, Pete – a St. Paul's graduate himself – hoped that such an exciting occasion would not be completely ruined by the fear and anxiety he knew Todd was dealing with.

Before Todd and Lindsey fired up their night together, they posed for a photo under an archway decorated with celebration flowers in Corbett's foyer. In typical Todd fashion, he whispered a joke in Lindsey's ear that had her keeled over in laughter, then posed proudly for the photo with a big laughing smile on his face. He was still beaming as he headed with his friends into the banquet room, wanting so badly to enjoy the night to its fullest without worry.

*Todd with Lindsey Parkes (MacDonald) at Corbett's pre-game before Grad.*

And, for a short while, everything was so good! After cruising through south Winnipeg towards downtown in a stretch limousine with some of his closest friends, Todd stepped into the Winnipeg Convention Center like a boss. He had a beautiful girl on his arm and his favorite people by his side. He knew this was a big night, and there would be no sparing of celebration.

After eating dinner and enjoying the festivities with his family and friends, Todd glided with Mom around the dancefloor during the Mother-Son dance, mingled with his classmates, and seemed to be having a good time. All was well in that moment.

*Todd dancing with Mom at the St. Paul's High School Graduation Dinner in June 2004.*

As the evening proceeded, however, and despite his best efforts to silence his worries and any negative internal chatter during the celebration, the scared voice in his head reminded him of the looming threat of the tumors inside his body. The thoughts were too loud for him to completely tune out. His underlying fear and anxiety slowly crept in and grew as the night went on. Lindsey (who, incidentally, would go on to become a sports doctor herself) knew there was cause for concern and avoided the topic. She could read Todd well enough to see his internal confusion and anxiety brewing, and she didn't want to fuel his worries. She just wanted Todd to have a great time and enjoy the night; and, for the most part, he really was! But as the night went on and great moments of laughter came and went, an undercurrent of dark emotion was lurking beneath the surface.

At one point in the evening, Alan Carruthers, then St. Paul's Vice President of Students, came up to Todd and told him that he had been praying for him. Todd appreciated Mr. Carruthers' kind words and prayers in that moment, but Lindsey could tell that Todd's energy had shifted by then, and not for the better. Todd looked at her with worry etched on his face as he fought back those heavy thoughts. Lindsey looked back at him with sympathetic eyes that suggested Todd could trust her. And he knew he could trust her – hell, he trusted her so much that he'd told her the password to his "pegcityplaya69@hotmail.com" email account, and he knew the password to her email account as well. That was a big deal in those days. More importantly, though, he knew he could be completely vulnerable in her presence, and as they sat apart from all the excitement and celebrations he finally stepped out from behind his facade of fearlessness, looked directly at her, and said, "I'm so fuckin' scared, Linds . . . "

Lindsey might have been the only person in the world to ever hear those words come out of Todd's mouth. Sadly, however, she knew that there was nothing she could do to really help ease his fear. All she could do, like the rest of his friends and family, was love and support him throughout this process. And, considering what was to come, he would need a LOT of both.

As evidenced by many great photos of Todd and his friends, he had an absolutely epic night that lasted well into the early morning hours. But, as the sun rose that next day, his personal *reality* set back in. While all his friends likely woke up with hangovers, Todd woke up with the looming fear of what was in his shoulder. The worst part was, unlike hangovers, which typically wear off throughout the day, Todd would still have to wait several days for the official diagnosis.

## After Grad Sad

Monday, June 28, 2004 – one week after Grad – proved itself to be one of the most significant and tragic days of Todd's life. One reason was that it was the day his St. Paul's class officially graduated; the other was that he underwent the biopsy that would change our family's world.

Only hours before Todd was set to change into cap-and-gown and walk across the stage at his convocation ceremony, he found himself in a hospital room, nauseated and dizzy, recovering from the one-and-a-half-hour procedure. A small incision was made into his left shoulder blade so Pete could extract the tissue to be examined. The incision would leave a new scar on Todd's body, marking ground zero. While the capsule-type tumor was removed in its entirety, the grape-like tumor was determined to have already penetrated the nerve sheath and therefore could not be fully removed. This was not a good sign of things to come.

The tissue samples holding Todd's future were sent across the city to a pathology lab at the St. Boniface Hospital. Now we would all have to wait seven to ten days for the results – far too long when one is already struggling to remain positive.

After regaining consciousness from the procedure, Todd threw up many times – a reaction to the anesthetic. When his clear mind returned, he remembered that he had big things to do that day – like attend his own high school graduation ceremony. Despite being shaken up from the procedure, and though he was supposed to be recovering in bed, Todd was adamant that he'd be walking across the stage when his name was announced. He wasn't going to miss out on sharing this milestone with his friends as they all received their diplomas.

He got dressed and left the hospital as soon as he could. At that point, he was still quite weak and weary, and his shoulder was frozen from the biopsy; he wouldn't regain full function for twenty-four hours. Mom took Todd to her house to quickly clean him up before the big ceremony. She washed his hair in the kitchen sink and scrambled to pull him together, then rushed back across Winnipeg through rush hour traffic to Church of the Rock, the site of the ceremony. With only minutes to spare, Todd, with help, walked in to join his classmates and friends in the staging area while the excited relatives and friends of the graduates eagerly filled the ceremony room. Todd played it cool and pretended that everything was fine, but he was surely uncomfortable. He also might have had quite a buzz from the pain meds.

While most of the crowd wasn't aware of what Todd was going through, enough of his classmates and faculty at the school knew, which created a subtle tension of worry in the air when his name was called. While most high school students proudly strut across the stage with a big smile on their face as they receive their diploma, Todd needed help as he slowly and diligently made his way. Though it may have taken longer than the others, and though he may have struggled to hold his head up, Todd eventually crossed the stage as our family held back tears of joy and worry.

After receiving his diploma, Todd took his seat amongst young men who were at a monumental stage in their lives: the beginning of life beyond high school! Todd too was at a critical juncture, but one that was filled with far more uncertainty. Things were happening fast for him, and he couldn't hit the brakes or the pause button.

I cannot remember a single word from the convocation speaker or valedictorian, although I presume their words were inspiring. A graduation speech is supposed to be, to leave graduates with a sense of power and confidence from their accomplishment as they take the next step of their journey. I've often wondered, what if Todd had spoken that day?

What if he knew how his story ended, and decided to relay a message? Perhaps his words would have gone something like this:

*Today I had a biopsy on my shoulder, which in the next few days will reveal that I have synovial sarcoma — a rare and aggressive form of cancer with low survival rates. Over my next days, months, and years I will learn what pain is . . . and what anguish is, coupled with loneliness, doubt, anger, sadness, and fear!*

*We live our lives in our minds, trying to plan out every step of our future in detail. But the truth is, nothing in this life is guaranteed. Life can come at you without a warning, and turn your world upside down. However, beyond all the pain and suffering I will endure, I will learn that love is the only thing that is real, and the most joy and peace I ever felt was during times of serving others.*

*The biggest lesson I can pass on to you is this: Live your life with no regrets. Live like you are playing your last shift. Live like you are dying.*

But of course, that didn't happen, and all of us, including Todd, still had hopes that within a week the scare would be in the rear view, nothing more than a bad dream. And so Todd turned his tassel with the rest of the young men and marched out of the amphitheater to loud cheers and clapping from the crowd. After the photos were taken during the reception and all the many great snacks were eaten, Todd seemed to be in good spirits. And, surprisingly, he was looking really good by the time the ceremony ended. Considering the severity of the procedure that had taken place only hours earlier, Todd needed rest, but he felt pressure (and the desire) to attend the after-party with his friends; not to drink or party, but just to be there with everyone in that space of joy and celebration, instead of by himself in a state of pain and worry. He was never the type to want to miss any of the action, and though they were concerned Mom and Dad didn't push it; they didn't want to deprive him of the opportunity of being with his closest friends on that monumental night.

Our older brother Joel was appointed Todd's chauffeur, ensuring that he got to and from the party safely, and his friends would look after him while he was there. We expected he would be out for a while, but within a couple of hours he returned to Mom's completely exhausted. Also, the freezing agent was wearing off, and the pain was setting in. To avoid putting pressure on his shoulder wounds, he slept in the living room in a black leather lazy-boy recliner – a soft spot that would become his retreat over the next two and a half years.

Todd slept much of the next day and was in pain and discomfort for all of it. He was more helpless than ever, stuck in the in-between of biopsy and diagnosis. When he woke up, he slowly moved around the house and yard, aimlessly trying to get himself to a place of peace, but nothing was helping. Again that night he slept – or at least tried to sleep – in the big recliner, but by then the pain came on full-force, worse than he had ever felt before.

## D-Day Shocked

Though the biopsy had only happened two days earlier, the pathologist at St. Boniface made Todd's case a priority and reviewed it as soon as possible. When he examined the tissue under the microscope he was shocked, and passed the news on to Pete: "I think this is synovial sarcoma . . . "

Knowing how rare synovial sarcoma was – it occurs in one or two out of every million people – and how serious, Pete was hesitant to accept the pathologist's finding. He hurriedly jumped into his vehicle and drove from Pan Am Clinic to the St. Boniface lab to personally examine the tissue. He needed to be absolutely certain before breathing a word of it to my family.

When Pete entered the lab and looked into the microscope, his gut sank when his own eyes confirmed the pathologist's diagnosis. He knew this was not good.

Across the city, Mom woke up that morning feeling that things would turn out alright. In those morning hours she felt peaceful and happy, carrying hope and faith that her sleeping son would be fine. She walked out into the yard and felt the sunshine on her face, looking around at all the beauty in the world. But as bright as that day started, it turned dark as soon as the phone rang around one p.m., with Pete on the other end of the line.

Mom's stomach sank as Pete tried his best to graciously pass along the delicate news:

"Things are not as I hoped. It is synovial sarcoma . . . "

Not knowing what to do or think, Mom immediately called Dad, who rushed over to her place in absolute shock.

As Todd slept, Mom and Dad spent the next hour discussing what to do and how to break the crushing news to Todd. With each passing minute more unease set in.

"My head hurts so bad," Mom later wrote in her journal as she reflected on those moments. "This is the worst thing of my life . . . "

When Todd awoke, Mom and Dad approached him as gently as possible. Surely his initial confusion at Dad's presence turned to fear when he saw their faces and their eyes filled with helpless tears. It was then, with their hearts breaking, that Mom and Dad told their youngest son he had cancer.

Todd just stared off, deflated, as if the life had been sucked out of him. All previous hope that this was nothing to worry about had evaporated with that one awful word.

In that moment, his life had officially entered a state of chaos. He was supposed to be training for hockey; he was supposed to be playing hockey at the highest level in only a couple months; he was supposed to be carelessly celebrating life and graduation with his friends; and he was supposed to be lost in big dreams of his days ahead. But he wasn't . . . instead, he was seized by sadness, fear, and anxiety.

Everything in Todd's life, and all of our lives, had changed in that instant. Nothing would ever be the same.

Mom then called Joel and me separately. I had just finished a work-out with Richard Burr at the old Winnipeg Stadium across the city. I instantly heard the pain and distress in her voice as she said, "Come here now!" and I jumped into my car without asking any questions. Clearly, something really bad had happened. My heart sank and my mind raced as two scenarios came to mind: either Grandpa Cherniak had died – which was always a concern at that point – or Todd's results had come back positive.

I walked in the door and rounded the corner into the living room, where I saw Todd lying on the couch in a fetal position. He looked up at me just long enough for me to see his eyes were filled with tears. Mom, Dad, and Joel sat around him, all in tears, looking distraught as well. I stood still in the entryway for a moment, trying to appreciate how serious this situation was; then I stepped into the living room as softly as I could.

"Your brother has cancer," Mom whispered, "Go give him a hug ... "

I moved towards him as we both burst into tears. We were *all* crying hard, as if our family had just been hit by a bomb – which it had. I cannot recall the moments after that. It all kinda went blurry for a while. Without warning, Todd was skating on the thin ice of life.

# CHAPTER 13

# A NEW OPPONENT

After our family cry – the worst of its kind since Mom and Dad broke the news of their separation years earlier – we knew we needed to move forward with strength, and Todd needed to be bombarded with love and support. Mom directed us to call every single friend we knew over to the house immediately. She didn't want to prolong the process of telling others; nor did she want it to turn into an ongoing pity party.

Joel and I spent the next hour on our cell phones calling everyone we could think of, and before we knew it the house and backyard were packed with people – it would remain so for the rest of the day and the night. Every person who came to visit brought love and healing energy. Todd had a whole new battle to fight, but it was made clear that he would have an army of loved ones at his side. He was not alone.

## Left on the Front Step

In late August, as the 2004-2005 hockey season was set to fire up, players departed their hometowns and headed to whichever team's training camp they were attending … but not Todd. Instead of getting ready to crack the Brandon Wheat Kings' roster, as was the plan only a couple months earlier, Todd was getting ready for his second week of chemotherapy.

He sat on the front step of our house on Ranch, watching as I packed up my Chevy Blazer for the trip west without him. Though it was one of the toughest things he had to endure, he spoke of it with his usual brave stoicism in a newspaper interview. "This year [Wade] left without me. It was pretty sad to see him go but that's part of dealing with what's happening here."

Todd's pain wasn't about me leaving, but about the fact that he couldn't go. He was supposed to be going to training camp like every other junior hockey player, not sitting on the front step with a PICC line, covered with white mesh gauze, just off the middle of his left bicep. He was like a stressed tiger being held captive in a cage. The most frustrating part was that he didn't feel sick. "I still feel like I could be playing hockey right now," he told the reporter, "I feel pretty healthy. But I can't do it so it's pretty disappointing."

Somehow, despite his sadness and inner torment that day, Mom got him to crack a smile for a photo; well, it was more like a slight smirk, but still a captured "highlight."

*Todd (with Molly), left on the front step in Winnipeg in late summer 2004, as I headed west for Red Deer, Alberta.*

I hit the road to Red Deer with a heavy heart and a mission in mind. Todd couldn't play, so I was going to try to make it for us both. It seemed that so much was riding on me making the team and I was very nervous, mentally and emotionally. The head scout basically said that if I showed up in good shape I'd have a great chance to make the team. Over the summer I had continued training with Richard Burr – who had trained countless NHLers over the years – four mornings per week at the Winnipeg Blue Bombers Stadium. After a six-a.m. workout in the Blue Bomber's locker room, I would head to Fountain Tire, where I earned money changing tires on cars and semi-trucks for the rest of the day. I was in fantastic shape and felt strong and confident going into training camp. Now it was time to perform.

## Rebel On

The Rebels' top veteran players were guys like Dion Phaneuf and Colin Fraser – both NHL prospects at that time. I was on Phaneuf's team and was lining up against Fraser during face-offs on the wing. Knowing it would instantly get me noticed I asked Fraser to fight, but he respectfully declined. He would be attending the Chicago Blackhawks camp the following week and probably didn't want to mess up his hand on my face. I did end up fighting another veteran player, with Phaneuf cheering me on with a comment along the lines of, "Fuck him up, Davison!" In the end, I did not "fuck him up," but it was cool getting a quick pre-fight pump-up from a player like Phaneuf.

Brent Sutter was the Rebels' General Manager and Head Coach that year. He is a legendary coach – most known for his success as head coach with the Team Canada World Junior team. He had coached the boys to gold medals at the 2005 and 2006 World Junior Hockey Championships, followed by a victory in the 2007 Super Series, a U20 event involving eight games versus Russia. Canada dominated the series with seven wins and one tie. This Rebels training camp in 2004 took place just a few months before that winning streak began. With Sutter behind the bench, the Rebels always seemed to have a solid squad, and they were always known as a tough team to make. Despite the encouraging words I had received from the scouts before camp, I knew my spot was far from solidified on that roster. I had been billeted in a house upon my arrival in Red Deer and welcomed in by the veteran players, but no playing contract had been signed yet. I was so close to becoming a Rebel, but the puck was still a stick-length away and I was in a foot race with several other very solid guys, like future NHLer Derek Dorsett, and Boston Bruins draft-pick, Jordan Knackstedt.

On the last night of camp I saw the writing on the dressing room whiteboard. It came in the form of a newspaper article, in which Sutter stated that I was battling for a spot against the Rebels' top young prospects. Considering those young guns were highly-touted draft picks who would be developed by the team if they were ready, I knew this was not a good sign for me. The next day, after the intersquad game, I was the last guy in line to meet Brent Sutter in his office. There, my worst fears were confirmed.

Sutter commended me on my effort and said that cutting me had been a really tough decision for him to make. That was a compliment in my book. He told me the Kitchener Rangers in the OHL – then coached by Peter DeBoer – might be interested in me, and that I should go make that team and "shove it up [his] ass." DeBoer was Sutter's assistant coach for Team Canada World Juniors that year, and only a few months from that day they would be winning a gold medal with players like Sidney Crosby, Patrice Bergeron, Mike Richards, Jeff Carter, and Ryan Getzlaf. I was also able to relate to all those Team Canada World Junior hopefuls, who, despite being so close to making the team, would be receiving that infamous three- or four-a.m. hotel room phone call from Brent Sutter and DeBoer notifying them that they were cut. The message is almost always the same: "We thought you had a great camp, but we had tough decisions to make, and we are going to have to let you go." To me, this was hockey heartbreak.

# Brothers share strong bond

## Rebel hopeful Davison has brother's battle on mind

By GREG MEACHEM
Advocate staff

Wade Davison fires a shot during training Friday at the Centrium. After spending last season skating in the Alberta Junior Hockey League, Davison is glad to have another shot at the WHL.

Photo by JEFF STOKOE/Advocate staff

His focus is on cracking the Red Deer Rebels' lineup for the 2004-05 WHL season, but part of Wade Davison's soul is back home in Winnipeg.

It is there, in the Manitoba capital, that his 18-year-old brother Todd is waging a battle with cancer.

"He's getting ready for his second week of chemotherapy. He's in Winnipeg for a couple more sessions of chemo and then he goes back to Toronto for another diagnosis," Davison, 19, said Friday following a Rebel training camp scrimmage at the Centrium.

The Davison brothers skated with the Regina Pats two seasons ago, but both were released last fall and spent the '03-04 campaign with Lloydminster of the AJHL.

Todd underwent surgery last month after being diagnosed with a rare form of cancer in the joint of his left shoulder. Surgeons, however, were unable to remove the entire tumour because cells had spread to the nerves.

Todd was scheduled to attend the Brandon Wheat Kings' camp next week. Instead, he's locked in a perilous struggle while Wade tries his luck with the Rebels.

"It was really tough leaving that situation. This is the time of year that we both leave for hockey camps," said Wade.

"It's a tough time for Todd but everyone is thinking of him. He has a lot of support and hopefully he'll get through this just fine.

"By all accounts, Todd Davison is a fighter who is facing this challenge in a positive frame of mind.

"He's definitely one of the toughest kids I know," said Wade.

"He just sees this as a little bend in the road. He's just battling right through it and I think he'll be OK."

Wade Davison learned the Rebels were interested in his services shortly after returning to Winnipeg following the end of his AJHL season.

"I got a phone call from Lorne Goulet, the (Rebels') Winnipeg scout, then head scout Randy Peterson called me a couple of times and expressed an interest. I was pretty ex-

**Training camp**

cited to learn about that," said Davison.

The five-foot-11 winger is anxious to return to the major junior ranks.

"Coming down from the WHL to junior A last year was such a huge drop," he said. "Even though I got a

lot of ice time in Lloydminster and was able to develop a bit, nothing compares to the intensity and emotion of the WHL game."

The fact he's played in the WHL should work to Davison's advantage during his quest to regain employment.

"I knew what to expect coming into camp," he said. "You have to be in top shape and be prepared to give it all you have. They don't take any prisoners in this league.

"It was a long summer waiting for this camp to happen and hopefully everything works out and I can get back in the league and play for a great team."

The answer could come soon. Most of the main-camp players will suit up for Sunday's Black and White intrasquad game, with the axe coming down at the conclusion of the 2 p.m. contest.

"He's a hard-working kid, and up-and-down guy who has to bang and crash and work his butt off," said

Rebels GM/head coach Brent Sutter.

"We'll see after Sunday whether he'll be able to fit in here.

"A lot depends on our younger kids. We might have a 16- or 17-year-old who can give us that same role. There are no guarantees with Wade and he knows that. We'll make a decision on him after Sunday's game."

● Veteran forward Joel Henituik has been unable to participate in training camp due to the lingering effects of a hand injury he suffered in the East Division final last spring. The Spruce Grove native should be cleared to practise in three weeks.

● The main-camp players were on the ice at 8 a.m. today for a 90-minute scrimmage, to be followed by rookies from 10-11:15 a.m. and a combined session from 4-5:30 p.m.

● The Rebels' open their preseason schedule Sept. 8 in Airdrie against the Calgary Hitmen.

*Photo by Jeff Stokoe, courtesy of the Red Deer Advocoate.*

After I was snipped, Jesse Zetariuk – a veteran Rebel and one of Todd's good friends from Manitoba – and some of the other vets brought me out for more than a few sympathy drinks. Some had hovered around the third and fourth line and noticed my performance. Playing on a line with Ted Vandermeer and Blackhawks' draft pick Jared Walker – another good Winnipeg boy who was always one of the elite players in the 1986 age group – I knew I'd had a great camp and put some of the veterans on edge. One, who watched camp from the stands due to a shoulder injury, witnessed my games and admitted he'd been nervous that I was going to take his roster spot. Just as someone replaced me in Regina's depth chart, he thought the same thing was going to happen to him. I was that close. But a lot of guys get close . . . sometimes it just isn't meant to be.

Though I put on a strong face for the boys, I was absolutely devastated. This was supposed to be my return to the WHL, and it was the only thing my mind and heart were set on. Getting cut from the Rebels at nineteen years old had essentially put me on notice that high-level professional hockey was likely not going to happen for me. As my professional hockey dreams faded away, confusion and depression set in. What was I supposed to do now?

In the weakness and defeat of that moment, I strongly considered quitting hockey altogether. I know that is dramatic, but it's just how I felt. Then I got a call from Carling MacDonald – Pete's youngest daughter and one of my closest old friends. Carling and Todd also had a tight and special connection. She knew what was going on with me, and what was going on with Todd. She talked me through the situation and snapped me out of my depression, confusion, and victimhood. I remember her stern words and sassy tone coming through the phone:

"Todd can't even play, and you're thinking about quitting…!?" In my fuzzy memory of the exact exchange, she may have even mixed in a "Like, are you for real right now?"

Carling was absolutely right. She brought me back to reality and made me realize how ridiculous my mindset was. Whether I played in the WHL or Junior A didn't matter; what mattered was the fact that I was able to play the game I love in one of the coolest ways to experience it: the Canadian junior way!

Once I got over my pity party about not returning to the Dub, I decided to look for a new Junior A home in the BCHL. While I had enjoyed my time in Lloyd and loved my teammates, I only had two seasons of junior hockey left to win a championship, and I certainly didn't want to burn that time with the Blazers in the quiet middle of the AJHL. I faced one major issue, though: despite teams calling the Blazers to make trade offers, the Blazers' coach refused to trade me.

I stayed in Red Deer for a few days, weighing my options and having discussions with close friends about my hockey future. One of the people I spoke with was Andy Zulyniak ("Zinger"), one of my lifelong best friends. Despite being one of the most talented defensemen I have ever known, Zinger had been released from the Prince Albert Raiders of the WHL only days after Todd and I were released from the Pats. Zinger ended up in Vernon, British Columbia, playing for the Vernon Vipers of the BCHL, and was absolutely loving it there. In addition to living in the Okanagan Valley, one of Canada's most beautiful areas, he was playing on a team with a long history of winning league and national championships. In fact, as of the time of this writing, with six national championships (1990,1991,1996,1999, 2009 & 2010), the Vernon Vipers currently stand as the winningest Junior A franchise in Canadian hockey history.

Zinger, being the great friend he is, pumped my tires to Mike Vandekamp ("Vandy"), then head coach and general manager of the Vipers, and convinced him to try to trade for me so I could help the team make another championship run. Like any other business, sometimes it's just who you know in hockey that gets you in the best spots. Vandy – one of the biggest beauty coaches of all time –called Lloyd to discuss the trade, but his calls were ignored. When a team has your rights, they are the ones calling the shots, and the player is often powerless regarding those types of executive decisions. Be careful who you sign a player's card with, kids. The Blazers demanded that I drive across Alberta to report in person before any trade deals would be considered. Fair enough. I reported, against my will, but only on the promise that I would be traded shortly after my return.

When I returned to Lloyd, I was billeted with NHLer Clarke MacArthur's parents, Dean and Deborah, who showed me how they raised a professional athlete through meals and their mindset. Though I only stayed with them a short time, I quickly learned how a certain physical and energetic environment established by parents or caregivers can provide the foundation for excellence. After I'd played some exhibition games and stayed in shape with the Blazers for a week or so, Blazers coach Dale Jackson granted my wish and traded me to Vernon. The trade was part of a three-way deal between Vernon and Powell River of the BCHL, and Lloyd. But the deal had a weird condition attached to it: though I was technically not on the team anymore, I had to play the first two regular season opening games for Lloyd, against the Bonnyville Pontiacs. Also playing one of the games was the player I had been traded for, coming from Powell River. That was an odd situation.

After playing the first game in Bonnyville, we returned to Lloyd for the Blazers' home opener the following night. In a very classy move by the Blazers, Todd was honored at the game during the opening ceremonies. He, accompanied by Dad, had made a special trip to Lloyd to be part of the team's action. Todd was called to the ice and was cheered on by the fans and our team. Todd was still shy talking about or acknowledging his cancer, but he was confident of his hockey return at some point! By making him feel as if he were still part of the team, the Blazers provided a massive source of motivation and encouragement for him. In retrospect, I was really happy and blessed to have gone back to Lloyd for those days and to have that exchange with Todd, and I felt like an arrogant asshole for not immediately reporting after I got snipped from Red Deer.

## Fight, Fight, Freedom

In the second period of the home opener, I was ejected from the game after I got into two back-to-back fights with the same Pontiacs player, who had just crushed one of our players from behind. When a player hits a teammate from behind, a beatdown is always deserved. The linesmen broke up my initial fight then started skating us to our respective penalty boxes, only to release us about twenty feet away with tempers still running high. Knowing it was my last shift with the Blazers, and that I was playing for Todd, I grabbed the guy again and went in for the second fight. Deemed the instigator and aggressor in both fights, I was given the boot from the game and received something like sixty-one penalty minutes in that single play, which surely put me into the AJHL record books. My antics may have been a little over the top, but it also gave Todd and Dad a little bit of a show while they were watching from the crowd. Knowing my time to exit the stage had come, I gave the crowd a slight wave and skated off the ice to the Blazers' dressing room. I still remember the smirk I shared with our Blazer teammate Brett Yeo – one of Todd's favorite guys and a former roommate – as I made my way off the ice at the gate beside the team bench.

Though the Blazers were capable of killing off the minor penalties, some of which were offset by some of the other team's penalties, Jackson was furious and blamed me for the loss in the media. I respectfully disagreed. I then packed up my bag, said goodbye to my teammates, gave an exit interview with one of the Lloydminster TV news reporters, and met Dad and Todd. The next day, in the center of Western Canada, right on the border of Saskatchewan and Alberta, Todd and I had another exchange of good-byes, much like weeks earlier at the front step on Ranch. I was heading west with a lot of excitement for hockey back in my heart, and Todd was heading back east for treatments, to battle hard in his heart and body, just to have the chance to play the game once again.

*Me and Todd, in Lloydminster during the home opener for the 2004-2005 season,
right after I got ejected from the game. The next day, I would be heading west to Vernon,
BC, and Todd would be going back to Winnipeg for his second round of chemo.*

# CHAPTER 14

# INNER PAIN

The first phase of Todd's treatment included five rounds of chemotherapy, carried out over the course of fifteen weeks. The oncologist decided that Todd would be receiving two of the strongest types of chemo available, given to him in intervals of seven straight days followed by two weeks off. The oncologist bluntly told Todd that those chemo treatments were his only chance of stopping the tumor, and that if they didn't work, nothing would.

In the car on the way to Cancer Care for his first round of treatment, the Universal DJ took over again when "Live Like You Were Dying" came on the radio. Dad, who was driving, quickly reached out and shut the radio off; he didn't want the song to upset Todd. Todd wasn't having that, though, and as if wanting to fully embrace the significance and meaning of that moment he turned the radio right back on and cranked the volume up. When life got the loudest, Todd turned it up even more! Todd opened up his heart and took in some deep breaths, and received all he could. He wanted to feel that song fully in that moment. He leaned right in.

Todd was hopeful and confident that his cancer issue would be healed up right away after those chemo rounds. He entered his first round with fresh eyes and an eager attitude. The first session took place in a private room that was nicely arranged by nurse Kim Zerkee, one of Mom's cousins assigned to Todd's care. She put extra love into making the hospital room feel as special and warm as a hospital room possibly could. Over the course of the next days that room hosted up to fifteen or so people at once – far beyond the visitor limit – showering Todd with love and support. Mom stayed during the nights, sometimes sleeping on just an aluminum chair in the hospital room. Dad and his then-fiancé Michelle would arrive early in the mornings, and other family and friends would come and go throughout the day, so Todd was well surrounded by the people closest to his heart.

*Pa (with a shaved head) and Todd during Todd's first round of chemo in August 2004.*

## Super Mario's Boost

Todd also received an outpouring of support from the hockey community at large, including from various high-profile people in the NHL. The hockey community is made up of some of the best people on the planet, including so many selfless individuals who aim to provide incredible support to those undergoing personal challenges. In contrast with the violence and intensity often witnessed on the ice, off the ice we see heartfelt displays from players and personnel who reveal their love and compassion for the less fortunate.

Primarily coming in the form of uplifting phone calls, the generous acts that certain members of the hockey community directed toward Todd helped him keep his spark during the toughest trials of his life.

One of the coolest calls Todd received during his chemo treatments was from none other than my childhood idol, Mario Lemieux. Mario – no-doubt one of the world's most legendary hockey players of all time, who led the Pittsburgh Penguins to back-to-back Stanley Cup championships in 1991 and 1992 and who has way too many individual accomplishments to list here – found out about Todd's condition through the hockey grapevine and got a hold of his mobile number.

Mario knew firsthand how scary going through cancer treatments can be. On January 12, 1993, when he was only twenty-seven years-old, Mario was diagnosed with Hodgkin's Lymphoma after an enlarged lymph node was discovered in his neck. At the time he had been leading the NHL in points and had to take two months off for intense radiation treatments. On the day of his last radiation treatment, he returned to play in the NHL, scoring a goal and getting an assist in his first game back. With Mario's return, the Penguins went on to win seventeen consecutive games – an NHL record. And, most incredibly, despite the two-month break during which he missed twenty games, Mario won the league scoring title, finishing with an incredible one hundred and sixty points (sixty-nine goals and ninety-one assists) in sixty games. Mario's cancer comeback is one of the greatest sports stories of all time.

Todd was asleep in the hospital room when the call came, so Dad reached over and grabbed his phone. When he saw the caller ID he blinked several times to make sure his eyes weren't playing tricks on him; then, unable to contain his excitement, he woke Todd up to tell him that "Mario Lemieux was calling!" Not quite waking up in time to answer, Todd accessed his voicemail to hear a heart-warming message from Mario wishing him good luck; he also left his personal cell number so Todd could call him back. When Todd gained composure he did so, and the two of them had a nice little chat. Dad said the look on Todd's face was absolutely priceless.

Todd described the call with Mario as "awesome" and as one of the coolest things that ever happened to him. He went from feeling like trash to being given a powerful boost from one of the world's best hockey players. During the phone call Mario shared his story with Todd, which Todd described as "positive energy" to him. For Mario this may have been a simple phone call, but for Todd it was incredibly special, a lifeline. While we may not all be Mario Lemieux, we can certainly follow his example of how to uplift those who might be facing tough times. Todd proudly stored Mario's number in his phone contacts, and though he showed it to me briefly for a few seconds, he refused to let me have it, smirking as he declined my plea.

With the help of all the external energy and encouragement being offered, Todd made it through the dark parts of this first chemo week with his spirit still intact. But his painful journey was just getting started, and he had a long way to go. Worse, no one could physically carry Todd through this treacherous next stage; he would have to face the pain and struggle alone. He had absolutely no idea how hard things would get.

## Surviving the Darkness

Todd's second chemo session was a much different story than his first. No longer was he going in there with an indestructible or naive attitude;

he knew he was going to get the shit kicked out of him. Knowing what was coming for him and the effects it would bring, Todd entered the hospital in a much more anxious and fearful state. His hesitation to be readmitted to the hospital set the stage for what was to come. In that second session, the chemo pushed his mind to its limits and challenged him beyond belief. He dealt with depths of darkness and mental anguish that he had never before experienced or imagined.

Todd was kept isolated during his chemo in a small hospital room without any fresh air or sunshine. Per doctor's orders, he was to be totally confined to that ward of the hospital for the whole seven days, without any breaks to go outside. Within a couple of days, things really intensified for him as he began to go stir-crazy. He began experiencing awful mental and emotional side-effects from the non-stop chemicals that were being mercilessly pumped into him without reprieve. Far beyond the expected physical effects such as nausea or complete fatigue, the chemo had a massive effect on Todd's mental and emotional states, and intense anxiety overtook his reality. And that anxiety grew with each new bag of chemo that was connected to his PICC-line.

The drugs continued to mess with him until a breaking point came: Todd began seeing horrible images in his mind's eye. On the third or fourth day he became absolutely terrified when he saw a vision of himself holding a gun, followed by flashes of an image of him shooting himself in the head. In those moments, the idea of death by suicide was his only way to escape the pain and torture. Battling tears of fear and confusion, Todd tried to express to Mom the wild running of his imaginations and the darkness that gripped his reality.

Desperate for the torment to end, he cried out and begged: "Please get someone to help me!"

Mom went running out of the hospital room to talk to the nurses, who, upon recognizing Todd's severe distress, gave him a sedative and allowed Mom to take him outside for fifteen minutes to get some fresh air. He sat on the bench outside the hospital door, breathing deeply to calm his thoughts. Those fifteen minutes under the sun's glow meant more to him than you or I will ever know. After that reprieve, he found the strength to carry on for those next days.

Things would not get easier from there on out. Todd absolutely dreaded the fact that he had to return to the hospital for three more week-long sessions. His apprehension before going in for subsequent chemo treatments grew so severe that he needed to be given a sedative before being taken to the hospital for the third, fourth and fifth rounds. Those were sad times, and I can't imagine the heartbreak Mom and Dad felt when they witnessed Todd's fear and intense anxiety on the rides back to the hospital.

The two-week breaks in-between those seven-day chemo sessions were difficult too. Though Todd wasn't in the hospital, he felt terrible. He was very weak and tired, and his body – which had looked so healthy and strong only months earlier – now seemed frail. There was no hair on his body and his skin was very pale. For the most part Todd was isolated during those days. He stayed quiet and wanted things around him to be quiet as well. He didn't have energy for visitors; he just wanted to rest by himself. Hanging out with the dogs, he watched a lot of TV, and stayed somewhat nourished by eating cheese quesadillas – certainly not a health food by any means but the only thing that didn't immediately make him nauseous.

I can't imagine a lot of the things Todd went through, but I certainly cannot relate to the roller coaster of confusion, doubt, hope, disappointment, and despair that he experienced throughout those chemo treatments. If you have a friend or family member going through chemo, be gentle; for they are fighting an internal battle that we simply cannot relate to, and their bodies need a peaceful and healing environment to rest and attempt to recharge. And remember, just because you can't physically see someone's pain and struggles doesn't mean they don't exist.

## Hockey Player Pain

Though it doesn't do any good to dwell on what could have been done differently, it is troublesome to think of the fact that Todd reached out in quiet desperation to so many people for help when something was clearly wrong with his body. Unfortunately, Todd's story – while much more severe than most – is not uncommon and sheds light on the darker side of injury and/or illness within the sports industry. All too often an athlete reveals that they are experiencing pain, or that something is off in their bodies, yet they are inadequately examined or are prematurely dismissed without adequate inquiry. They are told they *should* be fine. Moreover, unless declared injured by the trainer or coach, players are expected to play through the pain. It wasn't too long ago that you were a "pussy" for missing a shift after getting your "bell rung" – old-school speak for suffering a concussion.

Perhaps even more than most, hockey players tend to hide their pain so as not to be seen as "soft." Hockey players are supposed to be tough; and tough people don't show pain, right? "Pain is weakness leaving the body," we were always told, and we simply accepted it as truth. We were conditioned from a very young age to think this way. In the hockey world, "playing through pain" is not so much an option as it is a motto.

With these types of thoughts ingrained in his mind, Todd tried so hard to hide his pain from others, in both hockey and cancer. He also didn't want others to hurt from seeing that pain. Because of this, most people close to him, including me, didn't quite know how much he was suffering. While Todd's intentions were noble, they were also unnecessary. Todd wasn't weak, needy, or a complainer; he was sick, pure and simple. When pain is real, it shouldn't be ignored or suppressed.

Along with hiding their physical pain, hockey players typically don't talk about their feelings. In recent years, I have come to learn how many hockey players are suffering in silence in some way, especially with mental health. There are many things that can keep a junior, college, or professional player sleep-deprived and ridden with anxiety: a missed empty net; a missed pass; a costly turnover; pressure to fight; a bad goal against; a stupid penalty at the wrong time; getting healthy scratched; getting reduced ice-time; contract negotiations; family pressures; and so on. Couple this with the personal trauma, stress and pressures everyone experiences, and disastrous results can occur, all buried deep below the surface.

Mental illness can stem from a wide variety of things, including past emotional traumas, negative mental thought patterns, improper nutrition, and, as only recently discovered, chronic traumatic encephalopathy (CTE) – a disease linked with recurrent concussions. These mental injuries or conditions, whatever the cause, need to be understood better and treated more professionally by the hockey community at large. An NHLer diagnosed with cancer would be bombarded with support and love. However, if that same NHLer came out or was exposed as struggling with some form of mental illness, he would likely receive some sympathy, but not nearly enough to make him feel fully supported and connected to others. Todd had a team of professionals around him at all times supporting him with these internal struggles, who presumed he was facing depression, anxiety, and other related issues based on his cancer situation, but other guys aren't so fortunate. From here on out, we must be on the lookout for one another.

## Be a Light

We are all capable of being a light to others. Sometimes, the simplest action or word can make the biggest difference. This light alleviates our pain and darkness within. This light can save lives.

During our rookie junior season in Regina, we knew we would have to take our proverbial licks in order to earn the respect of veterans on the team. This meant doing lots of rookie shit, be it slamming consecutive warm beers at the rookie party or carrying the skate sharpener and team equipment trunks down the narrow and icy death-stairs of the visiting team entrance of the Swift Current Broncos arena. On our team, the *rookie-ing* was relatively light and harmless – the thing that pissed me off most was not being able to walk to the bathroom on the back of the bus without getting punched in the arms or legs by vets trying to sleep.

Trends in the *rookie-ing* department have changed for the better over the last decades, but there can be many tough days for a rookie on any junior hockey team, or any team for that matter. Beyond the collective *rookie-ing*, which wore off early in the season, there were a couple of veterans who made life very miserable for me at times during my rookie year. This wasn't *rookie-ing*, though; it was bullying.

After one winter afternoon practice and team workout, I was approached by one of the guys who gave me a hard time. That particular day, I sat in my dressing room stall with my shirt off, exhausted from the practice and workout. I was already tired, sweaty, and cold. He came over, sat in the stall next to me, and, proceeded to make fun of me for my chest (Todd and I were both born with a slight inversion of our chest at the sternum). He then started slapping me across my chest with an open hand and chirping me in my ear. This was far beyond a friendly buddy-to-buddy chest slap. And, as this player was one of our team's best, if I defended myself – say, with a punch to his nose – I no doubt would have been reprimanded, maybe even released. A fourth-liner does not dare step up to one of the team's stars. So instead of causing a big scene and getting called into the coach or general manager's office, I decided to soak the assault and ridicule. Eventually, after a few minutes, everything stopped. The slight physical pain was one thing, but emotionally I felt like a powerless piece of shit. That moment in the middle of a frigid Saskatchewan winter was a lonely and dark one, and at its core was confusion and shame.

After quickly showering and dressing, I waited for Todd and we walked out of the rink together to get in the truck to drive home. Todd sat beside me in the passenger seat of my truck, unaware of what just transpired. Still, he could probably tell that something wasn't right. Then, out of the metaphorical and literal darkness, the brightest light was literally shone into my life, which changed everything in an instant.

Rick Rypien, or "Ryp" as he was known, was one of our favorite teammates with the Pats. He lived just down Broad Street from us, a block or so away, and drove the same route to and from the rink when we didn't drive together. He was the kind of guy who would look you in the eyes and give you a big smirk or a smile as he greeted you. Rick loved Todd, and Todd loved him back. Some of my favorite memories of him are when he would look at Todd and say "Bitty" – a shortened version of Todd's Pats' nickname – with a nod and a smirk as we walked into the rink. Like Todd, Rick was the kind of teammate that naturally brought light to others around him.

Being from Coleman, Alberta – a small town in the Rocky Mountains within the Municipality of Crowsnest Pass in southwest Alberta – Rick had a giant, old green Ford pickup truck that allowed him to drive around one of Canada's most beautifully rugged areas. That evening, as we waited for the streetlight to turn green, Rick's truck made a turn and was pulling up right behind us in the same lane. We were deep in winter, and it was pitch black outside at the time. Rick pulled that Ford monster truck as close as could to the bumper of my tiny Mazda truck, and then blasted his high-beam headlights into my tiny truck's mirrors.

Todd and I were instantly blinded and jumped in our seats. It was the type of brightness that Clark Griswold's neighbor experienced when Clark finally got his Christmas lights to work in *Christmas Vacation*. After the initial shock wore off, we turned around and looked behind us to see Rick with one of his classic giant smiles beaming as bright as his high beams, laughing his ass off. Todd and I burst out laughing too, and I momentarily forgot the bullying incident that had been plaguing me just seconds earlier.

On the ice, Rick was bar-none, pound-for-pound, the toughest player that I ever played hockey with. I say that despite playing on the same team as Orrsy, who as mentioned before was one of the NHL's toughest of all time. While Orrsy was a big guy and a natural heavyweight; Rick was a breed apart. Though he was smaller than some bantam players, he was also the son of Wes Rypien, a Canadian boxing champion. In the words of Pats teammate Jordan McGillivray, Rick "could throw six punches at once," and often beat the shit out of guys who underestimated him. During one game against the Prince Albert Raiders, Rick challenged their captain Greg Watson, who was also a second-round NHL draft pick and one of their biggest players. Other Raiders mocked Rick when he dropped his hands alongside his body and shook his gloves – the universal symbol in hockey for, "You wanna go?" Thirty seconds later, the Raiders were no longer laughing when Watson skated off the ice with blood dripping from his face after Rick landed those six hard punches in rapid succession.

Rick, for all his toughness and great sense of humor, had also experienced great trauma and moments of darkness when his girlfriend was killed in a car accident on her way to our game in Lethbridge, Alberta. Her loss shook Rick to the core and triggered deep depression and anguish. After a brief period of time off, Rick returned to our team and played hard through his internal pain and suffering.

When Rick's hands were actually in his gloves, they were magical with the puck. Todd and I were witness to some of his beautiful plays, including a home game end-to-end rush followed by a dirty backhand post-and-in snipe from the slot that could have easily contended for WHL goal of the year. After his third and final season with the Pats, Rick was not drafted to the NHL but was given an amateur tryout with the Manitoba Moose of the American Hockey League at the end of the 2004-2005 season and into the playoffs. At the time, the Jets were not yet back in Winnipeg, and the Moose were affiliated with the Vancouver Canucks. Rick played well enough to be signed to the Moose for 2005-2006. Within months of the start of that season, Rick was called up to the Vancouver Canucks in December. In what could only be described as a Mario Lemieuxesque power move, Rick scored a goal during the first shift of his first NHL game! It was nothing short of a true Cinderella hockey story for an undersized and undrafted player.

Unfortunately, Rick broke his leg after only five games with the Canucks, resulting in being sent back down to the Moose for rehab. This was the start of several severe career-threatening injuries, which always held Rick back from excelling in the NHL. Rick played the next seasons between Canucks and the Moose before returning to the Canucks full-time in 2009-2010.

In 2011, in what was supposed to be a bright new start to his career, Rick signed with the Jets for their inaugural season return to the NHL. However, in an incredibly sad turn of events, Rick never made his pre-season flight to Winnipeg and was later found deceased in his home in Coleman. Apparently, he had missed his appointment with the Jets team doctor, Dr. Peter MacDonald – the very same who treated Todd – who notified the team's head therapist, Rob Millette. Rob in turn called Craig Heisinger – the Jets' Senior Vice-President & Director of Hockey Operations/Assistant General Manager and one of Rick's biggest supporters – who flew out to Alberta to check on him only to find it was too late.

Although his professional hockey future was looking better, Rick had been fighting a dark and loud battle inside his head for a long time. Like Todd, Rick did not want to burden others with his pain and suffering, so many were unaware of how bad things had gotten for him. Those who did know and wanted to offer assistance were often not able to reach him. I know some really caring individuals, like Heisinger and Vancouver Canuck teammate Kevin Bieksa, tried as hard as they could to help him, to no avail.

I will be forever grateful to Rick for giving me the gift of light and laughter during what had been one of my lowest moments of that season. His goofiness on the road that night lifted me out of the shame and self-pity I was feeling so I could share a great moment of true laughter with my brother. I am not being melodramatic when I say that Rick literally lit me up and changed the course of my life that night, just by being himself. Just like the power of a passing stranger's smile on a lonely person, Rick's actions were so natural to him that he didn't even realize how much he helped me in the moment. Unfortunately, for all his light Rick was unable to lift himself out of his darkest and loneliest times. I wish I could have somehow returned the favor to him when he needed it most.

# Lookout Light

It would be a cliché and borderline ignorant to say that Rick just needed more "loving energy" in his life. What I'm trying to say is that all of us – even the toughest – need consistent love and support, especially when we are not at the top of our game or are dealing with silent inner pain, as this is crucial to our wellbeing and even our survival. We should also be on the lookout for how we can help others when they need it. Sometimes a call or a text is all it takes to charge someone up out of a very dark place.

Of course, it's often not easy to recognize when someone is in emotional pain, especially if, like Rick or Todd, they are always joking around and making others feel good. That's why it's so important to look into a person's eyes when you engage with them. The eyes reveal the internal state of being, so if there is emotional or mental suffering you will find it there. We are all connected, we all have sorrows and challenges, so whatever they are dealing with – be it cancer, depression, or something else – bring them light as often as you can.

Humans can truly thrive only when they feel connected and loved, when they feel supported by the world and people around them. Todd was blessed to receive this support throughout his battle with cancer. As soon as they learned of his diagnosis virtually every friend, family member, and neighbor reached out in a powerful way. He literally couldn't get away from all the love and support, which at first was overwhelming and almost unbearable. All the focus on his well-being made him feel self-conscious and uncomfortable. However, when he finally surrendered to it, his heart was blown wide open by all the love being showered upon him. This love encouraged him and gave him the strength to carry on through his toughest moments. Everyone deserves this type of love and support. A candle used to light another candle does not lose its strength or power; it only creates more light!

# CHAPTER 15

# BELIEVE IN ME

## The Hidden Gateway

Everyone has that thing that opens a hidden gateway within; a gateway that leads to excitement, passion, and love for life. For some it's music, for others it's science or sports, and so on. For Todd, like so many other young Canadians, that thing was hockey. Todd lived his life with the power and pureness of hockey surrounding him at all times. He did not just play it for something to do, he lived for it. He was connected to hockey more than any other thing or activity, and he thrived within that world. When thinking back upon his relationship and passion for the game, he said, "Hockey was my life, plain and simple."

In an interview six months before he died, Todd described the "rollercoaster of emotions" he'd been on since his diagnosis. The highs and lows he experienced were strongly tied to whether he would be able to play hockey at the highest levels again, and his emotional and mental health were directly connected to the answer to that question. Early on in his treatment, the highs of the roller coaster came when the slightest possibility of returning to play hockey existed; the lows came when doctors held him back from playing, or cast doubt on his future in the game.

After receiving initial chemotherapy and radiation treatments, Todd was adamant that he would return to play at a high level once again, despite what he was hearing from some on his medical team. "They told me that I'd never play hockey again," Todd said as he recalled those tumultuous first days after diagnosis. "I find it hard to believe I'm not going to be able to do something I've spent my whole life doing."

Despite all the chaos, confusion, and doubt he perceived from certain doctors, Todd refused to let go of his hockey stick so easily. He truly believed that he would soon be as good as new and returned to play within a few months. During this early stage of his cancer, Todd's visions of healing his body of disease and pursuing a professional career remained strong, and these thoughts inspired and empowered him. Using the energy of the words of support and encouragement of others, combined with his own willpower, Todd found a way to change his state of mind and resurrect his life force. He would not let this diagnosis destroy him; he was going to find a way to beat cancer and get back to the game. His inner strength and composure were easily recognized. This was a comeback story.

## The Climb

After all the chemo sessions, Todd had to go to Toronto for five straight weeks of radiation, with a short Christmas break in Winnipeg as his only reprieve. Dad accompanied Todd to Toronto the first time and got him acquainted with his new surroundings and treatment schedule. Always the disciplined athlete, Todd quickly adopted a daily routine.

At ten a.m. he would walk from the hotel to Mount Sinai Hospital where he'd punch his treatment card and undergo radiation for fifteen minutes. Then he and Dad would walk a few blocks over to Eggspectation – Todd's favorite breakfast spot on Yonge Street. After returning to the hotel, he would sit on the couch with his laptop and watch DVDs like Napoleon Dynamite for some comic relief. Once he got some strength back, he'd head down to the hotel gym for a workout, pushing himself to regain his strength. Radiation, food, movies, and exercise . . . day after day.

After a short, bittersweet Christmas break in Winnipeg, Todd returned to Toronto, this time with Mom. On New Year's Eve, the two of them walked to City Hall and, underneath the bright, booming fireworks and amongst the crowd of thousands of people cheering and kissing each other, quietly rang in 2005. Todd looked around at all the carefree people around him; then, managing a smile, he gave Mom a hug. For her, seeing her son's slight smile was brighter than any of those fireworks, and it was the only thing that mattered. And, just as those fireworks were exploding high in the sky, strength and hope were bubbling up again in Todd's heart and mind.

At that point, we were all still very optimistic that Todd would make a full recovery and return to playing hockey. He had started to look healthier and stronger. He was happier and more confident.

Todd's mood and spirits were especially lifted when Hubby – our old fan-favorite Pats teammate whose skates Todd was supposed to fill – visited him at the hotel. Hubby was in Toronto at the time playing for the Marlies, the top affiliate of the Maple Leafs. Hubby and Todd had a special connection, both in the dressing room and on the ice, and now they reminisced about old memories, like the time they were paired up together during a flow drill and got caught up in their own little world – wheeling around, dangling, making passing plays, and taking multiple shots on net – oblivious to the fact that the rest of the team was waiting on them to finish. Though the team thought it was fitting and hilarious for those two free spirits to be doing such a thing during a flow drill, coach Bob Lowes wasn't amused by the disruption to the drill, and let them know, very loudly and with his face red with fury. Todd and Hubby had tried to conceal their smirks as they sheepishly skated to the back of the line, with Lowesy yelling at them the entire way.

Such playfulness was regular practice for them. While the rest of the team was busy being serious all the time, Todd and Hubby were doing their own weird and humorous things, like sneaking up behind each other during water breaks and making exaggerated labored breathing noises as loud and as close as they could to the nape of the other's neck. The victim would eventually realize the other was behind them, and the two would break out in laughter. Just like old times, Hubby's hotel visit brought Todd laughter and energy.

Along with his spirit and mental fortitude, Todd's physical strength was returning to his body. He looked strong and fit, and was certainly mentally sharp. Aside from the radiation burns on his face, he appeared to be a healthy eighteen-year-old, ready to return to battle! And he had worked his ass off for it. Instead of sitting on the couch or in bed, giving in to the weakness and nausea, he had found a way to get himself into a strength-building mindset as soon as he was cleared for exercise.

In between his initial treatments in Winnipeg, Todd continued to work out regularly at Focus Fitness. Focus was like his second home, and he loved being there. He was also given support and encouragement by a great cast of people, which he would mentally carry with him when he had to return to Toronto and work out under very different circumstances.

To be close to the hospital and various other amenities while he received treatment, Todd and Mom or Dad stayed at the Delta Chelsea – a twenty-seven-story hotel. While it was a nice place, it certainly didn't have a state-of-the-art gym filled with bright-eyed and good-hearted friends Todd was used to, but as always, he took what he had and made the best of it. One night around one a.m., Dad was awakened out of sound sleep by someone shaking him. When he opened his eyes he was shocked to see a hotel security guard standing at the foot of his bed.

"Excuse me, sir, why is your door open?"

Dad told the security guard that his son must have left the door open, then he got up to look for Todd, but he wasn't there. They went out in the hallway and checked the entire floor, but there was no trace of my brother. Getting a little concerned, Dad went back to the room and thought about what to do. A few minutes later, Todd came through the hotel room door, huffing and puffing. Dad asked him what he was doing, to which Todd replied, casually and perhaps with a little bit of teenage attitude, "I was running stairs . . ."

"What do you mean you were running stairs?" Dad asked, confused. It was, after all, one a.m.!

"I have to train for when I go back to Lloyd!"

Todd knew the hard work that had to be done if he were to ever have a chance to play competitive hockey again, and he was going to use every tool at his disposal – even a staircase – to do it. In his mind this was all an absolutely necessary part of the process, and sitting and waiting around on the bench would be a waste of his most precious resource – time! While in Toronto he continued to run up those twenty-seven flights of stairs three times a day. Was he pushing himself too hard? Maybe. But that was Todd, and he was determined to get back into playing shape as quickly as possible.

He was still only eighteen years old at that point, which meant he was still eligible to play for the rest of that current season, plus two more full seasons after that. Once he finished radiation and was cleared to play, he could go back to Lloydminster in the AJHL and maybe even get another shot in the Dub with the Wheat Kings, or somewhere else. In his mind, all that greatness and glory was still within reach; all he had to do was make himself as strong as possible and keep moving toward his vision.

## Training With Tucker in T.O.

An incredible thing happened during Todd's comeback journey. The NHL was in the midst of the 2004-2005 lockout season, which kept the majority of NHLers off the ice with their NHL teams. While many went to play in Europe during this time, and some dropped down to play in the American Hockey League or other minor pro leagues, others, including several Toronto Maple Leafs players and other local Toronto-based players, just rode out the lockout. Instead of staying off the ice and getting rusty and out-of-shape, guys like Darcy Tucker, Shane Corson, Joe Nieuwendyk, and Igor Ulanov were scrimmaging and putting themselves through drills. Through Auntie Donna's friend Lynn and her connections in Toronto, Todd managed to get himself an invite to their ice times by none other than NHL legend Shane Corson.

Todd was absolutely elated. One slight problem existed, though: Todd didn't have his hockey equipment with him! An urgent call was placed to Auntie Donna, who rushed to the basement of Ranch to pack up Todd's equipment – per his very specific instructions, of course – and shipped it to him rush-overnight.

Now, instead of playing alongside junior-aged players somewhere in Western Canada as he'd planned, Todd would instead be playing alongside veteran NHLers in Toronto – an iconic hockey city that was home to the Hockey Hall of Fame and the Stanley Cup. Better still, one of those players was Darcy Tucker, one of Todd's favorites, and the one whose picture he kept in that leather folder and used to stare at on those long bus rides down the TransCanada Highway with the Pats two seasons earlier.

At first, he was nervous to be scrimmaging with all these legendary NHLers, but his nerves calmed quickly as he felt respected and accepted by these guys as a player and person. By the end of it all, Todd said, "We were all just buddies and I felt like I was one of the guys with them."

I am not sure what Tucker or Corson said to Todd during those ice times, but after that Toronto trip Todd was more determined than ever to make a big-time junior hockey comeback. He had a fire within him, and no one was going to tell him that he wouldn't play again. By that point Todd had been kept from competing and hadn't played a competitive hockey game with his peers for almost a full year. But this comeback was happening!

*Todd with NHL legend Darcy Tucker in Toronto, 2005.*

CHAPTER 16

# HIS LAST SHIFT

## The Comeback of a Lifetime

At the end of January 2005, after finishing his radiation treatments, Todd was temporarily cleared to return to play competitive hockey. He knew he may be facing a major surgery in March, but he had six weeks until it was even scheduled – six weeks to go back to doing what he loved! And, knowing him, he was likely counting on not needing that surgery after all. I picture him envisioning the phone call saying that the chemo and radiation cleared up all the tumors, and that he was totally healthy again. Of course, that was wishful thinking, but Todd had that type of faith and hope.

It seemed he had no sooner arrived home to Winnipeg before he was traveling again, this time in his little green Dodge Neon, bound for Lloydminster. After braving an intense snowstorm that stressed him to his limit, he finally arrived in the tight-knit hockey community that welcomed him back with open arms.

Before he could play for the Blazers, however, there was a major roster and regulation issue to contend with. Since it was well past the Christmas break, all of the Blazers' AJHL player cards – or formal roster designations that are limited to a certain number per team, per season – were already used. In other words, the Blazers' roster was completely full, with no room for Todd. What injustice and cruelty! As if having cancer wasn't enough, he faced being barred from play by nothing more than league red tape.

Fortunately, a solution was found: Todd could sign on with an Alberta Junior B Hockey League team and be *leased* to the Blazers for five regular season games; and, if the Junior B team missed the playoffs, he could stay until the end of the Blazers' season. While playing games in a Junior B league may have been a slight blow to Todd's ego, he didn't hesitate before signing on with the St. Paul Canadiens. He just wanted to get back on the ice; plus, as mentioned, he hadn't played an official game in almost a full year and was not quite in "game-shape," so playing in Junior B hockey would be a great opportunity to ease back into Junior A. Just like NHLers recovering from injuries sometimes play games in the minors to help them reacclimate to the pace and action, playing Junior B would allow Todd to find his skating legs, timing, and skill in a familiar arena. Sure enough, after playing games with the Canadiens and sniping a few goals, he moved up to rejoin the Blazers.

All-in-all, Todd's willpower, determination, and effort allowed him to make one of the greatest low-key sports comebacks of all time. Against all odds, Todd climbed his way back to the top of the Blazers' roster and was right back into the mix. Despite missing the entire first half of the season, he found a way to jump back into full stride quickly. He wasn't just getting pity ice-time either; he was getting as much ice time as any other guy on the team, and he was looking great! Through a combination of positive visualizations, an intense workout schedule, and sheer determination, Todd had succeeded in manifesting his return. After all he'd gone through, he would not be denied his chance to compete once again. And, when he got that chance, he was not going to waste it away or take it for granted.

Any trepidation Todd felt before that first game he pushed aside, saying he "was more excited than nervous." He wasn't concerned about hurting or embarrassing himself; he just wanted to play! And he didn't take long to make an impact, either. "I was expecting to have a good game," he said later when talking about the Blazers' win, "but I wasn't expecting to score a goal . . . " Seeing that red-light flash on when he scored, Todd felt that familiar dopamine rush that was now even sweeter after having been away for so long.

Beyond helping the Blazers on the scoreboard, Todd uplifted his teammate's spirits. According to Josh Aldrich, then sports editor of the *Lloydminster Meridian Booster*, Todd's "effect on the team was an immediate one, displaying the leadership and spirit he was famous for" in his previous season. Fellow Blazer Branden Gay stated, "With Todd back, it was just pure inspiration."

While Todd's teammates appreciated him being back in action and helping them win games, Todd was ecstatic about being back with them. This return to Lloyd was not just about hockey; it was also about rejoining a team and being surrounded by others that all support each other in a common mission. He had upgraded from a hospital room to a hockey dressing room and was back to being a part of something bigger than himself. He was back with the boys.

In that spark of time, all was good again in Todd's life. This comeback was supposed to be just the start of big things to come. After all, he had paid the price and climbed the mountains dropped directly in front of him, and he was ready to move on from being someone with cancer back to being a hockey player. And he was doing it!

Todd played his heart out in every single shift and cherished every moment he experienced. Every moment driving to the rink instead of the hospital; every time he geared up in the dressing room with the fellas instead of changing into hospital attire; every time he felt his steel hit the ice for those first few strides on a clean sheet of ice; every time the puck first hit his blade as he started to dangle; every time he heard that post ring when he went bardown; every time he felt and heard the fans filling the arenas to watch the big show in town; every post-game victory hangout with the boys; and so on. Every moment of the comeback became special for Todd, and he charged it up with intense gratitude. He let no moment on the ice slip by unappreciated.

But, as with all things, especially those we enjoy, the time went by so fast. After what must have only seemed like a few shifts, Todd's comeback was cut drastically short by the news that he would definitely have to return to Toronto for a major surgery. The Tikhoff-Linberg procedure involved the removal of his scapula and the suspension of his arm against his upper rib cage, which would leave his body deformed and substantially weakened. No longer would he have the chance to return to "normal."

It was a colossal blow, and nearly as shocking and surreal as the initial diagnosis. Just as he was starting to find his top speed on the ice again, just as the glorious comeback looked to indeed be the rebirth of his career, his dream was ripped from his hands. It was official: his playing days were done.

I can't imagine the intensity of pain and confusion that Todd felt at that time. Beyond the fear, panic, and anxiety that came with the news that the cancer was back and spreading, he was dealing with the devastation that he could no longer do the only thing he really loved. I *can* imagine that among those emotions was an intense rage at the unfairness of it all. To put the devastation in perspective, Todd said learning that he would never play competitive hockey again was "way worse" than learning that he had cancer. No pharmaceutical painkiller had a chance of easing the agony he felt over that loss. In an instant, Todd went from eagerly anticipating the next game with his teammates to the fear and dread of the upcoming surgery.

However, in what would be one of the most bittersweet moments of Todd's life, he was given the chance to play one last competitive hockey game. Still reeling from the news, and with so much fire for the game still burning inside of him, the only thing he could do was savor every moment before cancer benched him for good.

## There Comes a Time

The night of Wednesday, February 23, 2005 was a bitterly cold one in Fort McMurray (the "Mac"). This city in northern Alberta loves its oil and hockey in equal measure, and as the blizzard began and the temperature plummeted, all that could be seen through the white hazy sky were the refinery lights. For Todd, it was as if nature had intentionally set the stage for this game of a lifetime.

That morning he had boarded the team bus in Lloydminster for the six-hour trip to Fort McMurray. As any hockey player knows, a lot can be thought about during such a long trip, and those aren't all just happy thoughts. This was especially true for Todd as he barreled toward his final game; surely, he was trying to process all that had happened and wondering what his future, which had once seemed so certain, now held. When the bus finally arrived at the Oil Barons' arena his heart must have been pounding out of his chest. This was one of those big-time moments, and all he could do was to soak it all in and appreciate everything in front of him before it was all gone.

By the time they unloaded the equipment off the bus and entered the visitor's dressing room, Todd must have been feeling like he was in a real-life movie. Small moments no longer existed for him; every little thing a hockey player typically takes for granted now held great meaning and significance.

Home to one of the best Junior A hockey programs in Canada since 1981, Fort McMurray was a righteous place for such a monumental event in Todd's life. As he entered that Oil Barons rink, Todd would have felt the greatness beaming down on him from the team pictures that lined the walls of the arena and the Royal Bank Cup national championship banners strewn across the rafters. He would have seen and felt the pure energy of hockey excellence and excitement that existed in such a legendary place.

As he did before every game he played, Todd would have looked over the fresh sheet of ice and empty seats of the arena, soon to be packed with cheering fans, and visualize success in the game to come. He would have gone through his typical game preparation routine, only this was no typical game. The joy of the little things, like the smell of a hockey dressing room or that fresh tape carefully being rolled onto a stick, or the feeling of tying the laces of his skates and pulling that jersey over his head, now came with an omnipresent reminder that these experiences would never be had again.

Mom and I were fortunate enough to attend and witness Todd's last game of competitive hockey. Sadly, Dad, who was long out of vacation days by then, could only send his love and energy to Todd from Fire Station #1 in downtown Winnipeg, two provinces and sixteen hundred and twenty-three kilometers away.

One of the hardest things about being a full-time firefighter is the number of holidays or special occasions that you are forced to miss because it is your turn to work the shift to keep others safe. Whether it be Christmas morning or your cancer-ridden son's last hockey game, the risk of fire and the danger that comes with it never goes away, and firefighters are bound to their duties. In fact, years later, in May 2016, the residents of Fort McMurray would learn that lesson in the harshest way possible when the city and its surrounding areas suffered one of the worst wildfires in Canadian history, which destroyed over twenty-four hundred homes and buildings and caused nearly ten billion dollars in damages.

Mom and I were only able to attend the game thanks to the efforts of two people: Auntie Donna, and a man named Stafford Gorsalitz. Throughout our junior hockey careers, Auntie Donna was one of our all-time biggest fans. Wanting to make our time away from home as comfortable and enjoyable as possible, she would send up biweekly or monthly care packages loaded with goodies like gift cards to Tim Hortons and Boston Pizza. She was also active on our team and league's online message boards and listened to every game broadcasted over the radio, cheering as hard as ever for her two nephews.

Initially, despite the significance of the game for Todd, we were not going to be able to attend. Last-minute flights to Fort McMurray in the dead of winter were extremely expensive, and by that point, Dad and Mom had spent tens and tens of thousands of dollars during Todd's treatment trips, especially during the six-week stay in downtown

Toronto, which came with very high hotel and food bills to keep Todd as comfortable as possible. To anyone who thinks that Canadian healthcare is completely *free* you are sorely mistaken, especially if you want the privacy and comfort of a semi-private or private hospital room. Unfortunately, as so many families of cancer patients know, the costs of treatments and the travel associated with them can cause severe financial distress during an already extraordinarily stressful time. Any disposable income and savings Mom and Dad had were pretty much wiped out.

Through the hockey fan forum website www.hockeytalk.net, Auntie Donna – operating under the pseudonym "Joe W" – contacted a Fort McMurray fan who operated under the pseudonym "Booster." Auntie Donna's initial request was quite simple:

*Hello Booster,*

*I wanted to know if you will be at the game in Ft. McMurray on Feb. 23rd.*
*I am wondering if you will be taking pictures that night?*
*I will explain more if you are planning to.*

*Thanks,*

*Joe W*

Having viewed his previous postings, Auntie Donna knew that Booster took action-shot photos of Fort McMurray Oil Barons' players. All she wanted was to arrange for a photo or two to commemorate Todd's last game. However, after sending that initial message, a heart-warming series of events unfolded.

Booster was actually Stafford – attorney, Oil Baron fan, hockey dad, and, as it turned out, an incredibly caring individual. Once he learned of Todd's illness and that it was his last game, he, with an open heart and open checkbook, offered to pay for our flights to Fort McMurray. And as if that wasn't enough, Stafford also offered to host me and Mom at his home. A stranger to us prior to that game, Stafford was actually an angel in disguise who blessed our lives in a very special and completely unexpected way.

As Auntie Donna and Stafford arranged the flight details, he sent one final, uplifting message:

> Life truly is a freaky thing, Donna. Last night when we were discussing the possibility of getting Wade up here I told you "Make it Happen." Lo and behold, as I was driving through the drive-thru at Tim Hortons, a young man was walking into the coffee shop with a jean jacket on. Imprinted in bold letters on the back of his jacket were the words "Make it Happen." What is the likelihood that someone in Fort McMurray would have a jacket that says that *and* secondly that would decide to walk into the coffee shop as I am driving in through the drive thru? Some things are just meant to be, Donna, and I truly believe that this is one of them.

As a special surprise, neither Mom nor Todd knew that I was also going to be attending the game. While Mom would be flying from Winnipeg, Auntie Donna and Stafford secretly arranged for my flight from Kelowna, through Edmonton, to Fort McMurray. I could hardly wait to see their faces when I arrived at the arena. First, though, I had to get permission from Vandy, my coach with the Vipers, to miss practices. A less caring coach might have refused, but not Vandy. He knew how important this was to me and without hesitation sent me on my way.

Everything had fallen into place to make this trip a reality, but for a while it seemed Mother Nature had other plans when due to snow and blistering winds my connecting flight from Edmonton to Fort McMurray was delayed. I sat nervously in the airport, repeatedly checking the time, knowing that the minutes until puck drop were rapidly ticking away and trying not to think about how much of a shame it would be to miss such an occasion. After what seemed like an eternity in the airport terminal, my flight was finally called to board. I took my seat and sat anxiously, not knowing how much of the game I would miss by the time I arrived. I calmed myself down, and my thoughts turned to Todd sitting in the Blazers' dressing room, experiencing his own internal storm of emotions.

After my plane touched down in Fort McMurray I sprinted out of the airport and flagged down a taxi driver, who did his best to navigate the snow-packed highways from the airport to the arena. I finally arrived at the game during the first intermission. Of course I was disappointed that I missed the warm-up, anthem, and opening period, but I was just thankful to be there for the last two periods. I made my way through the fans and spotted Mom with her back to me, standing with Stafford. I casually snuck up to her from behind. Already emotionally amped-up from being there, Mom burst into tears when she saw me. Having me there with her made things that much more intense and special, and more emotionally bearable. Stafford stood back and smiled, seeing the love and appreciation in front of him, and knowing he played a part in a very cool thing.

I got the first period summary from Mom and Stafford, then the three of us made our way back to the seats, across the rink from the Blazers' bench, to soak in the rest of the action. As if flying us in and hosting us wasn't enough, Stafford had staff from his law office make and hold a big banner with "BELIEVE" written in bold caps to be draped down during the game, which caught our eyes with impeccable timing. That word, "believe," held power for Todd and our family, and was displayed especially for us during that game as a beautiful act of solidarity and support to Todd and our family.

As the teams returned to the ice, I saw Todd walk out of the tunnel with his team and the grim reality of the situation hit home – hard. In that moment, I was watching my younger brother – who I had breathed the game with since we were toddlers – playing his very last hockey game. To say it was emotional for me was an understatement.

With the Blazer logo on his chest and #9 on his back, Todd hit the ice in a fury and played with absolute fire in his heart. There was not going to be another comeback down the road; this was his last game forever. And, though it was not for any sort of championship or trophy, this game on a Wednesday night in northern Alberta would be the biggest of his life.

From the stands we watched nervously and in awe every time Todd hopped the boards and his blades hit the ice. Shift after shift, Todd took possession of the puck, hit top speed in a flash, and created some sort of scoring chance. There was more than one shift when he took the puck and flew past or dangled three or four Oil Baron players, only to be stifled by the last defender, or the goalie. We could clearly see how badly he wanted to score just one last highlight reel goal – to feel the glory of one more end-to-end rush finishing with the puck being sniped top-corner, or make a great offensive play leading to a Blazer goal.

Todd was absolutely relentless, playing more desperately and intensely than I had ever seen before. Every shift he got was treated as if it were his last, and, with full intensity and fierceness, he competed with everything he had inside of him. His focus was obvious, not just to me but to everyone there. He left it all on the ice! Everything that he had ever played for – his love of hockey; every practice, every workout, every game – culminated in those very moments. For in those moments he was still a hockey player, and then he never would be again.

As the game clock ticked down, Todd's very last shift grew nearer. The fact that he was playing competitive hockey was magic enough, but we held our breath and prayed for something magical to happen just one more time. Despite his best efforts, and some incredible chances in his last shifts, no such highlight moment came. After all the close calls, near-misses, and the accompanying emotional drama, the final buzzer rang to end the game. The Oil Barons had won quite easily, yet, out of all the players who went on to play Division 1 college and/ or professional hockey, I can say with certainty that Todd was the best player on the ice that game. Had there been any scouts in the crowd, you better believe that they would have had a major asterisk besides Todd's name on the roster page; and, after his talented display, I can only imagine how stunned they would have been to learn that Todd was battling for his life.

To corroborate this, one of the Oil Barons' fans, "Hockeymom," wrote on the game's message board: "Man you lit up the ice when u were here . . ."

A Blazers' fan known as "The Man" responded, "Yeah, without a doubt in my mind (especially in the last few games). Todd had been hands-down our best player with regards to skill level and intensity. This plug convention could learn a thing or two from this little big man."

At the end of the game, the hometown fans went home satisfied. Almost all of these fans were completely unaware of what was happening inside the heart and mind of #9 on the visiting team, or that he was facing a much different future than his fellow players.

## For Those That Know

As the arena began to clear out, Mom and I sat crying in the stands as we watched Todd skate somewhat aimlessly around near the players' boxes. He didn't want to leave the ice, but the game was over, and there was nowhere else to go. After regular season games, most junior hockey and professional leagues do not have players shake hands after the game, so they usually just quickly leave the ice surface. However, after this particular game – in an act of pure class – the Oil Barons' head coach at the time, Gord Thibodeau, had every player and coach of the Oil Barons step onto the ice and shake Todd's hand, one-by-one.

Thibodeau was a cancer survivor himself, and Todd's situation hit close to home for him. In fact, he was one of the few people who really understood the emotional rollercoaster Todd was going through. According to Donny Kerfoot, a Winnipeg friend who played for the Oil Barons at the time, Thibodeau was pretty emotional as he announced in the dressing room before the game that Todd's situation didn't look great, and this would likely be his last game. He also explained how awful it was to go through cancer treatments, even saying how chemo can make you feel like you want to die. This situation is one "beyond hockey," he said, then he announced that the team would be shaking Todd's hand and presenting him with a card signed by all of them.

When the entire team surrounded him after the game, Todd initially thought the Oil Barons were trying to start a brawl. Imagine his surprise when instead of fists he was greeted by more than twenty outstretched hands in friendship and support. After each player and coach shook his hand, Todd was presented with that signed Oil Baron card, which wished him strength and courage for the rest of his journey. It was such a small yet very powerful gesture, one that marked the occasion with the ceremony and reverence it deserved. At the very least, Todd exited the ice with blessings from his worthy opponents, and his situation being recognized and respected.

We gathered down by the players' dressing room areas to wait for Todd, and when he finally emerged he appeared stoic, unfazed, and certainly not looking for sympathy. We hugged him and shared a moment by the Zamboni gate. Unlike us, who had clearly been crying, he didn't look like he had shed a single tear. I can only guess what was going on inside his mind and heart, but on the outside he was business as usual. Then, just like that and without a backward glance, he boarded the bus with his teammates for the ride home through the blizzard. His last game had been played, and tomorrow he would be facing a whole new day. Right now, though, he had six hours to reflect on his last game, and all of the games of his life.

## Beyond the Scoresheet

When it was all said and done, Todd had played eight games for the Blazers during his comeback. And in those eight games, he scored two goals, got two assists, and received twenty-three penalty minutes. Considering the Blazers won only seventeen games all season and were the lowest-scoring team in the league, those numbers were pretty solid, especially for someone playing through cancer. But I'm guessing that Todd didn't care so much about wins and losses those days, or even points, for that matter; he likely only cared about playing the game he loved at a competitive level. Eight games are only a sliver of a full season, but Todd had found a way to play junior hockey again, on his terms, with all of his heart. And, as I can personally attest, my brother's last game was nothing short of a world-class showing of courage and a pure moment in hockey history.

"Canadiangirl14," an Oil Baron fan who also posted on the hockey talk chatrooms, summed it up perfectly: "I thought Dynasty was just all talk about Davison . . . until I saw him play . . . he is truly an amazing hockey player . . ."

Todd's junior hockey comeback was remarkable and inspiring. It showed his inner strength and determination, his dedication to hockey, and his belief in himself; it also silenced the doubters, including those on his medical team, who said he would never play again.

A last game is inevitable for every hockey player; for Todd, it just happened to come at a very young age and due to a devastating illness. Even the cockiest young hockey star destined for NHL greatness is really only one freak injury away from never playing competitively again. The human body, though miraculous and resilient, is also very fragile, no matter how big or strong one is. So, in reality, one never really knows when they'll be playing their last shift! This would be the biggest lesson Todd imparted when he moved from player to coach: play each and every game – every shift, in fact – as if it were your last and, at the end of it all, have no regrets!

## Playing for Todd

Seeing Todd play his last game gave me an incredible amount of inspiration for my own hockey career. My first game after rejoining my team in Vernon was against our ultimate rivals, the Salmon Arm Silverbacks. In

*Top banner: Todd in action for the Lloydminster Blazers of the AJHL; Middle: Todd,
in Lloydminster for the opening ceremony, after his first chemotherapy session.
Photo courtesy of Lloydminster Meridian Booster; Bottom: Banner made
by Stafford's staff, for Todd's last game in Fort McMurray, Alberta.*

the middle of a sold-out arena of impassioned Vipers' fans, I soaked in the energy of the atmosphere and felt joy. I played that game with a whole new appreciation for what I had as a healthy young junior hockey player who was still able to play the game that I loved.

With that inspiration and gratitude, I ended up scoring the game-winner on a breakaway after my Winnipeg friend and former Mustang teammate, Dustin DeGagne, blew a tire in the neutral zone while I pressured him. I still remember faking the shot and pulling the puck across to my backhand before going top-shelf on the tendy, who just happened to be Decks! For some quick context, Decks was traded from the Pats to the Tri-City Americans in the 2004-2005 season before being released, so he spent time in the BCHL with the Salmon Arm Silverbacks before closing out his junior career back in the WHL with the Prince Albert Raiders. Decks was a phenomenally talented goalie back in the day, who was good enough to get called up to the Charlotte Checkers of the AHL before hip injuries forced his retirement. Anyway, the fact that the goal in honor of Todd was scored on Decks made it that much sweeter. The situation couldn't have been scripted better any other way.

# 3rd PERIOD

# CHAPTER 17

# ON THIN ICE

The seven-hour Tikhoff-Linberg procedure was performed in Toronto by Dr. Jay Wunder in March 2005. Pete described Dr. Wunder as the premiere orthopedic tumor specialist in Canada. Knowing of his work and skill through their friendship, Pete called Dr. Wunder and helped facilitate this procedure for Todd. Pete knew that Dr. Wunder first and foremost sought solutions designed to preserve limbs and their function, and knew that Dr. Wunder was Todd's best chance to maintain his arm and its use.

After that grueling surgery, Todd spent nearly a full month recovering in Toronto. All of this shit was really starting to take a toll on his spirit. He grew frustrated and angry. He, like so many other cancer patients, grew to despise being in the hospital. He would try to be upbeat, but he was really struggling inside. That was a long month for him.

When he returned to Winnipeg he wanted to be as social as possible. This was a major turning point in his life. His previous seclusion during chemotherapy made him realize and appreciate the importance of human connection and community. He wanted to be with his friends. He wanted to be around his family. He wanted to interact with those closest to him. He was doing his best to adapt to his arm's limited function and his new life.

But things quickly took a turn for the worse when Todd's operation wound became horribly infected. At first, the infection was tolerable. He could still live his daily life as usual, so long as he was extra diligent about caring for his wound. Mom found the perfect place to pop a hanger through the basement ceiling and let his IV-line drip into him while he sat in comfort, watching hockey or whatever else. But every day he woke up to a larger infected area on his left back side and, at the worst point, his collarbone popped right out of his skin. Thankfully Pete was able to fix it, but it would continue to happen over and over again, with Pete having to cut the collarbone shorter and shorter each time. Todd was so powerless in those moments.

Todd's situation was also worsening beneath the skin, as revealed by one of his periodic CT scans at Pan-am clinic. Pete, who was monitoring the cancerous infection and its spreading, told Todd that three spots had appeared on his lungs. Then, during his next appointment, four spots were found. Then, somewhere around May, seven! This wasn't good. Todd initially wanted a lung transplant, but he wasn't a candidate. The best the medical professionals could do was to perform experimental lung surgery, which took place over May Long Weekend. While most other nineteen-year-olds he knew were at lake cabin parties as they celebrated the kickoff to summer, Todd was being cut into right down the front of his chest.

Once the bone was cut through, the surgeon accessed his lungs. They deflated one lung at a time and hand-felt for tumors – taking them out one at a time. In the end, twenty-one tumor pieces were removed from his body. At this point, Todd's spirit wavered harder than ever before. Just like his lungs during the surgery, Todd was totally deflated. In what Mom described as "one of his weakest moments," Todd wanted to give up, telling her "I just can't do this anymore," with a distraught and defeated tone. If self-directed euthanasia was a thing, he may have begged for it in the state he was in.

After that pneumothorax operation, he just wanted to get back to Winnipeg. "I'm going!" he demanded. Restless and isolated in Toronto, he just wanted to be back with his friends, at the place where he still had a life outside the hospital. When they finally returned home, life began again, but things were slowly but undeniably getting worse and the chances of healing seemed to lessen with each blow.

## Cancer Kid

Right from the start, Todd didn't want any special treatment; he hated the idea of being seen as a victim. In one instance, shortly after receiving another blow about the severity of his condition from his doctor in Toronto, he left the downtown hospital and walked down Yonge Street with Mom and Auntie Donna. As he processed the update, which confirmed that things were going to be getting much more serious for him, he ruminated about his future days. Suddenly, and in reaction to an innocent question, he turned around to Mom and Auntie Donna and said, in the sternest tone possible, "I don't ever want to be treated like a cancer kid!"

But the truth was, no matter how hard we all tried to normalize any given situation for him, he was, indeed, a "cancer kid" in those moments. And when he returned from Toronto, despite his best intentions of getting back to a normal life, he just didn't get one. He just couldn't escape the outside world that refused to let him forget that he wasn't "normal" anymore. This took a toll on him mentally and emotionally.

One of the most heartbreaking moments I ever witnessed occurred during what should have been a comedic escape from reality for Todd. One Sunday evening, we sat together in the basement on Ranch and watched a new episode of *Family Guy*. Watching Sunday night sitcoms together, beginning with *The Simpsons* in the early 90s, was an off-ice ritual for us. Usually these were great times that brought a lot of laughter; however, that night our mouths hung open in shock when one of the characters, baby Stewie, made a tasteless remark that alluded to cancer patients being gross and abnormal. I cringed as I watched Todd process the statement. I saw his spirit dim and his confidence plummet as he instantly became uncomfortable and insecure about his condition. I could tell that he was really hurt, and I was heartbroken for him.

He couldn't even count on his favorite TV show as a safe space, where he could just laugh and be a carefree person again for thirty minutes on a Sunday evening.

Though he usually displayed a positive face for the world, Todd also had bouts of anger, and when they came, they came on hard! This anger was more than justified. It was the pure expression of mental anguish that had no physical outlet. Before cancer, when Todd was angry at something going on in his life, he could easily blow off steam with a shift or two of hockey, throwing a hit, slashing someone, or throwing out a few well-deserved chirps. But this anger was different: it had nowhere to go. Though he tried to fight it, Todd's internal rage needed to come out, somehow. Healing would not begin with this type of poison inside. Then out of the blue one day, Todd's anger came out on me, and the situation escalated into a disaster so powerful that it almost destroyed our entire relationship.

## Brotherly Currency

Todd and I had an interesting communication style, especially in later years playing AAA and Junior hockey together. Our mutual friends and teammates would agree. We had lived together and had been in each other's space so much and for so long – we even shared bunkbeds for a decade – that words didn't mean all that much sometimes. We knew of the silent energy between us, and we were strong and secure in that silence.

We rarely if ever made small talk, nor was there a need for inauthentic pleasantries. We didn't talk on the phone a lot, because we didn't have to; I didn't have to call him because he was around, or would be soon enough. We didn't have to catch up, because we knew exactly what was going on. We'd wake up and go to sleep around the same time; we drove everywhere together; we were in the dressing room, on the bus, and just about everywhere else, together. We experienced the same funny moments, in daily life and during special occasions such as holidays or celebrations. We watched the same TV shows and laughed at the same times. Our primary currency was humor and laughter – worth far more than anything else.

And then, of course, we had hockey. As mentioned, to play on the same team as your brother, especially at a high level, is a very rare occurrence. Many things have to align for that possibility to play out, and I am forever grateful that that's how it went for us, and more than once. Not including our first few "7 & Under" seasons, we were fortunate enough to play on the same team four times, including three consecutive seasons from 2001-2002 through 2003-2004. In those years together, many highlight moments and great memories were made, both on and off the ice. Though most brothers and friends get to glimpse each other's memories through stories, we had forged a lot of the same memories because we had made them together.

Once in a while we'd take a trip down memory lane and relive some of those great times. Starting with, "Remember when . . ." we'd go one-for-one, sharing highlight moments from our collective past. These memories ranged from things we'd witnessed in our family or amongst friends to just replaying and quoting our favorite moments from *The Simpsons* or *Family Guy*. Sometimes reminiscing on those memories made us laugh until we cried. We were closest during those times. But, like most siblings, our relationship certainly wasn't all laughter. Sometimes – as was the case with our one-on-one mini-stick battles – there was pain and anger. And, as any brother knows, sometimes bad brotherly shit just happens. At times he angered me, annoyed me, or just frustrated me, and I did the same to him. In the end, I had to forgive, as he had to forgive me – many times. However, on one particular occasion, the forgiveness he gave me was monumental.

## Creator, Sustainer, Destroyer

We often play the archetypal roles of creator, sustainer, or destroyer in each other's lives. Sometimes we play one at a time, other times we play two or three. Sometimes we offer someone an insightful idea that motivates them to better themselves, or an encouraging word as they pursue a goal. In that case we would be playing the role of creator, for the idea, and sustainer, for the encouragement. It feels good to be a creator of love and good energy, and a sustainer of the same. Sometimes, however, we get so caught up in an exchange or argument with someone that we say destructive things we just don't mean; or, if we do mean them, we say them in a harsh and hurtful manner that creates pain in the moment and can leave deep wounds. Enter, the destroyer.

Most of us avoid playing the role of destroyer because we don't want to deal with confrontation and don't want to feel lower emotional vibrations that can come out during such circumstances. Or, we act as the destroyer subconsciously or reactively, without realizing the full effects of our words or actions. Often in these situations it feels as if we lost control, or were thrust into a role we didn't want to play. Playing the role of the destroyer is not "bad" per se; however, as the word suggests, it comes with breaking down or altogether destroying someone else's energy, whether that be in thought or action, for better or worse. Whether the thing being destroyed is someone's attachment to a material thing or part of their ego that they have grown to like, the process of destruction typically brings about resistance and pain.

I played the role of destroyer in Todd's life in a significant way, at least one time. I still cringe when I think about the exchange which led to me reacting in a way that crushed something inside of him. My words were like daggers thrown into his body and spirit. I knew that I really fucked up as soon those thoughtless reactive words came out of my mouth. We all miss the mark in our lives; below is one of my worst examples.

It was early June 2006. I had just turned twenty-one years old, and on a sunny Sunday afternoon the Davison side of the family came to the house on Ranch to celebrate this milestone. Though I tend to drop toward depression, on that day I was flying high, super-excited for my birthday gathering with everyone. I can still remember the feeling of joy as I bounded up the basement stairs and out the patio door to join

Grandpa Davison for a beer in the backyard. That's when an abrupt exchange occurred that, in a minute or less, changed our lives.

I was wearing a brand-new t-shirt that I really liked, recently purchased from Royal Sports – our favorite Winnipeg store. The brand was "WESC" (We Are the Superlative Conspiracy), a Swedish clothing brand influenced by skateboarding and snowboarding. While at that time in my life I did not skateboard or snowboard – mainly for fear of getting hurt and being unable to play hockey – I wanted to at some point. I also just liked the way the shirt looked.

Just as I was exiting the house I crossed paths with Todd, who was heading inside. I smiled at him, but his attention was focused on my new shirt.

Out of nowhere he blurted out, "Nice shirt, you fuckin' poser!"

*Whoa,* I thought, completely caught off-guard. His words were aggressive, uncharacteristic, and had anger behind them – as if seeing me happy and smiling in my new shirt had triggered something in him. I was so stunned at the unexpected comment that I'm not sure I got a word in before he proceeded to verbally assault me. Somehow, the t-shirt translated right to hockey, which is where things got real. I remember the confusion as his offensive continued. Apparently, Todd had some grievances or problems with me that needed airing, and *Festivus* had come early that year.

I initially accepted the words calmly; then he said something that struck a chord of pain within me and sent me into a weird place:

"You suck at hockey!" he snarled, "You fuckin' suck!"

A storm of emotions instantly swirled inside my head and body. After all the years of competing against each other; all the seasons battling alongside each other as teammates; after all of the joy and pain experienced on the ice and in the dressing rooms; and all that the game of hockey meant to us . . . was this really what my own brother and lifelong playing companion, who knew my game better than anybody, thought of me as a hockey player? By that point I knew I wasn't going to make the NHL, and I knew, deep down, that I didn't have the pure natural ability that certain others had. But I'd worked as hard as I could when I was on the ice, and I absolutely poured my heart and soul into my game, just like he did.

Perhaps these verbal daggers were just another way of releasing the pain and anger that were overwhelming him, or maybe this was his actual opinion of my ability as a hockey player and he was just now expressing it. Regardless, it stirred up a feeling I'd never experienced before; it was a whole new level of disruption and provocation, and it revealed a side of myself, insecure and emotionally immature, that I didn't even know existed.

In that moment, that self was in full control, and its primary objective was to protect and defend itself, which it did so as hard as it could, and with reckless disregard.

"At least I'm still playing . . . " I muttered under my breath, just loud enough for Todd to hear.

I regretted those words instantly, almost before they left my mouth, but it was too late. Yes, I had been provoked, but it didn't matter. It was the worst possible thing I could have said, and given the context, a far worse punishment than my brother ever could have deserved. Even all these years later, I still shake my head and feel like an absolute piece of shit when I think about how I reacted in that moment. And, at that time, it was a Level 10 potential relationship-ender.

## Forgive Your Brother

I recall Mr. Praznik – our seventh-grade teacher at St. Alphonsus School – saying that the biblical commandment "Thou Shall Not Kill" could also apply to killing someone's spirit with words. If that is the case, I killed my own brother that day with five simple, thoughtless, heartless, ignorant words. I committed a cardinal sin.

Grandpa Davison was only ten feet away while the whole situation played out, and he was wise enough not to engage and just let us deal with it ourselves. There was no doubt that Todd was both instigator and agitator, but I certainly should have taken a second to breathe and gather composure.

I hadn't done that, and now I saw the consequence: a pain and rage in Todd's eyes like I had never seen before. "If you ever say that again," he said in a quiet but deadly voice, "I'll stab you with a fuckin' knife!" Then he stormed inside the house, leaving me stunned and trying to process what had just happened.

In less than two minutes our lifelong relationship was shaken, badly. I looked at Grandpa for some sort of guidance, and though we didn't exchange words his eyes showed compassion and pain. It had to have been heartbreaking for him to see. There was a chance, I knew, that he hadn't heard a single word; he was damn near deaf at the time and way too stubborn to listen to his doctor's strong recommendation that he get hearing aids. But he didn't need to hear the words to see that emotional bombs were just dropped and serious damage was done. Friends-off; relationship over; "I want a divorce"; red-alert level, emotional fucking bombs.

By that point, Todd had undergone several rounds of chemo, several surgeries, and radiation treatments; the back of his shoulder was mangled, and his arm was in a sling. He was not getting better, period. His body was getting weaker; it was shutting down, and whether he recognized it or not, a recovery would have been considered miraculous. He was also mourning the loss of hockey, which had been the source of pride and passion for so long. Most of all he felt powerless, and that powerlessness often manifested as anger and sadness.

I, on the other hand, was the picture of health and had a bright future ahead of me, with or without hockey. And in that split second of seeing me smiling in my t-shirt, Todd may have subconsciously compared our situations and questioned, who was I to be living a healthy life while he had to get sick? Who was I to have both arms working; to be physically able to still play sports; to be active and strong; to be happy and celebrate my twenty-first birthday, while he was feeling weaker by the day and most likely living on borrowed time?

As soon as the initial shock wore off, I knew I should have never reacted to Todd's words, no matter how much they hurt me. I should have recognized his pain, and not taken his words personally. I should have been able to detach from the situation, recognize his anger and agony for what they were, and forgive him, instantly. Instead, I would be the one seeking forgiveness.

A few minutes later, after I had regained some composure, I went downstairs to find Todd. He was sitting on the couch alone, staring ahead into nothing, engulfed in a swarm of anger and on the verge of a blowup. He had his arms crossed, and his body language said, "Get away from me." Ignoring this, I walked up to him and earnestly apologized, telling him how sorry I was. But it was too late, and the damage had been done. He didn't respond at all. He did not accept my apology, in fact, he pulled away from me, hard. I was used to silence between us, but nothing so heavy and cold as this.

Despite several attempts over the next days and weeks, Todd refused to talk to me or work to heal the situation. He smacked away the olive branch that I was desperately holding out to him with disgust. At that moment he was over me, and he was not going to care. I had betrayed him, and about the thing we held most sacred, and the heavy doors to his heart and inner world were slammed shut.

Part of me actually started to worry that we would not heal this situation before it was too late, that the awful exchange in the yard that day might be our last. What a terrible play that would be to end it all! I experienced intense anxiety, shame, and guilt in those days, but despite those low, shitty moments, I still held on to the hope that we would find our way back to each other. Surely the story of our brotherhood would not end with such a scene.

Several weeks after the incident, the 2006 Canada Day long weekend rolled around. I went west to Dauphin, Manitoba for Countryfest – a country music festival that was one of the biggest parties of the summer. Todd was going to be there too. I arrived at the Countryfest campground on Friday afternoon and began to set up for the weekend. As I worked I saw Todd briefly from a distance. He saw me too, but turned away and did not come over. We were both with our own friend groups, doing our own things. At that point it seemed like nothing would change between us that weekend, maybe ever.

Though I had fun with my friends on Friday night, something was missing. The rift with Todd would not allow me to fully enjoy myself, and I was reminded of our torn relationship every time I saw him around.

The following day, July 1, 2006, was Canada Day, and everyone was looking forward to seeing Montgomery Gentry, who were headlining that evening. Montgomery Gentry is a country group from Kentucky with a bunch of powerful songs about life and love, including "Something to Be Proud Of" and "Some People Change," which play upon themes of growing up in the world, working hard, being a good family member, and just being a good, loving person in general. Todd and I both ended up in the front area of the amphitheater for that show, very close to the stage in a sea of charged-up fans. He was up a few standing rows in front of me to the left. We saw each other in passing at the start of the show, and I nodded to him, so he was aware of my general location. We had friends in common spread out around and between us, and everyone was soaking in the show.

Montgomery Gentry was well into their set when they finally played some of their most powerful songs, the ones that pull at people's heartstrings. These are the types of songs that don't just entertain us; these are the songs that make us feel something real inside, if only for a fleeting moment. During one of those songs – in what turned out to be the beginning of one of the most emotionally charged moments of our lives – I looked up to see Todd breaking down in tears.

Something had happened inside of him during that show. The vibrations of the music were like waves of healing and love being poured through him when he needed it most. They destroyed the high walls he had constructed around his heart. The time had come for certain emotional traumas and anguish to be dealt with. The pain and anger inside of him needed to be released. And, something in him was triggered to forgive me and love me again.

In a rush, he turned around and started to push through some people to make a beeline for me. Then, with his head facing down to hide the tears in his eyes, he charged up to me and gave me a giant, tight hug. In that moment tears from both of our eyes were pouring down. My heart broke open in a rush of love and relief. All of the pain that existed between us evaporated with that hug, an act of surrender to the other. I had been waving my white flag to Todd for weeks, and he finally recognized it. He no longer wanted to carry that burden of pain, nor did I. No more war.

He squeezed harder as he told me he loved me. The moment was rare and pure. To the ignorant observer it must have been an odd scene – just two dudes hugging it out and crying intensely in the middle of a country music concert. To us, however, it was a moment of true forgiveness and deep healing of a severe emotional wound that had taken its toll on both of us for a month. The observer wouldn't have known that we were two brothers, making up after the fight of a lifetime, and that one of us would be exiting the world when the winter came. The observer wouldn't have known that if this conflict did not resolve at that moment, it may never have. They wouldn't have known or understood the context of that hug, or its significance of saving our relationship before Todd died.

Forgiveness can be one of the toughest things to do, but it is often the most powerful. It leads to love. In that moment, Todd finally forgave me, and love took over. The only blessing and beauty from the pain was that it allowed for our brotherly love to grow and expand more than ever.

## CHAPTER 18

# LIFE IS NOT FAIR,
# BUT LOVE IS REAL

After our relationship-saving moment, Todd's healing crisis continued. There, amongst the crowd of ten thousand-plus people, he turned to Katie Moe, one of his closest friends, and with tears in his eyes and a heavy, defeated heart, blurted, "Life just isn't fair!"

The next morning, Todd woke up embarrassed and ashamed. He apologized to Katie for his emotional display, which he perceived as personal weakness. But Katie wouldn't let him off the hook so easily: she told Todd that he needed to understand the trauma of what was happening to him. She told him that he needed to learn how to deal with this trauma and process it, instead of just bottling everything up and pretending he had everything under control.

"People can't just see you as this positive human being all the time," Katie continued. "You need to have these real moments!"

Katie's words were raw, real, and just what the doctor ordered. Despite the pain and confusion that had built up over two years of tortuous medical treatments and their unsuccessful outcomes, Todd had been trying so hard to stay strong and composed. Katie's words in that moment allowed him to take off the mask and finally accept his situation for what it really was.

This moment of unconditional love was so badly needed, and led Todd to further release the anger and angst that were consuming him. Ultimately, Katie's words allowed Todd to know that he would be surrounded by loving friends and family no matter how he emotionally reacted to his disease. This led to another profound breakthrough: love and connection are real, and perhaps all that really matter in this world. Regardless of how unfair life can be at any given time, love can heal even the deepest wounds. Through these types of moments, Todd began to feel how real the love around him was, and realize that it wasn't going away.

World-renowned author and healer Dr. Joe Dispenza has said, "We are all bound by an invisible field of energy, and that connection is called Love." Todd echoed this sentiment in a Mother's Day letter to Mom around that time: "I know I haven't been pleasant to deal with, mostly because I am confused about life . . . but at least I know that one of the most important things in life is love, and with all that I have lost, I know you'll always be there to love me."

Aside from Mom and Dad and his many friends and family members, true love was introduced to Todd, in significant part, by Rosie Wilson. Dad's wife, Michelle, is a nurse who instead of working shifts in a hospital decided to foster medically challenged babies and raise them up as her own in a loving and fun family environment. Rosie was Michelle's precious foster daughter who touched our lives immensely, along with those of everyone she met.

Born January 13, 2004, Rosie developed a severe lung disease early on and had to have a tracheostomy. She was an incredibly adorable baby, and a ball of brilliant light who brought joy to all who met her, especially my brother. Todd met Rosie when she was about six months old and, through her, felt an intense connection to the field of love. Todd once told Michelle that even if he were able to have his own kids someday, he didn't know if it would be possible to love them any more than he loved Rosie. The intensity of his feeling for her taught Todd a great deal about the power of love.

With that monumental discovery also came the realization that he was responsible for creating and giving love in this world. He looked to himself first to see how he could live with more love, and what he could do to share it with others. He started to *be* love. In a Viktor Frankl-esque way, Todd found meaning and beauty in his brutal situation.

After two years of intense bouts with fear, pain, anger, loneliness, uncertainty, and hopelessness, Todd recognized the blessings that had come into his life as a result of having such a terrible disease. He reframed that terrifying roller coaster ride as a journey to a blessed life filled with moments of love that trumped the suffering he was going through. After all the traumatizing events that had happened to him, and the bleakness of his human situation, Todd still found a way to acknowledge and accept that he was still winning in the game of life, through his connections with others. Now it was time to spread his own love out into the world.

CHAPTER 19

# BELIEVE IN THE GOAL

After Todd's last shift as a player, it seemed his relationship with his first love, hockey, was over forever. And, as he had said, the pain of this was as great, if not more so, than learning he had cancer. None of us, certainly not Todd, could have anticipated that a space would open up within him that allowed something new and beautiful to arise. As his external "normal" world of fun and familiarity was crumbling down around him, his inner world was being built up stronger than ever.

One of the methods Todd used to balance his inner and outer worlds was writing down words that inspired him. In a little orange notebook held together with thin coil binding, he wrote down his favorite quotations. These were taken from books he was reading, posts he saw, things he heard, or seminars he attended. The words he wrote give us a glimpse of his consciousness in what would be his final months on the planet. This was Todd's sacred "quote-book" – his playbook for life.

One of the quotations, taken from Caroline Myss' *Invisible Acts of Power: The Divine Energy of a Giving Heart*, spoke specifically to the end of Todd as a hockey player:

> The ending of any relationship necessarily forces you down a new path . . . when you finally surrender to it, you will be able to see your new circumstances as a blessing after all. You can

choose to view crises as arbitrary and antagonistic, or as inter-
ventions that are part of a greater plan . . .

Wow.

Todd *chose* to see the end of his playing days as part of a greater
Universal plan. Now it was time to let that greater plan reveal itself
even more.

## Giving Back

After being diagnosed with cancer Todd initially struggled with how he
could contribute to making the cancer-world a better place. He felt a
duty to lighten the burden and ease the suffering of those in similar situations, especially the younger kids, but he didn't really know how to go
about this.

Then, after seeing Lance Armstrong speak in Vancouver at a
Livestrong Foundation event, Todd had a chat with Glenn Carnegie, his
former hockey trainer, current boss at Focus Fitness, and close friend.
They had a special connection – one of those true-blue bonds where each
sparks something in each other. Todd believed in Glenn, and in all that
he was, and Glenn believed in Todd just the same. Glenn was one of the
major players in Todd's life, and the person who made him believe in
*Believe in the Goal* before it was even named.

They discussed options of how they could turn Todd's vision of contributing to the cure of cancer and easing patient pain into a reality. As
they neared the end of their brainstorming session, they came up with
the idea of putting on a big charity all-star hockey game with all of Manitoba's best professional players. While cool in theory, however, this would
not be easy to orchestrate. They would have to ask the various NHLers
to donate their time and effort, in the middle of their summer vacation,
to play for an unknown charity - a task Todd initially thought was far too
challenging. And, though Glenn encouraged him to pursue the vision,

he figured it was just an awesome idea that ultimately wouldn't get done because of laziness, distraction, or something else coming up. Such is the case with many great ideas, and with most people.

Todd wasn't most people. He had that mindset and extra gear of determination, and a tendency to set his sights on big goals and work towards them with relentless focus. In this case, what started as a lofty but improbable notion took root in his mind and began to grow. In the words of Glenn, "Todd took it from there and was on it!"

In the spring of 2006, Todd founded *Believe in the Goal* – a foundation aimed at providing support and comfort to children and adolescents dealing with cancer. Despite fighting for his own life, Todd wanted to reach out to others and give them some energy and love, and to remind them that they were not alone in their cancer journey. The foundation included programs such as building custom hospital rooms for patient and family comfort and entertainment during grueling treatment stays; a hospital blanket program, whereby patients were visited by NHL stars and presented with a comfy fleece blanket; and sending patients on "NHL dream experiences," which were similar to the *Make a Wish* program but exclusive to NHL hockey trips.

When introducing *Believe in the Goal's* "Sizzlin' Summer Showdown" hockey game at a press conference to Winnipeg's biggest media outlets, Todd said the following words:

"I graduated June 26th, 2004, from St. Paul's High School as a young confident hockey player, thinking my future would turn out exactly as I planned, without a worry. I was ready to jump into the real world, and grow up and live a long life. Two days later my whole life and future was put on hold after having to watch my parents struggle to tell me that I had cancer. I had plans ahead [to go to] Brandon to fight my way onto the Wheat Kings roster. Instead, however, I was stuck at home, fighting for my life. More bad news kept coming [with] each visit to the doctor as two weeks later I learned that I would never be able to do what I spent my whole life doing: playing competitive hockey. For me, it was worse than learning I had cancer . . . way worse, because hockey was my life, plain and simple . . .

"After figuring out what it would take for the doctors to get me back to a young, healthy teenager, I began to actually, for the first time, feel like a cancer patient. Shaving your head and watching your hair fall out from chemotherapy is a devastating experience. Perhaps it was the first time in my entire life that I realized that I wasn't invincible. Since this was my first experience with chemotherapy I didn't know what to expect. I read a lot about what it was like, and what prepared me the most was Lance Armstrong's first book. After three straight months of chemo and thirty days of in-hospital treatment, chemo easily became my biggest fear.

"This past September, once again, my plans to attend university and have a job would be put on hold to resume my battle. After eight grueling months of chemotherapy, doctors finally decided that I was ready for surgery. Three weeks ago I completed what was hopefully my last cancer treatment ever. I cannot put my last two years into words, but I can truthfully say that cancer has given me more blessings and a better life, in a way that only so many people can understand.

"So how did cancer bring me to today? My favorite experience was going to see my new hero and inspiration, Lance Armstrong, speak in Vancouver. I finally felt that someone else in the world knew what it was like to go through what I went through. Part of his speech was about his commitment to the cure. He could go about his regular life and keep to himself, or he could share his experience with others and make people aware or try to find a cure for cancer. He chose to fight back and to this day he has raised over half a billion dollars for cancer research. Lance speaks about how, as a cancer survivor, how you have an obligation to the cure, and it was these words that gave me the idea for this hockey game, and from the beginning of this idea people have supported it completely.

"Word quickly spread to Lyle Bauer and his Never Alone Foundation. He wanted to meet with me and immediately put his full support behind our hockey game. I'd also like to thank Shirlee Preteau, who has worked closely with us, guiding us through the process.

"An idea was only the beginning of this journey. From the moment I started to talk about this game, people have come onboard easily and willingly. I am so thankful for all of the help and support I received since I was diagnosed, and the only way I thought that I could say thank you is to in return help somebody else."

While the entire speech was moving, the statement *"I cannot put my last two years into words, but I can truthfully say that cancer has given me more blessings and a better life . . ."* is most revealing of my brother's state of being at that time.

Things really started to come together when, in addition to Glenn, a small group of inspired people surrounded Todd and helped lift his vision to reality. One of those people was Colleen Deckert – Decks' mom – who was a major ally for Todd right from the jump and knew she could rile up support from around the Manitoba business community through her professional relationships. Another major player was Ray Kuik – father of fellow former Winnipeg Sharks Midget AAA teammate, Brent Kuik – who was a master emotional brander and marketer for the foundation. Ray teamed up with Colleen and Auntie Donna – who played a managerial role and was the person to do whatever needed to be done at any given time – and they got to work firing up the event in the real world. Ray still remembers the look on Todd's face as he sat in the lounge at Q-Power in St. Boniface, staring at the proposed jersey logo – a cartoon mosquito with a hockey stick, basically Manitoba's spirit animal – that was presented for his viewing. Todd was both stunned and ecstatic. His internal vision was coming to life, for real.

*Believe in the Goal* brought together some of Manitoba's best talent of all time. Fittingly, a bunch of the participants were Todd's friends, either as past teammates, training partners, or league opponents. These guys were more than willing to support Todd and eagerly joined his mission. Beyond Barks and Boyd, the *Believe in the Goal* rosters for the inaugural game included NHL stars like: Jonathan Toews, Travis Zajac, Mike Richards, Colton Orr, Jordin Tootoo, Nigel Dawes, Eric Fehr, Dustin Penner, Ryan Craig, Tyler Arnason, Derek Meech, Nolan Baumgartner, J.P. Vigier, and Ian White.

This group of players have contributed to countless highlight-reel goals, assists, defensive plays, and heavyweight fights at the highest level of hockey in the world. It is lit up with several Stanley Cup Champions, and Olympic, World Championship, and World Junior goal medal winners. Winnipeg and its surrounding areas in Manitoba have always been known as being a hot spot for spectacular hockey talent, and this local event proved and validated that for all to see.

Todd's vision for how the game would play out had been set months earlier in Auntie Donna's basement: "I see a sold-out rink that's crammed with people," he said, "where everybody comes together to watch the game. And everyone knows they're helping the cause."

The inaugural *Sizzlin' Summer Showdown* was held on the hot, sunny evening of August 3, 2006, at the Selkirk Recreation Complex arena. Selkirk, Manitoba, is a city twenty-two miles north of Winnipeg, and its modern style arena, which holds approximately three thousand spectators, is home to the Selkirk Steelers of the MJHL and Selkirk Fishermen of the MMJHL. It also holds the energy of decades of hockey excitement and victory, and was one of our favorites to play during our minor hockey days. We thought we were in the show when we stepped on that ice! When Winnipeg hosts major events, such as the World Junior Hockey Championship, or is the filming location of movies, such as *Keep Your Head Up Kid: The Don Cherry Story*, that Selkirk arena is utilized and appreciated for the classic hockey rink it is. With Don Cherry's voice and tone, I'd say that this rink is "a beauty of a barn!" – and the perfect intimate and historically charged venue for the game.

A couple of hours before the crowd started rolling in, Todd and Glenn drove out to the arena together. Glenn recalls Todd being "all fidgety; chatty; [and] all over the place. He was so nervous and asked, 'What if no one shows up?'"

"Who gives a shit? We did it!" Glenn had replied, snapping Todd out of this pre-game anxiety.

Glenn vibe-checked Todd hard, and they amplified their excitement and positive thinking. The truth was that neither of them knew if anyone would in fact be coming; but that was now out of their control, and it was time to enjoy the fruits of their effort and intention!

Todd entered the lower level of the arena and walked into the staged dressing rooms. He saw beautiful jerseys, bearing the names of hockey champions at the highest levels, hung up in the individual stalls, and decided that Brian Hamilton, the Vancouver Canucks' Equipment Manager, had outdone himself. In truth, Todd was pleasantly surprised with the top-shelf quality the game had taken already, and his face lit up with a big grin. He was in the dressing room again, buzzing with energy that lit him up. As the players started to roll into the room, Todd greeted them and hung out. He was back in the room with the boys. He was back in the game, only this time with bigger stakes at hand.

By the time the ceremonial face-off puck was dropped, thousands of eager hockey fans packed the stands to fulfill Todd's vision. Todd took the microphone at center ice and said words of gratitude and appreciation for all those who had helped him. He conveyed a short and simple message about what the game was really all about for him: helping others. Then he stepped off the ice, turned the microphones over to the radio personalities who called the game and engaged the crowd, and let the professionals put on a light show for the fans.

The game was an absolute hit and an incredibly rewarding night for Todd. He expressed that in his post-game interviews with the local television stations and other media, including "Canucks TV," who attended the game and captured some of the highlights of that special night. As he had done with every hockey game in his career, my brother had poured his heart and soul into that event, and, if only for a few short hours, made the world a better place that night.

## Difference Maker

After the game there was a social event at the arena in the conference rooms, and then an exclusive after-party social at a rented-out nightclub in downtown Winnipeg. With NHL training camps sneaking up as the summer drew down over the end-of-July hump, the boys were ready for a party. The limos were called, and the night went on raging with a celebration that capped off a phenomenal night.

That next morning, Todd was absolutely spent. The alarm chime on his Motorola Razr flip-phone played again and again, but he lay on the downstairs couch, where he had fallen asleep after returning home from the after-party, lacking the strength to even reach over and shut it off. The alarm went off for what seemed like an eternity, until I, who was asleep in my basement room, finally woke up and shut it off for him. I looked at him sleeping in front of me, so desperately in need of deep rest. Just as when he was playing and left everything on the ice, all of his energy had gone into that game, and now there was nothing left. But though Todd was tapped, he had also been transformed by the experience and the rewards of his efforts for others.

When it was all said and done – through the sale of admission tickets, t-shirts, hats, and proceeds from various donated prizes for auctions, including an awesome piece from Jersey Chair made out of one of Todd's game-worn official Pats jerseys, the event raised over $50,000. But the game wasn't just about raising money. The game was about connecting with others and making a difference in the world through unselfish acts and concerted effort and intention. Todd had a vision, and he pursued it to the end. He put in the work through thought and action, and he experienced his creation, and knew it was good. And though maybe insignificant in the eyes of the larger world, he had done something great for his community, and affected real people's lives in real, positive ways. Through *Believe in the Goal*, and all that he imparted to others during his life, Todd was a true difference-maker in the world. And, by example, he encouraged everyone around him to be one as well.

*From left to right: Glenn Carnegie, Travis Zajac, Todd, and Colton Orr ("Orrsy"). Believe in the Goal Press Conference, 2006.*

# SUDDEN DEATH OVERTIME

# CHAPTER 20

# THE LAST MONTHS

Though the inaugural *Sizzlin' Summer Showdown* was a major success, the game was now long over, and winter was coming for us all. As the players moved on to their respective teams to resume their professional careers, Todd, again, was left back in Winnipeg without any definitive good news. He just wanted things to stabilize and get better for once. He didn't want to be the cancer kid anymore; he was sick and tired of being sick and tired. He just wanted to be healthy again. More so, he just wanted to be free from pain. Little did he know that his real pain was just beginning.

In early September 2006, on what was to be his very first day of university, the final blow was delivered: Todd was told by his oncologist that there was nothing more they could do to help him. He was told that the cancer was very bad, and that he had about six months left to live. In essence, he was told to go home and get ready to die. Despite being an innocent being, having committed no wrong, he was given an early death sentence. Worse: he would be a prisoner inside his decrepit body until the very end.

As soon as Todd was not "saveable" in the eyes of modern allopathic medicine, a younger resident, who just so happened to be named Joel, took over Todd's case. The two had formed a bond, and Joel was almost in tears as he delivered that heartbreaking message that nothing more could be done. Typical of my brother, he expressed concern for another's pain even in the midst of his own, saying, "It must be really hard to tell people that they aren't going to live…"

Then, in an admirably stoic way, Todd realized that he had to adapt his game plan. Even more than before, he really began to dig into life in that moment. The potentialities of his future had radically changed in a short period of time, but he didn't shut down in the face of death. In fact, even as his weakened and diseased body continued to shut down, Todd's life force seemed to intensify. He figured out a way to get up, move forward, and refocus his lens, living each day he was given. In a way, every day became Todd's last day; at least that is how he seemed to approach it.

Just like the game clock ticked down to zero during Todd's last game, he knew that the game clock of life was not going to stop or slow down for him. So Todd began squeezing absolutely everything out of each twenty-four-hour period. He didn't want to waste a second. Todd could have spent his days wondering and worrying about, among other things, whether he was going to lose his arm completely, how many new tumors were growing, which bone was going to snap next, whether he would suffocate in his own bodily fluids, or whether he would even wake up the next day, or whatever other baggage he had at the time. But he didn't. Mom's words on this topic, which have helped me out at various times in my life, and which Todd abided by, are appropriate here: "You can't waste your day on the worry. When you worry about things, you waste the moment you are in." So Todd woke up each day and went to the hockey rink and coached; or he went to the gym and moved around and saw his friends, and lived the moment he was in with all that he had.

Todd's willpower was so strong that he was in full control of where his body vehicle would go, even when his body didn't want to do anything except lay down. He planned each day and made commitments, then used his mind to demand that his body tend to whatever he deemed necessary. Anyone who has reluctantly dragged themselves to the gym or yoga studio knows how tough this can be, especially when it's forty below outside or when we aren't feeling a hundred percent. Todd knew that he'd be exhausted at the end of the day, but accepted that as the price to pay for living as *hard* as he could. He wasn't going to tone down his daily life to save up for tomorrow. He knew, as we all too often ignore, that his tomorrow wasn't guaranteed.

Every Monday and Wednesday he'd wake up at five a.m. to head to the Winnipeg Winter Club, where he worked on-ice with the Focus Fitness adult men's hockey group – attended by a bunch of hockey-loving guys who just wanted to get better and have more fun playing. Though he couldn't do much for demonstrations at the time, he strapped on his skates and set up drills, gave helpful tips, and brought a great presence to the ice. Then, after the ice time, he'd come back home to shower up, get dressed, and grab some breakfast before heading right back out the door to his morning university classes. He paid attention in class and tried to be the best student he could be. Afterward, he'd come home for a short break, and it was off to the rink yet again in the late afternoon or evening, this time as an assistant coach with the Winnipeg Thrashers. Then he'd stop by Michelle and Dad's place to visit with the kids: Rosie, Carter, Sarah, Johnny and Blayne; and the dogs, Ben, and Todd's own puppy, Tess. He was living his life with urgency and purpose.

Todd ran those early Focus Fitness ice sessions with Glenn, and was sometimes a few minutes late to those six-a.m. ice times. When he arrived at the rink he changed in a private locker room, away from Glenn and the other guys. Though being a couple of minutes late or changing in a separate locker room wasn't a huge deal, it was enough for Glenn to speak up and give Todd shit in a lighthearted way. Glenn razzed Todd for the above offenses, and wouldn't let him off the hook just because he had cancer. Todd actually loved that, because Glenn was one of the only people who treated him normally, as if he weren't sick. What Glenn didn't know, however, was that Todd was late those mornings and changed in his own dressing room because he'd been throwing up in the parking lot or the dressing room and didn't want anyone to know.

If anyone was ever entitled to be a victim of their circumstances, it was Todd. He'd lost everything; at least that's how it seemed. He could have lulled himself to death in a storm of victimhood and pain, but he didn't. He fought through, and looked for the deeper meaning in the pain presented to him. While he could have wasted his precious time feeling sorry for himself, he looked beyond victimhood to find the higher meaning and power in whatever moment he was in. He had every excuse in the world to sleep in; to not get up and go; to call in sick, but he refused to give in to the voices of doubt or powerlessness in his mind. Not only did he silence those internal voices, he also never complained to others. He didn't leave clues for Glenn or the other guys to find; in fact, he did everything he could to prevent them from feeling sorry for him. These days, Glenn uses those thoughts of Todd battling through his nausea and fatigue without excuse or complaint to tame his own inner excuses, and as motivation to get up and put in the work even when he isn't feeling great.

At the same time Todd was getting up early and getting on with his day, I – a "healthy" person and student-athlete – barely had the energy to make it through my days. After staying up too late, I would peel myself out of bed after a few snoozed alarms, then rush across the city to the university to [maybe] make it on time for my morning class. Todd, who was in the same classes, would also maybe make it on time, but at least he had more of an excuse. I would be in class until mid-afternoon, then head on over to the MaxBell arena for team practice with the Bisons. After practice we'd workout, and by the end of that, I would be absolutely toasted. It was reasonable for me to be tired with a fairly demanding schedule, but I was always perplexed as to how Todd – with late-stage cancer by that point – had so much energy to live his daily life as he did, and without complaint.

In re-examining Todd's calendar-filled days and questioning how he maintained his high energy levels, I noticed a few constant things: first, Todd realized that his time was limited; second, he had a passion for what he was doing; third, he gave energy to others in the process; and fourth, he had extreme gratitude for the fact that he was still alive and free, and for the things he had in his life. The combination of these four things enabled Todd to wake up with energy and enthusiasm, and to be a light to the world every day he had the chance. No excuses were needed.

He was living his life to the fullest, and making excuses would only take away his own power.

But, make no mistake – he was playing through pain like you wouldn't believe!

## Life, Intensified

Of the nearly two and half years that Todd lived after being diagnosed with cancer, the last few months were especially brutal. Those days brought a whole new level of intensity to deal with; that is, when Todd's severe physical pain crept into his daily life, and was growing worse by the day. While he was still having really good days and could still be strong and independent much of the time, October and November brought terrible and regular waves of pain, fear, along with anxiety that crippled Todd at night when he was out of the public eye.

November 2006 was Todd's last full month alive, and it was especially harsh. Despite his peaking pain he carried on as strongly and with as little assistance as he could. This was his last shift of life, and as long as it lasted he would continue to play it on his own terms. But then more scary episodes began to happen.

On November 8, 2006, Todd came home after school with an excruciating headache. He laid down in an attempt to sleep it off, and when it was time for hockey practice he got up and answered the bell. After practice he came home and went straight to bed, and that's where Mom found him early the next morning with his left eye bulging out of his head.

"Oh My God!" she exclaimed, shocked and caught off-guard by the sight.

"Mom!" Todd snapped back, signaling her to calm down, but when he looked at himself in the mirror he saw why she had reacted as she did. Then he just went quiet . . . the same type of quiet he went into when he was initially diagnosed.

Todd was rushed to Cancer Care, where an axial orbits CT scan revealed a big tumor in his head had broken the orbital bone, which pushed the eye out. Frail bones and growing tumors make for an awful combination. He was given a strong dose of radiation and sent on his way to resume his life. Not missing a beat, a day later, Todd – with his eye still swollen – attended a press conference with Lyle Bauer for the Never Alone Foundation. He also marched onto the Winnipeg Thrasher's team bus before they were about to depart for a weekend road trip and matter-of-factly told the players that he had an issue to take care of and couldn't make the trip; he'd be back at practice the following week.

*Todd and Martin St. Louis in Tampa Bay, Florida, in October 2005, during his first trip down.*

There was also another trip coming up, and this one Todd was determined to make – to Tampa Bay to see Martin St. Louis and the rest of the Lightning team. He had flown down there the previous year to meet Marty and to soak in all of the energy that was around a Stanley Cup-winning team's locker room, but he had been in much better condition back then. Now, despite having apple-sized tumors in his lungs and elsewhere in his body, and regularly having liters of fluid drained from his chest, enough to fill up big glass jars, he was absolutely adamant. Mom was very worried at that point and begged Todd to let her join him, but he refused her pleas. This was to be one of his biggest trips, a pilgrimage he needed to make by himself.

After hanging out with some Lightning players in the dressing room and soaking in the energy of the game and dressing-room experience, Todd left the arena to return to his hotel room. At that point, the excitement of the trip and game wore off and his personal reality set back in – he began having trouble breathing, and he felt his body start to react in odd ways that it never had before. Thousands of miles from home, he became panicked and very scared. This was perhaps the first moment when Todd actually thought he might die.

He called to tell Mom, who felt absolutely helpless and powerless as she heard the fear in her son's voice and his short, urgent breaths. She stayed on the phone until he finally calmed down enough to go to sleep. The only comforting thoughts she had was that Jake Goertzen, the chief scout for the Lightning at the time and a good friend – was going to be picking him up in the morning, and he would be on the first flight home. Todd could no longer deny that his condition was reaching a crucial point. Shit was getting real.

When he returned to Winnipeg, he still somehow managed to hide this pain from his friends, the players he coached, and the public. He staunchly refused to give them any cause to feel sorry for him, and even during his toughest days, despite being riddled with pain, discomfort, and weakness, he would tell everyone he was fine. And they believed him too. His mind was powerful, his spirit was upbeat, and his voice was strong, so there was no reason his friends wouldn't take his word. But then, once his friends had left after a visit or he exited the arena after coaching, he would be alone at home, where the weakness and sickness would take over.

Todd even hid the severity of his condition from our father, saying he felt fine whenever Dad asked. Not wanting to be soft in the eyes of his father, Todd wore his "game face" when they were together. But in his moments of weakness at Mom's house, his true condition was revealed for her to see. Knowing that Todd was hiding his true pain from Dad, Mom called to tell him of the latest developments and how bad Todd was actually getting. Dad was surprised by what he was hearing because it was so different from what Todd was expressing or showing. One night shortly after that call, Dad went over to Mom's house to hang out with Todd in the basement, just the two of them. From that night on, Dad realized the severity of the situation.

Todd could no longer function independently for the full twenty-four hours; nor, despite his best effort, could he constantly hide his pain. Mom and Dad witnessed the worst by far. They were there during those heartbreaking moments when he had no other choice but to rely on them for help. Though Todd typically waved them off and said he was fine, other times he had no choice but to cry out when it all was just too unbearable. These moments often came late at night, after he had given all of his energy to the day; or early morning when he awoke to a body permeated by intense pain.

By the end of November Todd simply could not hide the fact that his body was not going to survive cancer. He could also no longer deny it to himself. I believe that even though his conscious mind resisted his imminent death for so long, he subconsciously knew but refused to give up without the most valiant effort. Now he was growing weaker by the day, and saw evidence each time he looked in the mirror that the doctors had been right.

Todd realized living with urgency was not going to make the days pass less quickly, or help him outrun death. So he cut out any bullshit and focused only on living and participating in experiences that he actually wanted to have. He avoided negative and low-vibrational people, and was attracted to positive and happy people who were living with purpose. Every second was precious, and he refused to waste even one on things that were not in some way creating happiness or positivity in his life and the lives of others.

His life became about living with a higher purpose and holding himself to a higher standard. He understood that following his passions empowered him and welcomed joy and contentment into his life. He liked who he was when he was doing the things he loved, so he did those things more.

# CHAPTER 21

# COACH TODD

Todd and I had several great coaches throughout our careers. Our best coaches were patient, understanding, knowledgeable, motivating, encouraging, and, most importantly, empowering. They also maintained these attributes whether our team was winning or losing, and whether an individual player was succeeding or struggling. Whatever the circumstances, they found a way to adapt and connect with us. And they never belittled or intimidated us or attempted to fuel us with fear. They never screamed in our faces or made snide and disparaging comments that only weaken a player's spirit, but instead built us up on a daily basis to make us as strong as possible. They would fuel us with inspiration, and make us believe in ourselves and our capabilities. The great coaches were the true leaders of the team, and we would play our hearts out for them, leaving everything on the ice. These types of coaches made hockey fun, as it should be.

One of our best coaches during the crucial transition period between youth hockey and junior hockey was Kevin Benson, who coached us with the Winnipeg Midget AAA Sharks. Beyond having the aforementioned qualities in spades, Kevin instilled within us a sense of deservedness that was earned through our effort at practice, and the confidence that accompanied that hard work and preparation. Despite having a storybook 2001-2002 season, our team had heartbreaking losses in both the Manitoba Midget AAA league finals, and the regional championship that would have earned us a trip to the national championship tournament. The only reason we got that far, however, was because of Kevin's coaching and leadership.

A few seasons after Todd played for Kevin as an underage fifteen-year-old, Kevin had brought him onto the bench to coach the Manitoba Midget AAA Winnipeg Thrashers, which had been formed after the Winnipeg teams of the League were restructured. Todd jumped at this opportunity and became an incredibly dedicated coach. He couldn't play the game, but that didn't mean that he couldn't still be involved in the game.

Since playing midget AAA hockey in Winnipeg was typically the last stop for the elite players before making the jump to a junior team somewhere in Canada or the US, coaching the Thrashers allowed Todd to stay connected to hockey at a high level. He also spent some time coaching the St. Andrews Aces – our cousin Mark Sutherland's 14A1 community club team. Unlike the professional prospects on the Thrashers, the Aces were community club players who mainly just wanted to have fun on the ice playing organized hockey. Accepting this community club coaching position showed Todd's level of dedication and love to the game, in whatever form it came.

Coaching gave Todd a creative outlet for his mental and emotional energy, and a platform to teach and inspire younger players who had a shot of playing professional hockey one day. It also allowed him to be in the present moment, far away from hospital rooms and worries about his health. When he was coaching he didn't focus on himself at all, but was instead fully engaged in the moment and immersed in love for what he was doing. More importantly, though, coaching gave Todd the opportunity to directly empower the lives of other humans, which in turn empowered his soul.

Todd did all that he could to help these players develop and reach their potential. Whether coaching some of the best young players in the world or kids who just loved playing the game, Todd taught and inspired his players as best as he could. He related to them as young men who were just getting through their days in this world as best as they could, and he dedicated himself to helping them become better, as both players and as people.

From all reports, Todd was an excellent coach. He knew the game far better than most, and he passed this knowledge and insight on to his players. Calm, collected, and encouraging, he fueled them from the inside and made them excited to be alive and playing such a fun game. And, though he always brought humor to their exchanges, he took his role as their coach very seriously and poured his heart out for them.

Todd was a tremendously inspiring figure to these young men, who recognized him as a special type of human and appreciated having him around. When Todd stepped on to the ice, dressed in his team tracksuit with shining eyes and a huge smile, he brought an infectious energy that uplifted the entire team. According to Kevin, despite whatever internal struggle he was facing that day, "Todd came to the rink every day wearing a smile and his work boots. For him, each day at the rink was a chance to be a part of a great game, to have some fun with the team, and help make the kids better players and stronger people. He believed what he said and he lived what he spoke . . . with those qualities it didn't take very long for everyone to appreciate and respect Todd's abilities as a coach, his passion for the game, strength of character, and most of all, his courage."

Leading by example, he inspired and motivated his players, making them believe they could be or do something great. He instilled within them a sense of power and confidence, energy and focus, and he recognized the individuality and natural gifts of each player – both in their game and personality – and made them feel special for having such gifts.

In January of 2006, the Aces went to Fargo, North Dakota for a tournament – about a three-hour drive from Winnipeg. Todd knew the tournament meant a lot for the boys and he wanted to be with them on their journey, so he rescheduled his blood transfusion and made the trip with the squad. He was supposed to return to Winnipeg for a big-time concert on the tournament's final evening. Todd really wanted to go to that concert – especially because Joel had given him tickets as a Christmas present – but the boys unexpectedly went straight to the championship game, which put a kink in his plans. Since Todd was just an assistant coach, he easily could have snuck away to hit the road back to Winnipeg early, but there was no way he was going to let the boys down. Demonstrating his commitment and loyalty to something bigger than himself, he prioritized the team and players over his own entertainment and chose to stay for the championship game. This is a perfect example of how he inspired his players, through his own actions, on how to approach hockey and life.

Perhaps the most important lesson he taught them was not to take hockey for granted, be it in games, practice, or just hanging out with their teammates and coaches in the dressing room. He taught them to appreciate their big and small moments with the game, and to enjoy their journey with it. Todd's ultimate message to them: play every game – and live every day – as if it were your last, and have no regrets!

## At the Rink

The rink, no matter if it was around the corner from home or thousands of miles away, was always home for Todd; it brought him happiness and peace, and continued to do so right up until the end. The players and staff of the 2006-2007 Winnipeg AAA Midget Thrashers were witness to Todd's incredible example of courage, strength, and dedication in his last months. Despite the intensity of his pain, and regardless of the physical, emotional, or mental stressors that he was dealing with on any given day, Todd would show up to the rink to coach his team, just happy to be there. Oftentimes he was very sick and weak for the entire day, but whether he was throwing up or could barely walk, he would muster up the will and strength to get to the rink and walk in with a smile.

In Todd's mind, part of caring for his players meant hiding his pain and suffering from them, just as he did with the other young kids in his life. They were, he said, "too young to be worrying about stuff like this, and they should just focus on living and being happy." He tried so hard to be strong for them, to avoid passing any of his pain onto them. Despite his physical body crumbling and his mental-emotional body warding off some dark and powerful attackers, he never let on that he was struggling. Whether he was battling an anxiety attack when he felt like he couldn't get enough oxygen, or when his orbital bone broke and his eye was bulging out of his face, he always kept his composure around them.

And in his last weeks, so many of his other bones were breaking. They were so weak by then that they were literally just crumbling and cracking. One night when Todd was especially restless, Mom heard a loud "crack!" as he tried to get out of bed. From across the hallway, she heard her son moaning in pain all through the night. The next day she took him in for an X-ray, which revealed that he had a broken hip bone. The X-rays also determined that part of his spine had deteriorated to the point that it was breaking off.

His overall physical condition rapidly worsened as well, and by late November 2006, it was truly dire. Yet, he stubbornly refused to stay home, leaving no doubt in anyone's mind that he'd rather die in a hockey rink than a hospital. And as much as he had already endured, it was hard to imagine things could get worse, but once again we were wrong. For Todd's very last week would prove to be by far his toughest to endure, physically, mentally, and emotionally.

It started on Sunday, November 26, 2006 when Todd woke up in debilitating and crippling pain. Mom and Joel were sitting in her kitchen, just down the hall from his room, when they heard Todd screaming. They rushed down the hall and found him in a very fragile state. His back was likely already broken, and Mom figured that it had probably fractured further as he tried to get himself out of bed. Yet, incredibly, Todd was still bound and determined to get to the rink. The Thrashers had an afternoon game scheduled at Gateway, and though Mom pleaded with him to stay home, missing it was not an option.

Realizing they were not going to change his mind, Mom and Joel lifted him out of bed and dressed him. Mom recalls standing off to the side, watching Joel doing up the buttons on Todd's dress shirt and helping him with his tie. Any other person wouldn't have even considered attending the game in that shape, but Todd was adamant that he was going to the game to be there for his players. Dad picked Todd up and drove him to Gateway.

Kevin recognized how weak Todd was at that point. As his coach in years prior, Kevin had seen Todd as a physically fit and powerful fifteen- and sixteen-year-old, when his strength and conditioning was simply impressive; and just a few years earlier, he had competed against some of the best hockey players in the world. But long gone were the days of Todd flying around the ice at the speed of light, and Kevin's heart broke as he watched him walking as carefully as he could, moving slower than some of the older grandparents who were attending the game. He was so weak at the rink that day that he needed to be helped up to stand on the bench of the players' box to coach the game. But, in classic Todd fashion, he played it off as cool as ever so as not to upset the players. It was only after they were in the huddle and none of them were watching, that, with Kevin helping him for support, he used all of his remaining strength to step up on that bench.

This was less than one week before his death, and though he didn't know it at the time, that game would be the last he ever coached.

Just over forty-eight hours later, on Tuesday evening, Todd called Kevin at home and told him that things had deteriorated rapidly and he probably couldn't come to the rink anymore. Kevin heard the pain in Todd's voice and knew that statement was probably one of the toughest things he'd ever had to say. With nothing he could do to help, Kevin had to accept that his assistant coach and friend would no longer be there to light up the team in the dressing room, or on the ice at practice.

Yet, somehow, Todd managed to find the strength to show up to the rink for just a few minutes and say hi that night. Kevin left the ice and stood beside him just outside the rink at the glass as Todd watched his team skate on the ice sheet he grew up on. Later, he would say how detached from them, and how frustrated he felt at that moment. He told Kevin it was probably time to tell them that things weren't going to work out. But then, after momentarily feeling the pain of what that future would entail, he changed his mind, saying how upset the guys would be to hear that news and maybe there would be a better time.

The next night, Wednesday, Kevin and the other Thrashers coaches delivered Todd's message for him. They did so because they knew Todd's life could end at any second, and they didn't want the players to be completely shocked. With heavy hearts, the whole team sat together in the dressing room and wept for their friend, their rock, who would be lost to them. The news was devastating to everyone, but especially to those guys who saw the light that Todd brought into their lives just by his presence.

And then, in the midst of this most sorrowful moment, to everyone's surprise, Todd showed up at the rink! He slowly entered the dressing room, surely feeling the energetic heaviness hanging in the room as a result of the recently disclosed news about his dire condition. He surely saw the tears in their eyes, and the saddest looks on their faces. Todd hung out with the guys for a bit as he usually would, likely just trying to compose himself to deliver the news on his own. During the team's pre-practice meeting, Todd took the floor and delivered a personal message to his players: he told them that he hadn't been feeling very well lately, and that he wouldn't be able to be around in the next while. But, as he always said, "they would get things figured out," and maybe he would be back . . . With that he told the guys that he loved being around the team, and that they meant a lot to him. Then he left.

Todd's eyes did not shine that day, nor did his face bear anything but a forced smile. He was weak and unavoidably anxious. As Todd stepped out of the dressing room Kevin joined him for a moment.

"I hope we can see you tomorrow," Kevin said.

Todd responded with hope and honesty: "Who knows . . . maybe I'll make it back."

He then left the rink and headed home. He shouldn't have been driving by himself, but like a stubborn senior citizen on the verge of losing their license for public safety reasons, he absolutely refused to have Mom, or anyone else, chauffeur him around. Mom had reluctantly let Todd use her car to make the five-minute drive. She recognized that he just wanted to be alone in his own space as he prepared to deliver the toughest message he ever had to give as a coach.

It was a cold late-November day, and a lot of snow had fallen. The roads were snow-covered and slick, and after having some close calls getting the car stuck in the Gateway parking lot, and sliding on the roads home, Todd returned home noticeably scared. His hands and face were blue from the frigid Winnipeg cold and his body's inability to pull in enough oxygen. Mom rushed him to the bathroom, where they sat with body warmers and a blow-dryer, trying to restore his warmth and stop his teeth from chattering. Todd paid a physical price for making that journey, but that final visit with his team was imperative for him to be at peace.

# CHAPTER 22

# REAL TREASURES

Todd experienced various powerful realizations as the end of this earthly reality drew near. One of the biggest was understanding the limitations of material goods in relation to happiness, and the hollowness that comes with attachment to things. Todd was showered with material gifts when he was first diagnosed, all given by people with intentions of easing his pain. As his treatments continued, more gifts came. There came a point in time when Todd had every material thing a teenager could need or want. But, by the end, he knew he needed none of it.

Around ten p.m. on Saturday, November 4, 2006, I received a text from Todd telling me that our house on Ranch was broken into and ransacked. "They took everything," he wrote. I was in Vancouver with the Bisons at the time, so there was little I could do except try to stop myself from succumbing to the sadness and anger threatening to engulf me. Hadn't my family gone through enough?

Apparently, Joel had come home from the bar to see the front door left open and the lights in the house on. He knew that I was out of town, Dad was working a night shift at Fire Station #1, and Todd was at Mom's house; plus, we rarely used the front door to enter the house, so Joel quickly became suspicious that something sketchy was afoot.

As he entered the house to check things out, he could hear people in the back bedrooms and basement. The piles of Mom's fur coats passed down from Grandma and the large basement TV moved upstairs close to the front door made this an even stranger sight. Realizing that he was entering the house in the middle of a full-out burglary, Joel yelled and ran out of the house. His yell scared the burglars, who then escaped the house and fled the scene through the back bedroom windows.

After getting outside and away from immediate danger, Joel called 9-1-1, then Dad, who in turn made a phone call to alert the nearby fire station on the corner; they sent a truck over to check things out and give Joel some backup just in case. Joel's next call was to Mom, who was at her own house on Evenlea. Leaving Todd behind so he was free from danger, she rushed over. She arrived within a few minutes, then she and Joel hid behind some bushes in the yard and waited for the police.

Soon after, the officers arrived and with guns drawn ran through and around the house, yelling, "Police! Police!"

Todd had never been one to shy away from intensity, so there was no way he was going to miss something as exciting as a break-in! He arrived a few minutes later.

After clearing the house, the police officers told us they believed the break-and-enter had been committed by several people working as a team. They had smashed in the front door and made their way through everything, including Todd's room. Thank God he wasn't home alone at the time.

The burglars then proceeded to pillage the entire house, going through every drawer and closet and snatching anything of value. Fortunately, Joel had scared them off; otherwise they certainly would have made off with just about everything. Still, the value and significance of what they did steal was quite brutal, including Todd's car! Then, as Mom, Joel, and Todd walked through the house to survey the damage, they found that Todd's laptop was missing – another devastating loss, since, as is the case with most people, Todd's *life* was on that laptop.

Later Mom would tell me she hadn't started crying until she noticed the missing computer. That, she said, was one of her saddest times.

## Storing Your Treasures In Heaven

In the days prior to the break-in, Todd had continued to run himself ragged in an effort to squeeze every last moment he could from life. You could say that he was fearful that he would be laying on his deathbed, wondering what else he could have done with his time. He was so busy that he'd be driving all over the city, without taking enough time to rest and recharge. But who am I to say that he should have been resting? I wasn't the one running out of time.

Regardless, he'd continued to meet his commitments, and use his car to get where he needed to go. He was also keeping himself distracted from death and entertained online with his laptop. Through his car and laptop, he was still primarily focused on living in the external material world; that is, right up until the night that group of thugs stole them.

At that point in my life I was reading through the gospels of the New Testament on a nightly basis. The Bisons had a team chaplain who conducted weekly meetings, where we feasted on pizza while holding discussions about faith and the world. Roger Berrington, or Rog as we called him, had given our team beautiful leather-bound Bibles that had our name and team number inscribed in gold lettering on the cover. As Todd was going through his treatments, I was praying and seeking more than ever before. I was conditioned to pray and seek the "Christian" way, which primarily came by reading and studying the Bible. The night after the break-in, I returned home from Vancouver and sat in my rampaged room, with shit everywhere around me (though this was not too different from any other day), and flipped open the Bible to continue where I had left off. I started reading in the book of Matthew, at Chapter 6. Within minutes I read the following verse, and was in disbelief at the timing:

> *Do not store up for yourselves treasures on earth, where moths and vermin destroy, and where thieves break in and steal. [20] But store up for yourselves treasures in heaven, where*

*moths and vermin do not destroy, and where thieves do not
break in and steal. [21] For where your treasure is, there your
heart will be also.*

Imagine that: on the very next day after our house was broken into,
and only weeks before Todd would die, I had been led to the foregoing
passage, which teaches us to not focus on obtaining the material possessions of this realm, but instead on cultivating and storing spiritual
treasure in heaven, where it can never be destroyed. The message was all
about working on your eternal self, and recognizing what is true and eternal in this existence. The synchronicity of reading that particular verse
while in the midst of that situation blew me away.

With the theft of his laptop and his car, Todd was smacked across the
forehead by the Universal two-by-four. What I mean is, he was hit so hard
with a direct circumstantial change that he was forced to make changes
in his lifestyle. While he could have immediately gotten a replacement
computer, it would not be his, and would not be filled with his pictures
and videos and all of the memories of his *life*. And sure, he could have
immediately gotten another car, but at that point it just seemed unnecessary, especially considering that the stolen one might turn up and be
returned. And then there was the other thing no one wanted to think,
let alone talk about: that whatever car he had, Todd wouldn't be using it
for very long.

# CHAPTER 23

# THE POWER WITHIN

In the grand scheme of Todd's life, the robbers played masterful dual roles, both as villains of the scene and bringers of a powerful message that helped him release attachments to cherished material possessions before he died. The bright side of the car theft was that it forced Todd to be still, instead of always frantically rushing around. The bright side of the laptop theft was that he was led to go within himself for connection, instead of searching for it externally through a screen. Without the distraction of material things and all of the places to go and things to do, Todd was led to go into contemplation and reflection within himself. He was laying the foundation for his transition away from his physical body.

Ironically, the thieves' effort to steal as much stuff of "value" as they could had resulted in Todd's most valuable lesson: the material world and possessions one can attain within it don't really matter all that much. Truly, Todd didn't seem to care that his car and computer were gone. After seeing Mom's tearful reaction, which was really about her thinking that Todd had been violated and would suffer from his losses, he looked at her and in a calm and stoic manner said, "Mom, it's just stuff . . ."

Todd's response put the temporary material things in our lives into perspective. He knew he would soon be leaving this Earth without any material possessions at all. There was no time to waste grasping at dust. In that moment, Todd saw the fleeting nature and ultimate meaningless-ness of all those things the thieves took, knowing that they were replace-able items that had no real bearing on his internal state. A car was just a car, and a computer was just a computer, and he simply wasn't going to waste his energy on either of them. He knew material things could not make him happy, and were not empowering him in any true way, so he accepted the losses. He wasn't begging the cops to track down his car, nor did he start some online campaign for awareness of his missing laptop. Deep down, he knew that nothing *real* had been lost.

A side note: in true Todd fashion, after telling me about the break-in, his mind went to humor. In his next texts he convinced me that Molly had gotten so fast she was scouted at the off-leash park to become a rac-ing dog. This, by the way, was a completely made-up story.

## Ego Death

After the break-in, I noticed a definite shift in how Todd spent his time: he was much quieter, and much more observant. He was no longer so distracted, and often seemed to be in a type of meditation or prayer state. He also had no interest in mundane material things; it was as if he was over anything that wasn't eternal. It's like that break-in event triggered the realization that the external/physical/material world would never be capable of producing the emotions and vibratory states that he had started to glimpse and feel inside of him. He knew the truth he was seek-ing was not to be found somewhere out there.

By that point he was identifying with the immortal power inside of him much more than ever before. And how could he not? The alternative was to keep identifying with a deteriorating body that was destined to die and decompose. For me, it was like watching a caterpillar in a cocoon; my brother seemed to have undergone an internal transformation, and on the other side he had come out a changed man. He was no longer consumed with his body, his image, or his possessions; instead, he was focused on connecting to the truth of what this whole life thing is all about. In losing his body and his possessions, he had undergone what I now understand to be an *ego death*.

In essence, your "ego" is the collection of ideas that you think about yourself at any given time. It is the foundation of "who we think we are" that we build for ourselves to allow us to operate in space and time on Earth as a distinct entity. In other words, your ego is the collection of your personal "I AMs" – for example, "I am strong", or "I am weak"; "I am smart", or "I am stupid"; "I am wealthy"; "I am homeless"; "I am attractive" or "I am ugly"; "I am a doctor or a lawyer or an astronaut"; "I am a womanizing, booze-hound who is the best partier of all time"; and so on. In Todd's case, "I am a hockey player" was certainly one of, if not *the* most prominent "I AM."

Before his diagnosis, Todd was a typical seventeen-year-old male in many typical ways; he was as vain and self-conscious as any other teenager trying to find their place in the world. He was also physically attractive – with a chiseled body, flowing hockey hair, bright eyes, and a gleaming smile – and, that, combined with his natural magnetism and sparkling personality, allowed him to routinely attract beautiful girls with ease. He was the type of guy who was never afraid to ask out the hottest girl in the room. He could wheel on the ice, and he could wheel with the ladies. However, within weeks of his high school graduation party, when the cancer was discovered and treatments had begun – his looks began to change. Although these changes started gradually and were almost unnoticeable, by the end of his days, Todd's exterior form was a shadow of its former self.

With his first chemotherapy session came the loss of his hair. He shaved his head early on as a preemptive measure, rather than watching it fall out in clumps. This wasn't too alarming, as guys in the hockey world shave their heads all the time, yet as a showing of support, Pa, Dad, I, along with a ton of friends, all shaved our heads as well. Though he might have appreciated the gesture, it didn't really help his diminishing self-image. Our hair would all grow back with ease; Todd's might not. Things then went to a new level when he lost his eyebrows and eyelashes.

He lost power with those initial physical changes, which were, in his words, "a devastating experience." When he saw himself in the mirror he realized, perhaps for the first time in his entire life, that he was not in control of his body or his fate.

When his hair grew back after his last chemo treatments, it was radically different. No longer did it flow in thick, lustrous waves, but was thin and tightly curled – a look Todd was initially quite insecure and self-conscious about. He eventually rolled with it, but it was no easy adjustment. His hair – one of his favorite features – was changed forever. And that was just the start.

Fast forward to a year into his treatments and his body had lost most of its strength and muscle tone – this, due to not being able to work out. The most noticeable changes were with his upper body, which had gone from broad and strong to narrow and weak. His left arm was, for the most part, useless, and he had to hold it in an unnaturally shrugged position when it wasn't in its sling. While he had been dealing with his physical changes fairly well all along, I think he always believed his looks would eventually improve. But as the days went by and they continued to deteriorate, he started to lose that hope. Perhaps for the first time in his life, Todd began to feel really insecure. Negative thoughts about himself crept into his mind.

Aside from his arm, the most-heartbreaking physical change we witnessed was to Todd's face, which had lost its structure and was sunken in. By the fall of 2006, he just looked really, really sick at times. And by the very end, his eyes bulged out of his face, his skin changed from radiant to dull and grayish, and he looked frail. He was being forced to face the destruction of his physical vehicle, and all of his associations to his once-held image.

Fears that he was no longer "physically attractive" or "normal" in the eyes of others seemed to be confirmed when girls around his age, who'd previously been giddy in his presence, no longer paid him any attention.

Worse, the same types of girls who would have been aggressively trying to get his attention only two years earlier looked at him with worry, fear, and even repulsion at times. Mom recalls one heartbreaking scene towards the end, when Todd stood in line at Subway to order lunch. Some attractive girls close to him in age stood nearby, and instead of checking him out and smiling, they looked at Todd with concern and subtly distanced themselves from him. Mom was crushed inside when she witnessed that, and desperately hoped that Todd somehow didn't notice.

With the familiar surface version of himself long gone, Todd was forced to ask himself some really difficult questions. Who was he, if not the young stud, or star-athlete, or girl magnet he had always identified with?

Like all of us, Todd had undergone many ego blows before. When we got released from the Pats in the fall of 2003, for example, he could no longer identify with being a member of one of the most prestigious junior hockey teams in one of the best junior hockey leagues in the world. But those blows paled in comparison to what he was facing now. Who are we, he asked, when there is nothing left to cling to, no more masks to hide behind?

These types of introspective questions led Todd to go within, where he underwent the death of that egoic collection of ideas of who he was in this world. During this time of confusion and transition with his body and identity, Todd appeared to make major breakthroughs in his perceptions about life. As the walls of his external world were crumbling around him, Todd felt something inside of him start to grow. He became focused on his *inner world* and rose up. He was, perhaps for the first time in his life, coming to know himself as the true I AM, far beyond ego.

## Something Within

So many people from all over the world speak of sacred mystical experiences so powerful they erased any fear of death. Regardless of how they achieved this experience – be it prayer, meditation, religious ceremony, psychedelic experience, or getting struck by lightning – their message is the same: that something incredible and outside our limited human imagination awaits us beyond this physical world. They tell us that not only should we not fear death, we should embrace it as a miraculous next step in an eternal journey. These accounts, while varied in many ways, all point to God/Creator/Source and the spirit world existing in and around us, loving and supporting us always. Yet, despite these "five-star" reviews of the afterlife from those who had seen it, and the similar descriptions found in holy books of the various religions on the planet, we still lack faith; and most of us truly fear death.

Unless you consider hockey as a religion – which is perhaps the case in Canada – Todd was not a "religious" person. He didn't have a rigid or dogmatic belief system. We were raised Catholic, which is to say that we had been conditioned with a fair amount of guilt and shame, but Todd didn't buy in. He wasn't going to feel guilty and shameful just for being a curious kid; he was not going to be called a "sinner" based on someone else's standards. So, while he dutifully attended the mandatory masses and received the sacraments with the rest of the Catholic school students, he distanced and detached himself from all non-mandatory religious ceremonies. And, along with me and Joel, he silently rejoiced when Sunday morning church was replaced by Sunday morning hockey games.

As Todd grew older he did not speak outwardly about his faith – at least not to me – but I can safely say he wasn't into visiting a fancy building every Sunday to listen to a man wearing a robe preach righteous behavior. He made light of church, and seemed to have reservations about the intentions of so-called "religious" people who wanted to get too close to him. I think he saw through the mind-control systems that certain religions were operating under, and was also leery about the inauthenticity and hypocrisy of certain people he had come across in his life, so he stayed back. There was something about it all that just didn't sit right with him.

He was naturally discerning, sensing truth and authenticity, and his guard went up when he felt pressured by others to accept and believe as they did. He was an independent free thinker, and no priest nor pastor was going to tell him that he wasn't going to make the God-squad based on his lack of allegiance to a religious code or a set of specific behaviors. His actions revealed that he embodied compassion and love for fellow humans – which just so happens to be an essential teaching of nearly all religions anyway. It was his own organic way of operating in the world.

Though he didn't broadcast it to others, Todd was in fact quite spiritual. He certainly held reverence for a higher power, showed interest in spiritually-inspired people, had a deep reverence for the mysteries of life, and was curious. He was a seeker of Truth – the truth of who we are, why we are here, and what this life is all about. Any spiritual practices were conducted in the most righteous and proper of manners: in his room, with the door closed and lights off, on the altar of his heart, with his awareness as witness. His prayers weren't for others to hear and proclaim they were holy; they were for him, and him alone. I can only imagine the contents and intensity of some of his prayers throughout his journey, especially when things were getting rough. But through the ups and downs, Todd kept faith and trust that something beyond this world and life existed for him.

After the break-in Todd's search for the truth deepened, particularly with regard to what happens when we die. When I would walk by his room late into the evening, I would peek through the door, left open just a crack, and find him, not staring at the screen of his laptop or entertaining himself in some other way, but lying in silent meditation.

I did not realize Todd's level of consciousness or the depths of his seeking in those final days until several years later, when I looked through his quote-book and saw the authors and books he was reading. I was blown away. He was studying works far beyond the typical feel-good and fluffy self-help books. He was intrigued and absorbed in studying and aligning with some of the highest principles of living, as written by various mystics and people of faith and experience. From Christian mysticism to ancient teachings from Eastern traditions, Todd was seeking the Truth. One of the books that Todd resonated with was *Conversations With God* by Neale Donald Walsh. As you can imagine from the title, Todd, ultimately, was seeking God, the Source of all Life, the thing death cannot touch.

Despite never subscribing to religious dogma, while on this journey he intuitively trusted the teachings and clues of the saints, mystics, and masters who had come before him. I can't tell you exactly how you can find this Source yourself, because everyone's path is different, but I can say that I have glimpsed its existence, if only for a second, and Todd did too. Todd doubted God much of his life, but he refused to give up on the search. He knew there was too much power in this life for there not to be something more. And, just as he pursued everything else, he was going to do his best in reaching it.

I don't know where he went or what he saw or felt; what I do know is that something empowered him, and that something was big! A contentment came over his presence, which I presume was the result of a mystical experience – perhaps a contact with a spirit guide or maybe even God Himself! – that finally made sense to him. I don't quite know. But, from then on, he was a changed person. Something had been revealed to him that took his fear away. It was like he had tapped into a sacred vibration that showed him that true eternal life exists, and on a much different level that we can comprehend. This holy vibration of timeless power seemed to guide Todd into a deeper place of love and existence. Finally, he had accepted that he was dying and, more than that, he became a seeker of death, and he came out victorious.

Like the great mystics he studied, Todd came to realize that one's consciousness – one's awareness of themselves as a Soul being – does not end when the human body shuts down. The greats that have walked this planet have preached their faith in greater things to come beyond this transitory existence in this dense and heavy "reality." In his search for the heart and mind of a righteous man, Todd became a true mystic himself

– someone who sees and feels beyond the physicality of this dense reality and all the typical intellectual boundaries that are imposed upon us. And, by his last day, after all the darkness, pain, and suffering of his journey, he knew he was indeed going somewhere magical, far beyond the limitations of this life and physical body. Indeed, in the eleventh hour, he spoke out to let us know that "he knows he'll be okay." He knew that his inner light would continue to shine bright.

Whether we realize it or not, we all have glimpsed our inner worlds, and our own real power – be it in a dream, meditation, a mystical moment, or by introspection. The true masters are those who find their way to the Kingdom within and still manage to live in the *outer* world through this empowered *inner* place. Todd studied these teachings as he focused more on his *within*. As he wrote in his quote-book, he began to understand, as  Caroline Myss taught, that "The goal of human experience is to transform ourselves from beings who long to have power in the physical world to beings who are empowered within." Ironically, when he was at his weakest and most vulnerable – with little ability to move his body and no material wealth to show off to the world – he was at his most powerful, and was becoming his strongest as a spiritual being.

The darkness, suffering, pain, and loss of his body pushed him to the depths of his being, and he came out a whole new man. After the transformation brought forth by that *ego death,* Todd leveled up and didn't come back down. He developed a new way of thinking about himself and others, and went about living intentionally from the place of inner empowerment. Instead of operating in the world only through his small self's collection of ideas about himself – he saw through a different lens and acted accordingly. He realized that real power is the power within us – always there, waiting for us to connect to it and live through it.

CHAPTER 24

# HIS REAL LAST SHIFT

## Near-Death Experience

The first time I was exposed to the topic of near-death experiences ("NDEs") was late fall of 2006 in an introductory level Psychology course. Todd was enrolled in this class with me, and we typically sat together in the upper side rows of the lecture amphitheater, amongst a couple of cute female classmates. It was an interesting class that allowed us to peek into the workings of the human mind together and consider novel and challenging ideas. More importantly, though, it allowed us to be side-by-side once again, just like back on a hockey bench, for at least a couple of hours a week.

All semester long, our professor, "Dr. Bob" – whose teaching style revealed a dry sense of humor and a touch of arrogance – hinted about his infamous last lecture that he would deliver to us. He noted that in years past the nature and content of the lecture had been disturbing to many students. Most of us didn't give a second thought to it, but as the end of the semester crept closer, Dr. Bob repeatedly reminded us of the delicate nature of that future lecture, which served as a warning to the sensitive students to brace themselves for whatever was to be revealed.

By the time that class rolled around on November 29, 2006, Todd was simply way too weak to attend. He rarely missed class, but some days, especially as the harsh Winnipeg winter drew near and his body broke down more, he just couldn't make it across the city to sit in a brutally hard wooden seat of a lecture hall.

I took my seat that day without Todd beside me, and eagerly awaited the appearance of Dr. Bob. A few minutes later, the mysterious last lecture's topic matter was revealed: "NDEs and the Afterlife." The energy of the room intensified and a noticeable excitement hung in the air as the three hundred or so students – most of whom, I presume, had ever heard of NDEs either – seemed excited to explore these uncharted waters.

People who speak of their own NDEs generally describe an out-of-body experience in which they realize their awareness is separate and distinct from the physical form. Next, they often describe a sensation of total relief from all physical, mental, and emotional pain that was associated or tied to the body. Instead, they experience feelings of unwavering and unconditional love, peace, and joy sweeping over them and embracing them, as if they were instantly healed. Then, there is often the description of a glorious and immersive white light, the frequency and feeling of which is far different from any light we experience in this dimension. And, of course, there is testimony of seeing relatives, friends, and pets who had previously passed. Then it gets really cool: they speak about being met by angels, spirit guides, or some form of higher power; some even describe meeting God. Finally, some talk about experiencing a *life review* – an in-depth, play-by-play analysis of the emotionally charged or important moments that transpired during their time on this planet.

Only a few minutes into the lecture, the charged atmosphere seemed to quickly deflate as Dr. Bob puffed out his chest and began to "debunk" all of the phenomena associated with NDEs and the afterlife. Dr. Bob dismissed these spiritual testimonials away as mere physiological reactions of the body. He believed, in essence, that every reported mystical or metaphysical phenomenon perceived during an NDE could be explained away with materialistic science. One by one he hit his prepared teaching points and droned on in a rather depressive tone about why such NDE testimonies were utter nonsense.

Dr. Bob went on to say something along the lines that we were nothing more than our bodies and brains and, upon death, we would "power down" forever like any other machine.

The entire amphitheater went silent. Feelings of dull melancholy, restlessness, and subtle anxiety came over the group as the lecture came to a close. The teachings were atheistic and devoid of faith in an afterlife. They presented a dull explanation of the NDE material purely from the skeptic's point of view. Fair enough – Dr. Bob had the full right to think this way – but leave it up to a social scientist to forget that energy, including the life force energy that powers our bodies, cannot be destroyed.

To say I was fired up at that point would be an understatement – not only about Dr. Bob's message but his delivery. Believing that he was presenting his hypotheses as undeniable truths for us to blindly accept, I shot up my hand and waited to be called upon for comment. I felt a duty to at least challenge the dark and depressing narrative that had just been cast over the room. This was not "truth," but one man's guess about the end of life. When I was called upon, I reminded the class of this; I then went on to say that we should not consider the phenomena described by people who experienced NDEs as being categorically false because these were individual perceptions that were true and real to the experiencer. Dr. Bob acknowledged my points but appeared to remain convinced that he had a superior opinion.

When class was dismissed, a confused and uneasy blur of humans blended together to exit the room. Across the city, at that very point in time, Todd lay at home in bed struggling to operate. Considering that he was approaching death without return, I was relieved and thankful that he missed that lecture. Hearing some discouraged, and seemingly spiritually desolate professor disavow any sort of credence of near-death experiences and the afterlife would have been nothing but a waste of Todd's precious remaining time. Though we didn't know it at that exact moment, the sand in Todd's life-glass was getting down to the last particles; indeed, within three days, he would be learning, first-hand, what really happens when we die.

## A Last Goodbye

Before Todd died he asked Dad to explain to others why he didn't tell anyone that his cancer had been worsening. With a heavy heart and somewhat guilty mind, he said:

"As hard as it is for everyone to say goodbye to one person in their life, I have to say goodbye to everyone in mine. For me, it's like everyone I know is dying, and I need to say goodbye to them. I just wanted to spend the rest of my time with people treating me normal, not being sad or feeling sorry for me."

As Todd walked up the stairs at the old Focus Fitness, he greeted Glenn as he usually had every few afternoons back in those days. But in Glenn's eyes, something was different this time: Todd's usual spark was faded, and he looked extra tired and weak. His persona was different than usual, and he had a more reserved tone to him.

When Todd typically stopped in they talked about hockey and girls, not necessarily in that order. Glenn would do things like bug Todd about the lifeguard at the Winnipeg Winter Club, who he'd had a crush on but was too shy to ask out (kind of like Smalls' crush on the lifeguard in the classic movie *Sandlot)* until he made a big move and did, and then they talked about that. Or they'd lightly joke about other regular daily life stuff. But this time was different; this time their conversation was far more serious.

They talked about *Believe in the Goal,* and all that was accomplished. They talked about all Todd had achieved in hockey, and what he went through to get where he did. As a sixteen-year-old, he'd had to fight so much harder than everyone else, but he'd made it to the WHL, and he was proud of that. He was also proud of returning to junior hockey after surgery. Then he spoke of his love for the game, and his love for coaching. Then things got deeper: Todd talked about how he really wanted to be in love and be married; and how badly he wanted to be a dad, but was coming to terms with the fact that it wasn't going to happen . . .

Glenn didn't realize it at first, but somewhere in the conversation he understood that Todd was really close to the end. He then stopped joking around and took a mental snapshot of the essence of his friend who was in front of him in that moment.

The conversation ended all too soon, as the good ones always do. Then, with a handshake-hug, Todd was on his way.

"We'll talk to you later," Glenn said, as he watched Todd deliberately hold the handrail and slowly move down the first stretch of the L-shaped stairs. Halfway down, he stopped, turned around, and smiled.

"I'll see you later."

As he disappeared from view, Glenn knew it was the last time Todd would be coming by for an afternoon chat.

After the exchange with Glenn, Dad took Todd to the hospital for one more strong dose of radiation. By then, Todd didn't have any more strength to stand on his own, so he was carefully placed in a wheelchair. It was, just thirty-six hours until his death, the first time he had needed one. Despite all the pain and weakness he had endured through the last two-and-a-half years – including barely being able to walk at all with a broken back – he had refused to take a seat. As long as his legs could move on their own, he would use them, including to climb a big set of stairs to say a final goodbye to the guy who trained him, made him laugh, and motivated and inspired him to take action and do something to give back to this world.

If he had more time and strength to do so, Todd would have visited all of his friends like this. But time was ticking away for him faster than ever, and he faded a little more with every passing second.

## This Saturday

As mentioned, since his diagnosis, Todd had always downplayed his illness so as not to burden others. He felt the pain they felt when they found out, and he felt ashamed and powerless for being what he perceived to be the source of that pain. He wanted their relationships to continue unchanged by the fact that he was dying; he didn't want their exchanges – and certainly not that last one – to be dominated by sadness, fear, and pain. So he continued doing what made the most sense to him: he told others that he was doing well and fine.

Despite Todd's assurances, his physical appearance told a different story, and soon those who knew him couldn't deny the fact that the end was drawing near. One of those people was Linda Moe, mother of Todd's great friend, Katie, who had observed Todd bouncing around Winnipeg hockey rinks for years. Katie, who was attending flight school in Calgary, Alberta, hadn't seen Todd in a couple of months, but based on her conversations with him she presumed he was doing fine. So when Linda called and told her that she had seen Todd and didn't think he had much time left, Katie was left in utter shock.

"I saw Todd at a hockey game and something isn't right. You need to find out what is going on. You need to come home."

Katie called Hammy to inquire, and when he confirmed what her mother had said Katie immediately booked a flight. It was Thursday evening – a few hours after Todd had visited Glenn and went to the hospital for the radiation – when she, joined by Hammy, arrived at Mom's house. Katie spent some time catching up with Mom in the kitchen and asking questions about how Todd was doing, but before Mom could answer her Todd walked out of the bathroom and into her view. Katie was absolutely shocked by how sick and frail he looked and instantly knew his death was close by. She might have been even more blown away, however, by Todd's upbeat and positive mood.

"Are you feeling okay?" she asked.

"Ya, I'm fine," he responded as if nothing out of the ordinary was happening.

Katie was confused by the obvious contrast between the diminished outward condition of Todd's body and the usual joy-filled spirit and strong mind that was still inside her young friend. When she finally got her bearings and acclimated to the situation, she became angry that Todd hid how sick he was from her.

"You should have told me!" Katie said. "You don't have to tell everyone, but your good friends should know! You need to start telling your friends what's going on."

"I know . . . " Todd responded guiltily.

That's when he realized he was doing his friends a disservice by keeping the truth from them. They deserved to know how bad his condition was. It was time to tell everyone that he would be leaving the party a bit early.

Katie and Todd talked it out and agreed that they would get all his friends together. Perhaps coincidentally, or perhaps with his Soul's intuitive sense of the future, Todd said, "Okay, let's do it this Saturday."

A few minutes later, Todd slowly came up the basement stairs, clutching the side rail tight as he struggled to the top. He finally made it to the back landing, right near the kitchen where Mom had been standing near the sink. He was nearly completely out of breath. Moments earlier, Mom had told Katie and Hammy about the importance of not calling 9-1-1 if Todd were to suddenly stop breathing, or go into cardiac arrest. An official-looking piece of paper with the words "Do Not Resuscitate" sat on top of the fridge. Now she looked at her twenty-year-old son standing before her and instead of seeing a vibrant young man beaming with life, she saw a frail body, like that of a weak old man, fading before her. She realized that within just a couple of hours Todd's body and physical condition had drastically deteriorated.

Todd looked Mom in the eyes and said words that she never wanted to hear and that he never wanted to believe:

"I think I'm going to die tonight."

# CHAPTER 25

# FINAL MINUTES ON
# THE LIFE CLOCK

After resisting death and fighting for life for so long, Todd intuitively knew that this really was the end for him. We all knew that this day would come, but it came so much faster than expected. After all the ups-and-downs of his journey – all of the high hopes and dreams, and all of the lows of suffering and anguish – it was time for him to move on.

Mom lay awake and sleepless in the room across the hall from her dying son. She figured that Todd maybe slept for an hour or two that night.

With the strength he had left he started making calls to say his last goodbye to certain people. He wanted to thank them for all they had done for him and all they had given to him in this life. Since it was quite late at night, some people would wake up the next day to a missed call. For those who missed the calls or didn't answer for whatever reason, just know this: Todd called you for a reason. You were on his short list. Others were fortunate enough to have beautifully painful conversations with him.

Todd called Pete – the surgeon who had fought and cared for him with so much composure and devotion. Pete was much more than just a doctor to Todd; he was a pillar of knowledge, strength, support, care and comfort. Beyond that, he became a trusted ally of truth and possibility. When virtually every doctor who reviewed his case concluded that Todd's entire arm would have to be amputated, Pete dedicated time and energy to find a surgeon capable of removing the tumor while saving the limb. When Todd's collarbone repeatedly broke through the skin and needed to be fixed, Pete was the one to get it done, without blinking. When Todd needed a break from his treatment, Pete took him to Moose games, where they sat at ice level and hung out around the dressing room and players. Pete would do everything possible to help Todd through this situation and allow him to have a better quality of life, and Todd knew that. After their journey together, that last phone call in his final hours was Todd's way of saying the most sincere and heartfelt thank you.

Todd also called Michelle – a person he knew loved him and cared for him so deeply throughout his illness – and they shared one final, emotionally charged late-night/early morning conversation. Over the two previous years, Todd would go over to Michelle and Dad's house to hang out with the kids and the dogs. After the kids went to bed, Todd often joined Michelle by the fire for a late-night chat. They would talk late into the night, with Todd revealing his emotional state as he navigated cancer along with the challenges of being a teenager. Michelle, a nurse, brought her natural caring energy to Todd, and gave him a safe space to open up his heart and mind. They connected at a deep personal and heartfelt level. When it was apparent that his brighter future would not be happening while in physical form, he revealed his thoughts about things beyond this life.

Through the phone, Michelle listened one last time to Todd's thoughts and reflections on his life, their moments together, and about what may await him after death. Though Todd rarely, if ever, spoke outwardly of his faith of an afterlife, he did that night. He told her he knew that something more awaited him. In relaying part of that sacred conversation, Michelle told me that Todd passed a message on to me: "He said to tell you that he doesn't necessarily see things the way you see them, but he knows that he'll be okay!"

## Of Angels and Ancestors

The idea of angels and what they represent pervades the literature of humanity's past, particularly in Christian and Judaic traditions. There are also countless personal accounts from all over the world about miraculous encounters with what are described as angelic beings. Angels, understood as God's helpers and messengers, are viewed as benevolent spiritual beings that operate from the spirit world to help us here on Earth; however, most people who make reference to them do so in passing, saying such things as, "My angels must have been watching over me," when they miraculously survive what should have been a fatal accident.

Similar to the concept of angels is the idea of "ancestors," which is commonly derived from indigenous peoples or other tribal cultures. Ancestors are those in our lineage who have passed on but remain connected to us in soul and spirit, and are invested in seeing us thrive on Earth.

I like to think that our angels and ancestors are the "spiritual fans" in our lives, watching over us from the beyond and cheering us on. I like to think that they see the game of life being played out on Earth's grand stage, and wish to help us out. Whether it be a back-door pass for a tap-in goal or that glorious breakaway pass, maybe angels and ancestors are real, and are assisting us to score and succeed in powerful and miraculous ways. Like a coach watching from up in the press box with a microphone leading to an earpiece in our ear, perhaps they can guide us, help us, and give us a better idea of what is going on in the game of our lives beyond what our limited vision can see.

Though many will dismiss all this angel and ancestor talk as just a bunch of nonsensical bullshit made up by humans to make them feel all warm and fuzzy in a cold, harsh world, others have a strong belief that these types of forces exist in our lives and are here to watch over us and help us and guide us to greatness and God. As evidenced by the writings in his quote-book, Todd came to believe that angels are real; and, on his very last morning on Earth, I can't help but think that he met some of his angels and ancestors.

After a torturous night, Mom heard the sound of Todd crashing into the dresser in his room across the hall. Without knowing what happened, she jumped up and rushed in to help him. When she opened the door, she saw Todd looking around the empty room in bewilderment.

"Who are all these people here?" he asked in a confused and nervous tone.

Mom, who was very much grounded in the reality of the physical world at that time, looked around the room and saw nothing but furniture and empty space. Todd was seeing differently, though. His eyes moved all around, seeking different heights and levels. He was actively seeing beyond this reality.

"No one is here, Todd. It is just us," she responded, as she tried to calm him down and reassure him that they were alone.

But Todd wasn't buying it.

"There are other people here with us! How come there are so many people here?"

Todd's uneasiness quickly turned into fear as his *reality* started to blur. Imagine how freaked out you'd be if you woke up in a room full of strangers and had someone telling you that no one else was there? Todd grabbed his phone as he stumbled into the bathroom across the hall and called Katie. He wanted to get some sort of reassurance from someone other than Mom.

"People are beside me . . . people are in the bathroom!" he said frantically.

Katie, not trained in dealing with someone's end-of-life-transitioning or seeing invisible beings, didn't know what to do or say. She was stunned, but tried to calm Todd down. Then Mom came on the line.

"Katie, this is it!"

Todd's final descent to death had begun, and there was no turning back. He was seeing beyond the veil of the physical world. In retrospect, it is clear that Todd was then experiencing other dimensions – other levels of vibration not typically perceived by humans during day-to-day existence. His awareness and reality had started to move away from the dense vibrations of the "real" world. The ancestors and/or angels had arrived to help him transition beyond the physical plane, across the bridge to the other side.

Mom wasn't thinking about all this, though, as she grabbed the phone and frantically made another call. All she knew was that the moment she dreaded most had arrived.

"Come, please come," she shouted when Dad picked up the phone, "Todd's dying!"

# CHAPTER 26

# HIS LAST DAY

On Friday, December 1, 2006, I received the phone call that changed everything. I had just showered and was getting ready to head to the university to take my Psychology final. Todd was supposed to be taking that exam too, but he was too far gone for school at that point. His *real* final exam – the one that mattered – was just about to be submitted. When the call came around nine a.m., I was preoccupied with rehearsing the material I was to be tested on in my mind. I was not expecting any call; certainly not *that* call. It came from Michelle, and she had a very strange tone in her voice.

After a quick hi, she urgently said, "Todd knows about the letter that you wrote him, and he wants to hear it. Wade, come to your mom's place, now! He's dying!"

I had written the letter a few weeks earlier, but the timing had never felt right to give it to him. Far from a "get well soon" note, it instead acknowledged his terminal fate, so reading it at an inopportune time would have been more than awkward. The letter spoke of him dying and had some of those uncomfortable words in it – words like "cancer," "death," "heaven," and "God." It was personal and powerful, and I was waiting for the right time to give it to him, but sometimes that "right" time never comes. I didn't think I would be reading it to him . . . especially not like this.

I got into my car and rushed to Mom's place. What was normally a two-minute drive seemed to take twenty because of the foot of snow that had fallen overnight. Todd was visible as soon as I walked in the door. He was laid back in the black lazy-boy recliner. He was shirtless, wearing his navy blue Tampa Bay Lightning shorts. His eyes were closed, and the only ones in the house that were not filled with tears. I took my jacket and boots off and gently walked in.

Glancing at the faces of Mom, Dad and Michelle, I took a deep breath and pulled out the letter, then stepped next to Todd. He was really battling at that moment, and it took great effort just to look up at me. Then he became focused and serious. "Just give me a minute here," he said, as he tried to compose himself. He knew what was happening. The time had finally come.

I walked back around the corner into the kitchen to give him some space and time. I heard him take several deep breaths and saw him struggle to reach for the lime Gatorade that was beside him. He took a sip, slowly and deliberately; it was like he was gathering all the conscious energy he had to be present in this world.

A minute or so later he signaled that he was ready.

"Okay . . ." he said.

I sat down on the living room step that was just behind him, and leaned my body forward so we were side-by-side. This was one of those moments; one of those real-life moments. I felt a wave of overwhelming emotion and used all the strength I could muster so as not to burst out in tears. Then, with a slow, deep breath, I began to read.

I told Todd how much he meant to me; how grateful I was that he was my brother; how much I looked up to him as a person; and how I appreciated all of our moments together. I told him that his life was blessed and righteous, and that he was truly a gift to the world. I spoke of my faith in what awaited him. And, most importantly, I told him I loved him; something I hadn't done nearly enough before.

In one of the most powerful exchanges of our lives, Todd then weakly held out his right hand to me, palm open, and said, in a calm, labored voice, "That was really nice."

We made direct eye contact for just a moment – just long enough to signal a conscious connection and a response that went beyond words. Then he closed his eyes and laid his head back. Relief came over me as I finished reading. All that needed to be said was said, heard, and received. My word was all I could offer to him at that time.

I can't imagine how much effort it took him to stay present and pay attention to what I was saying, and to respond at all. That simple response was more than anything I could have asked for.

I grabbed his hand and held it as I wept. I sat there beside him in silence for a few minutes. There was nothing else to say.

His awareness seemed to drift away from his body shortly after that last exchange. Like a tether that was fraying by the second, it was only a matter of time before the cord that bound his Soul to this world would be released. After fighting for so long, his body had become too weak to hold his true power. It was time to retire for good.

We did our best to quickly spread the word through phone calls and texts that Todd's time had finally come, and everybody came running. I remember calling Lindsey to tell her that Todd was dying.

"I know . . ." she said, in a sad and defeated tone.

"No! He's really dying . . . like right now!" I responded, telling her and Carling to come immediately. They, along with all the others, also terribly shocked, rushed over as fast as possible. They knew he could go at any moment and didn't want to miss their chance to say a final goodbye in the flesh. After all the fears of the last two years, this was really it.

The next hours were filled with some of the people Todd impacted most in this world coming to see him one last time. They wanted to see his eyes for one last time. Friends and family flooded through the front door of Mom's place on Evenlea. Gathering in the living room, one-by-one they knelt at his feet, held Todd's hand in theirs one last time, and said their personal goodbyes. Tears were flowing hard that day. No one wanted to leave him. No one wanted to see him go.

Among the people who came to see Todd on his last day was a tall man dressed in black from head-to-toe, including a long black robe tied off at the waist with a rope. As he solemnly entered Mom's front door and surveyed the scene before him, it was as if the Angel of Death had arrived. The man was Brother John: a kind and loving man with a gentle disposition who our family had come to know through our involvement at St. Alphonsus School. Carrying a Bible, an old Catholic text, and a cross, Brother John was ushered to the feet of Todd. He had come to perform the Last Rites – a mysterious and seemingly fear-based Catholic ritual consisting of final prayers and ministrations. It is like a Hail Mary pass for the dying person's Soul, made by a priest and their loved ones as the final seconds of the game clock of life tick down to zero.

Brother John carefully approached the black recliner with awareness and appreciation for the fragility of the situation. As he moved close to Todd, the energy of the room shifted to one of hushed reverence. By this time, Todd had been fading in-and-out of consciousness for at least a couple of hours.

Brother John looked at Todd with sympathy for his body, but with faith in what awaited. Todd, not fully grasping the situation, looked at Brother John with wide eyes that told of wonder and confusion – similar to how an innocent child might look at a stranger they are not sure about. As if treading into unknown territory, Brother John gently began to engage with Todd. He looked at him quietly for a moment and then began.

"Hi, Todd. Do you remember learning about Jesus in school and church? Do you know of Jesus?"

Without flinching, and with the most casual, innocent tone and delivery, Todd responded with what would be some of his final words:

"Ya, I know Jesus . . ."

Though Todd had not met Him during his life – at least not to my knowledge – he had taken enough Sunday school classes and heard enough homilies to be familiar with the figure and the story of Jesus

Christ. By then, though nowhere near an evangelical Christian of any sort, Todd seemed to have intuitively internalized the essence of what the real teachings, and the real Christ, were all about. Todd knew there was power in those teachings about being a good person through intention and action: acting with love instead of hate; forgiving instead of holding grudges; seeking the true power within; and having faith that things are happening on a bigger stage. It's like he naturally understood that if you act from those places, you'd be doing the best in any given moment this life gives you, and would be living a righteous and holy life, worthy of entering any Holy Kingdom that may exist beyond this world. Todd seemed to embody the *Christ-Frequency*, just as he was. We all have this potential and this power within us to tap into this frequency, but Todd was a natural.

As if he was remembering an old familiar friend from the past, Todd seemed to be briefly reflecting on the idea of Jesus in his mind. He then closed his eyes and slowly faded back into his transition.

As Brother John continued, I sat in the corner of the living room and watched each person come to Todd's feet, one by one for one final exchange. Todd would make eye contact with the person before him, which seemed to trigger some memory or thought he had inside. On the lighter side of one of perhaps the heaviest days of our lives, as he drifted further and became delusional, Todd – like a great comedian telling one more killer joke before ending the show and walking off stage – brought laughter to those mourning his death. He rambled about things like skinny-dipping with the girls, not getting a "Jug" – St. Paul's High School's version of detention – because "he wasn't fully aware of the Fall dress code," and other random nonsense. While this material was just odd, anecdotal things that seemed to be pulled from the depths of his subconscious mind as it unwound, everyone lightened up just a bit. On a heavy and solemn day, those smiles and laughs gave us all some relief. Maybe, just maybe, he was aware that this life was all a great divine comedy, and that was his way of trying to show us that, even in the face of death.

After those brief laughs, reality set back in. Todd began to drift further away. His awareness flowed in and out of his body, but mainly out. Then, eventually, he just went completely silent.

His eyes stayed closed after that, and as the afternoon turned to evening it was clear that all that remained of Todd was the shell. With the help of oxygen tubes, it was clinging to its grip on this world, but the essence of him was ready to go. This showed me most clearly that Todd was the energy that operated his body, not his body itself.

He would struggle to inhale, pause, and then let out his breath with a deep exhalation. Then there would be silence for what felt like minutes.

*That's it, he's finally gone,* I would think to myself, only to hear him inhale . . . again! This sequence happened over, and over, and over again, for hours on end.

Over the course of the next few hours the only sounds we heard were our own sniffles, softly drowned out by the sound of oxygen flowing from a tank and into his nose through plastic tubes. That oxygen gave us the appearance of life, but that was just wishful thinking. We all just wanted the suffering to end.

By that point the hospice nurse had gracefully left, knowing there was nothing left for her to do. Finally, after hours of watching their baby boy suffer, after it was obvious that he was not coming back – in one of the most tearful and painful decisions Mom and Dad ever had to make – they removed the breathing tubes from Todd's nose.

Knowing it wouldn't be long now, we surrounded his body, kneeling around his chair. In the next minutes, shortly after two a.m. on that cold December morning, after nearly twenty-four hours of transitioning, we watched Todd die before us. We watched his skin turn cold and whitish-blue. There was nothing left for any of us to do.

Still, we all remained gathered around him for a while, feeling into that new reality, one that did not include Todd physically here with us. All that made Todd special – his laugh, his smile, his presence, and so much more – was gone for good. This was just the start of the real pain.

We carried Todd's stiffening body from the living room recliner to the bedroom at the end of the hallway. Joel and I each grabbed a leg, while Dad grabbed his back and head. Hammy was there and helped too. Mom guided the way, then watched her youngest son's body being laid down in his bed. Our job done, we then stepped back, weeping and praying as Mom washed and tended to him one last time.

I recall a subtle sense of relief that Todd's ordeal was over, but it was only for a split-second before grief in its most intense form swept over me – over the entire group. A brother, son, dear friend, and so much more was no longer here with us. This was real death. We had handed him off to those angels and the ancestors on the other side to take care of him now, and lead him onward.

"Two-o-one," was all Dad said as Grandma Davison answered the phone in the middle of the night. He repeated the time again, and broke into tears. By that point Grandma surely knew what Dad meant. It was a short call, but it was necessary. That type of call was repeated over and over again to our various relatives. It was a sad, sad time in our lives.

*He only lived his youth, but he always experienced his truth.*
*Maybe he was lucky this way, he left before the day-to-day got gray.*
*Before he ceased he held peace and faith,*
*No longer bothered by his body's fate.*
*What did he find in those final nights? Before he crossed over the bridge of Light.*

# POST-GAME

# CHAPTER 27

# THE SPIRIT LEFT BEHIND

Considering the person he was, the relationships he forged, and the reach of his message, it came as no surprise that Todd's funeral was a hot ticket. Indeed, nearly two thousand people attended the service on that frigid Winnipeg day in December 2006. Days earlier, while reporting on Todd's passing, a local television news anchor astutely predicted, "There isn't a church in Winnipeg big enough for that funeral."

And he was right. As there was not a Catholic church that could hold the number of expected attendees, Dad had to climb the Church's hierarchical ladder, seeking formal permission for a Catholic funeral service in a non-Catholic church. In a rare and surprising concession, the Catholic leaders granted the request. North Kildonan Mennonite Brethren Church on Gateway Avenue, just down the road from his all-time home arena, was chosen as the venue for Todd's ceremonial send-off. It was one of Winnipeg's biggest churches at the time, and still the movable walls at the back had to be removed and additional seating and audio equipment placed in the building's gymnasium. In the hockey world we call that a "sold-out barn."

People came from all over Canada for Todd's funeral. Family, friends, teammates, coaches, teachers, and complete strangers who had learned of Todd's story wanted to pay their respects to a fellow human being who had tried his best to live a righteous life and help others do the same. Though Todd kept his spiritual beliefs close to the vest, he believed that when you die you leave a piece of spirit inside of every person you connected with during your life. If that is true, Todd's spirit is alive and thriving in thousands.

## Be Your Highest Self

"Go now and change your world. Go now and be your highest self . . . For yours is a destiny larger than you ever have imagined. You have come to the room to heal the room. You have come to the space to heal the space. There is no other reason for you to be here." (Conversations with God, Book 3)

Todd wrote these words in his quote-book as they rang through him. Something about living out his destiny just by *being* as he was, in whatever state or place he was in, in any given moment, gave him comfort. He didn't have to be some superhero hockey player to be a special person in the world. He didn't need to be coaching hockey to be an agent of change in the world. He came to understand that the smallest actions, done in the subtlest ways, had true power. He came to know that his only mission in life was to *be* himself wherever he went. When he surrendered to this notion, his Spirit and Soul took over.

Todd was a master at being happy, and making others happy. That isn't to say he was never unhappy: he certainly had bursts of anger, sadness, anxiety and depression. He was human, and experienced the full gamut of human emotions, but he always found a way through the darkest ones. Even despite awful circumstances – through his cancer diagnosis and onwards towards death – he found a way to find real happiness and love in his daily situations.

He generally approached the world with joy and laughter inside of him, which showed in his relationships and exchanges with others. These relationships and exchanges were generally characterized by smiles, laughing, and happiness. He could make people relax quite quickly, and could lighten up the hardest characters, making them lose themselves in laughter. Somehow, someway, he would get right to their soft side.

According to Dad, "Todd had the goofiest laugh, the biggest smile, and the dumbest sense of humor." He was a master at subtly discovering what made someone laugh and would approach that person with that particular brand of medicine. He was a unique and complex individual in many ways, but operated simply through joyful and energetic actions that were filled with enthusiasm and humor. He was, in essence, just a really special guy who had the ability to light others up with just his smile, presence, and well-timed jokes or antics. His laughter medicine drew people to him anywhere he went.

Todd also had the natural ability to charge others up and amplify the energetic environment of any given place he was in. Be they friends, family, teammates, coaches, or strangers, he intuitively knew how to brighten people's days, both individually and as part of the same human team. It's like he saw people as light-beings – kind of like lightbulbs – and knew that he could affect their brightness, by dimming their light or increasing it. By his own nature he usually found a way to crank up someone's dimmer switch to full throttle and have that person shining brightly. That was just his effect.

Written in his quote-book was one of the principles (from the mouth of Dolly Parton) that he embraced: "If you see someone without a smile, give them yours." While that may be a cliche and soft quote, creating smiles is a powerful act, and it became part of Todd's mission. He just made people feel better about themselves. This was his personal gift to the world; it was how he shared his spirit and served others.

This gift allowed Todd to quickly connect with others and open up a space for real relationships to grow. It gave him a magnetism that attracted others with ease. He had a lot of great friends because of this, and was welcomed everywhere he went. He was constantly surrounded by friends who loved him and who wanted to interact with him. He was an in-demand person. Most importantly, children and elderly alike were drawn to his presence, and in my book, that means you are doing something right.

When Dad started dating Michelle, our families merged. Michelle's kids were between the ages of six months and eleven years old when

Todd came into their life. From the start, they felt the love he embodied and couldn't get enough of him. It didn't matter if they were playing with Play-Doh, carving pumpkins, watching TV, or just sitting around, each moment in each other's presence was beautiful, innocent, and loving. And when Todd was with the kids he was truly present and happy. Love and fun were what it was about for him.

Even before his diagnosis, and more so throughout his cancer journey, Todd didn't have the time or patience for dramatic bullshit; he cut right to the core of what true relationship was all about: manifesting joyful, fun, and loving encounters with others. He didn't want heaviness and pettiness affecting who he was or how he showed up in the world. With joy and laughter being the dominant energies inside of him, he had a ton of energy to make sure he was bringing all he had to the relationship.

Philip Rosario, a powerful and graceful yogi and one of Todd's great childhood friends, summarized their relationship in such a simple, yet beautiful way:

"We just had a lot of fun . . . "

Most of Todd's friends would say something along those lines about their friendship. That joyful and fun-loving behavior sparked relationships that were begun with ease, and built on a foundation of mutual respect and appreciation.

He was far from a stereotypical hockey player in this way, and certainly was not a one-dimensional player off the ice. Todd embodied love, peace, and truth, which allowed him to connect with others on a deeper, personal, and authentic level. Be it a wealthy businessperson, esteemed professional, or hockey fan who just wanted to talk after a game, Todd had the ability to elevate the conversation beyond just superficial pleasantries and make them feel good. He was rich with life energy, and used that as his best currency to give to others.

Todd was a nonviolent person by nature who typically avoided unnecessary and energy-wasting confrontation. That is certainly not to say that he would back down from others if he was challenged, but he operated at such a different vibratory frequency that he seemed to just avoid aggressive, violent, and evil situations. He was a peacemaker in many ways, and chose to exist around the lighter vibrations of life. He was an empath, and could feel the invisible vibes of social interactions in a vivid way. As Auntie Donna stated so beautifully during her eulogy: "Todd had the ability to feel your sincerity. He had a special compassion for the young, the weak, and the hurting..." – even that young doctor who had to deliver more bad news to him. But along with that sensitive and softer side, Todd had a strength, toughness, courage, and an edge to his personality evidencing his inner warrior; indeed, he could be fierce and furious; angry and temperamental; or downright dismissive if he didn't align with something or someone. But most of the time he knew when to fight and when to lay down his sword. Instead of acting out on any feelings of rage, hate or angst, he usually managed to deal with and express any of those emotions or urges in a healthy fashion that didn't hurt others.

Todd was independent, and to say he was strong-willed and stubborn would be an all-time understatement. This strong will and stubbornness were evident from a very young age. Dad recalls during one game at the Highlander rinks in Winnipeg when he first benched Todd for a shift or two. This benching was probably because Todd had earned a bad retaliation stick penalty – likely a slash, crosscheck, or high-stick, done out of frustration in the intensity of the moment – and likely very justified. Regardless, Todd was so pissed off that he walked down the bench, onto the concrete outside the rink, and got Mom to pick him up and take him home. If he felt he was right, he wasn't going to take shit from anyone, even Dad.

At six years old, when Pa told him that "no grandson of mine is going to get his ear pierced" and that there would be no more trips to McDonald's if he did so, Todd told Pa that it would be *his* loss, then proceeded to put a gold stud in his left ear without flinching. Pa had to accept his actions, and the McDonald's trips continued. Todd didn't really care if he upset or offended others because their reaction was not his concern; he didn't let the opinions of others about him shake his foundation. When he wanted to dye his hair red or bleach it blonde, or say what came to mind, he did just that, and with confidence. And when a group of old, conservative ladies pointed and gossiped about the young boy in the restaurant with red hair, Todd didn't slump down but instead proudly declared to Mom, "See, it's a conversation piece!" From an early age he knew who he was, and he knew the intentions behind his thoughts and actions are what mattered, not the way they appeared on the outside to others.

When the 2004 AJHL playoffs started while we were playing in Lloyd, Todd decided that he wanted to add a festive hairstyle to the mix to show his dedication to the team's playoff push – and he didn't ask permission. Though his hockey hair was pretty solid that whole season, he really dialed it in for the boys when he dyed his whole head blonde and shaved his sides into a very aggressive mullet. It was a surprising and bold play that lit up our entire team. While the fellas loved it, the team's general manager, "Skip" Crake – a good ol' boy who played in the NHL for the Boston Bruins, Los Angeles Kings, and Buffalo Sabres in the 1960s and 1970s – had a different opinion. When Skip stepped onto the team bus to wish us well (as we were about to travel west to St. Albert for our first playoff game), he caught a glimpse of Todd's hair and almost had a stroke on the spot. His face turned beet-red and he began yelling at Todd, demanding, in the tone of an angry grandfather, that he fix his hair. But underlying Todd's serious expression was a giant smirk, which revealed the fact that he simply didn't care what ol' Skip had to think about his playoff hairstyle of choice. Skip left the bus and the boys cheered for Todd. It was a great moment that showed his true colors and confidence, and uplifted our team. We wound up beating the St. Albert Saints – a huge win – and Todd sparked it all.

Ultimately, Todd was serious about living on his terms, through his own mind and heart, doing what he felt was right in any given moment. He later wrote in his quote-book: "So long as you are still worried about what others think of you, you are owned by them. Only when you require no approval from outside yourself, can you be yourself." (Conversations with God, Book 3, Chapter 1)

By now you know that Todd's convictions and personal security were not easily altered, which led to him being a consistent and stable force as a human. In an honest and authentic way, he was who he was, and he liked that person, as did nearly everyone he came into contact with. Some might say Todd had a really great *vibe*, but to me, that really doesn't do it justice. He had what I would call a great *energetic signature.*

## Energetic Signature

An *energetic signature* is the energy one naturally carries and shares, which leaves an impression on others and the environment. Like a person's handwriting, or the tone and frequency of their voice – which is unique and distinguishable from however many billions of other people on this planet – everyone has their own unique energetic signature that distinguishes them from everybody else in the whole world.

To validate this, try the following experiment: first, for a few seconds, think of anyone you really love and enjoy spending time with. Perhaps this is a beloved family member or a best friend. What do you feel inside of you when thinking of that person? You are feeling their energetic signature, as you perceive it; it is who they are to you – which likely comes with positive feelings of love and happiness. To contrast this, next think of someone you strongly dislike, who annoys you and bothers you, and who you forever want to avoid. What do you feel about that person? This same experiment can be done with anyone you know. Notice how each person you think of leaves a different impression on you. You are feeling their frequency – at least how you perceive and filter it.

Likewise, others can feel your energetic signature as well. The quote, "Your energy introduces you before you even speak," is appropriate here. Your energetic signature is essentially 'who you are' on an energetic level; it is the personal energy frequency that provides for meaningful connections and relationships with others and the Universe. It is the invisible imprint that allows others to feel you as a person and remember you when you're not around or have left the physical world. If you strive for anything in this life, strive to have a beautiful energetic signature.

Aside from your physical actions, it is the impression of your energetic signature, left on others, that matters most. Todd had a beautiful and powerful energetic signature, and that is why so many people cherish their memories with him. Far deeper than just his personality, it was like he had that something extra inside – an intense joyful and loving vibration that others could intuitively see and feel through his presence. But his real power was that he knew how to freely share this treasure with others to make them feel special. This, along with his ability to make almost anyone laugh, was of his greatest talents.

## Givers and Takers

There are generally two types of people in this world: those who charge the energy of others, and those who drain the energy of others. We can label them "givers" and "takers." Givers walk into a room and carry with them a sense of joy, vibrancy, and ease. They inspire and encourage others, and give words of support when needed. Their laughter and smile are contagious, and people feel lighter and more alive when they are around. They transmit something invisible to others, which raises them up. On the other hand, energy takers, also known as "energy vampires," do exactly the opposite. An energy taker is often a victim of the world and their circumstances. They complain, whine and will tell their problems to anyone who will listen, and deflate others' energy by turning everything into a problem or issue. Or, even worse, they deliberately hurt people and attempt to gain power over them.

But Todd knew what real power was, and where it came from. In his quote-book he wrote:

"The truth is that the more you empower others, the more powerful you become." Caroline Myss - *Invisible Acts of Power: The Divine Energy of a Giving Heart.*

There was no question that Todd was a giver. He charged up those he came into contact with. This was one of the many reasons that people wanted to be around him. Todd received an outpouring of love and energy from people by giving it out first. He gave his energy to others with an intention to empower them.

Being a giver or taker is a matter of awareness. It requires the realization that our energy impacts others. While all humans are co-creators in this manner – for better or worse – it takes a strong and powerful individual energy to be able to consistently uplift the vibration of others and the environment through their presence and action. Todd had this ability: he would enhance the energy of any space simply by being there. This life thing is a vibration game and, just like hockey, Todd knew how to play it well.

If you are on the fence about all of this energy talk, consider the following: Nikola Tesla, one of the most brilliant scientific minds that has ever existed on this planet, said, "If you want to find the secrets of the Universe, think in terms of energy, frequency and vibration." Tesla was a legitimate genius. His inventions, including the mysterious *death ray*, were said to be so powerful that they could be dangerous if used by evil people. *The New York Times* first reported about this in 1934. A core premise of Tesla's work was that we are living in an energetic/electric universe, and that *free energy* exists and can be tapped into for use to perpetually power our lives in extraordinary ways. Upon Tesla's death in 1943, the FBI seized his writings, documents — and everything else he owned. Considering this, it is safe to say that Tesla may have been onto something quite powerful on this planet, and understood the power of the invisible energy around us.

Tesla's quotation regarding energy, frequency, and vibration is in alignment with so many of the world's greatest scientists and spiritual teachers, both past and present. The common messages and teachings are simple: all is energy; all is vibration; and we are all creators in and of this Universe. Beyond our ability to build physical creations made of wood, metals, and plastics, we also create energetically through our thoughts, intentions, and emotions, in realms outside our human perception and far beyond what is able to be commonly seen with the naked eye. Though Todd naturally embodied a powerful frequency all of his life, he was consciously studying these concepts in his last months, and put them into action in his daily life. In a way, Todd was studying how to consciously be and act in this world; this made him even more powerful.

Although we are composed of physical matter – muscles, tissues, blood, cells, and so forth – we must not forget that there is something deeper – a source field – which underlies all matter. This is not just anecdotal spiritual speak. According to the leading quantum physicists, the "material" world is actually more than 99.9% empty space, despite us perceiving it as solid matter. Moreover, these scientists have stated that invisible matter is exponentially more powerful than physical form. The invisible energy that we embody and *carry around with us* is far more powerful than our physical bodies of blood and flesh. In other words, we are actually a composition of energy operating within, and inherently connected to, a field of energy all around us, and have capabilities and capacities far beyond what is currently known or thought possible.

Knowing this, there is no doubt that we can pick up on the energy of other people we come into contact with. Think of the last time you sensed someone was in a terrible mood before they even opened their mouths. As human beings, we have the natural ability to sense and feel the energy of others around us. When we come into contact with someone, or even when we think of them, we can sense and feel their energy as we have perceived it; we can also directly impact their energy, leaving impressions. As energetic beings, even just by our presence alone, we contribute to and affect the energetic environment that we exist in at any given moment. In this way we are co-creators in the energetic environment that we exist in. This is something that my brother had figured out: he could receive more joy and love into his own life by first giving that energy to others.

All of humanity could be considered a big team, with the energetic frequency of each contributing to the whole. Each person's frequency either enhances the team's charge and makes it stronger, or weakens the charge and leaves it weaker. Each newborn joins the collective human charge, and when they die they are removed from it. When a good light goes out, it leaves the room dimmer. When a good teammate gets injured, it leaves the team weaker. And when a good person dies, it leaves the world with a little less love. When Todd died, we lost his powerful charge, yet so much inspiration was gained. It remains through memory and the feeling of his spirit left behind in us, to fuel the creation of more love and care in the world.

# CHAPTER 28

# IMPACT PLAYER

In the days following Todd's death, Dad found a handwritten note in his hockey binder that stated, "A child doesn't care about how much you know, until they know how much you care." This was a major tenet of Todd's coaching, and so important to him that he carried the note with him as a reminder when he was at the rink or preparing for a game or practice. His care for others was the bridge for inspiration. What he passed on to his players is carried forth in the world by each and every one of them, and to all those to whom they pass it on.

Before Todd passed, Kevin was able to tell him how much he meant to all of them. He also told Todd that the Thrashers would be dedicating their season to him, and that they would never forget him. To this day, hanging from the rafters of the Gateway "blue" rink is a raised Winnipeg Thrashers banner with the number 34 and "Davison" across the name bar – a tribute to a truly righteous person whose special presence filled that rink for so many years. In addition to showing respect for and honoring their fallen teammate, the Thrashers hung that banner knowing it would serve to fuel and inspire them in practice and games to come.

And it worked. In the 2006-2007 season, the Thrashers made it to the finals, but lost in heartbreaking fashion to the Brandon Wheat Kings. However, the very next season, with so many returning players who were coached by Todd and wearing his "TD-34 Believe in the Goal" patch on their jerseys, the Thrashers became the Manitoba Midget AAA League champions. Moving on from the regional level to the 2008 Telus Cup – the annual Canadian national Midget AAA hockey tournament, formerly the Air Canada Cup – the Thrashers earned the silver medal.

Despite the team's narrow six-to-four loss in the gold medal game, Todd's impact was left on that tournament. Mathew Bodie, one of the players deeply inspired by Todd, was named as both the Most Valuable Player and Top Defenseman of that national championship. According to Mat, Todd's most significant impact as a coach was teaching the players to play every game with no regrets. "He always said to play every game like it's your last, because you never know when [your last game] will be."

After graduating from the Winnipeg Thrashers program, Mat played junior hockey in the BCHL for the Powell River Kings, and then got a scholarship to play NCAA Division I college hockey for Union College of the ECAC. While playing for the Union Dutchmen, Mat was individually named All-Team/All-American in every season. Perhaps most importantly, though, Mat's leadership skills were recognized as he was named the team's captain in 2012. Wearing the "C" on his chest, Mat led the Union Dutchmen to win the 2014 NCAA Frozen Four – the national championship tournament for men's college ice hockey in the United States. He was named to the tournament's All-Tournament Team.

After winning the NCAA championship, Mat, undrafted, signed with the New York Rangers. Though he did not end up making the Rangers' roster, he went on to be named team captain of the Rangers' affiliated AHL team, the Hartford Wolf Pack, in 2016. He would go on to have several great AHL seasons and is now playing professional hockey in the KHL. To this day, Mat attributes much of his success to Todd's teachings. In word and in deed, Todd planted seeds of inspiration inside his players: Mat said that Todd "didn't talk about his situation much, but knowing how he went through treatments and was able to play a few more games, knowing they would be his last, really stuck with me.

"I remember going to the gym, Focus Fitness, and seeing Todd there working out and shooting pucks," Mat continued. "This was after treatments and his shoulder wasn't in good shape, but he was still there working out and taking shots, his work ethic and love for the game was evident to every guy he coached and I'm thankful I had the opportunity to play for him."

Kevin delivered the following heartfelt words at Todd's funeral:

"Todd, right now it is hard to think of our world without you . . . But I want to tell you that we are truly better people for having had the privilege to be your teammate and friend. Thank you for sharing your life with us. We will miss you. No regrets."

*Todd's banner, hanging in Gateway "blue" rink - our home rink.*

## Waves of Inspiration

The energy created by Todd's spirit remains powerful today. Thoughts and memories of him can bring waves of inspiration, especially when hockey is being played.

As a perpetual underdog, Todd had a natural ability to inspire people by his play; this was especially so with younger, smaller players who saw him in action. One of the people he inspired most was our cousin, JC Lipon. As a Regina native, JC attended our Pats home games as a bright-eyed nine-year-old; and, because of our family connection, he looked up to us as players. Also, JC was always one of the smallest players on the ice growing up, so he had an automatic connection with Todd.

In fact, JC might have even been smaller than Todd during his WHL bantam draft season and did not get drafted. But he had the same tenacious mentality, and knew that his small size just meant he had to work harder to succeed. Three years after Todd died, JC–then as a five-foot-eight, one-hundred-and-fifty-pound player – cracked the Kamloops Blazers' roster and entered the WHL as a sixteen-year-old, just like Todd. The next season, in tribute to Todd, JC proudly wore number 34 on his back. He marked "TD 34" on the back side of his grip alongside the initials of his other family members. Each time he put on that Blazers jersey or looked at his stick, he pulled in a little extra strength and inspiration with thoughts of Todd.

Two short years later, JC began to absolutely dominate the Dub. Halfway through his nineteen-year-old season with the Blazers, he led the WHL, and the entire CHL, in scoring with twenty-two goals and thirty-five assists in thirty-four games. In case you missed the significance of that, by early December 2012, JC, using thoughts of Todd as inspiration in his pre-game routines, was the top-scoring major junior hockey player in all of Canada! His scoring lead was disrupted only because he missed several games when he was selected to attend the Team Canada selection camp for the 2013 World Junior Ice Hockey Championship in Ufa, Russia. He received the invite while he was riding the team bus from Spokane, Washington back to Kamloops; the date, December 2, 2012 – the sixth anniversary of Todd's death.

In a year when all the best nineteen-year-olds in Canada were available because of the NHL lockout, JC joined ten first-round NHL draft picks when he was selected to Team Canada and, as the team's "unexpected" player, he wore the red maple leaf on his chest for Todd and all of us back home.

## Leaving a Legacy

In addition to inspiring JC and other hockey players, Todd inspired others to act in some way for the care and betterment of all. Although this came naturally to him, toward the end he came more intentional in his efforts to help create change and healing in the world, especially as it related to cancer. Though disfigured and atrophied and facing death himself, he took action, and encouraged others to do the same, to help find the cure, or at least alleviate the pain and discomfort. *Believe in the Goal* was Todd's contribution to his mission.

Though not with the same fanfare or press, Todd followed in the footsteps and along the same path of fellow Winnipeg-born Canadian Legend, Terrance ("Terry") Stanley Fox. In 1980, at the age of twenty-one, Fox embarked on a run across Canada – from St. John's Newfoundland to Victoria, British Columbia to raise money – one dollar from each of Canada's then twenty-four or so million citizens – for cancer awareness and research. The most incredible part of this story: he'd be running on one leg. The other had been amputated in the treatment of his osteosarcoma.

Braving Canadian snowstorms, windstorms, heavy rain, and his own inner demons, Fox made his way west by running a marathon a day, refusing to take days off. After an incredible journey over 5,373 kilometers (3,339 miles), run over one hundred and forty-three days, Fox was forced to cut his "Marathon of Hope" short when – after an intense coughing fit outside Thunder Bay, Ontario – he learned that the cancer had spread to his lungs. Fox died in 1981 at the age of twenty-two. Though he fell short of his goal, by the end of the run he had raised $1.7 million – and that was just the beginning.

Since then, the Terry Fox Run has become a staple across schools and other places across Canada, as well as the world's largest one-day fundraiser for cancer research. Nearly a billion dollars have been raised in Fox's name since he started the Marathon of Hope. Most importantly, though, the survival rates for osteosarcoma have increased substantially since Fox's death, partly attributable to the awareness and money raised by his initiative. In a CBC article titled *Terry Fox's cancer now highly curable researcher says*, Dr. Jay Wunder – the very same sarcoma specialist at Mount Sinai Hospital in Toronto who operated on Todd and helped save his arm – stated that the cure rate for Fox's cancer is now as high as eighty percent in younger patients. So, though Fox lost his leg and, ultimately, his life, his heroism and determination helped save countless other lives and limbs.

In the years after Todd died – and in a controversial and bold move at the time – the students of St. Gerard School in Winnipeg participated in the "Todd Davison Walk" instead of the "Terry Fox Run." This change was initiated by our former St. Alphonsus School fifth-grade teacher, Miss Gilbert, who wanted to honor Todd's efforts and carry on the tradition of raising money for cancer research through the name of her former student and *Believe in the Goal*. As one of the most influential teachers of our youth, Ms. G sparked something in our lives; and, conversely, by the end of his days, especially through his mission with *Believe in the Goal*, Todd had sparked something in Ms. G.

St. Gerard School eventually rejoined forces with the Terry Fox Foundation, which still carries Terry's torch from the Marathon of Hope all those years ago. And though *Believe in the Goal* raised the slightest fraction of what the Terry Fox Foundation has raised, the St. Gerard school initiative put Todd's name in the same category as that of a legendary Canadian hero who fought and suffered to make a difference in the world. Todd, just like Terry, went down fighting for others he would never personally know and inspired countless others to make positive change.

In a *Winnipeg Free Press* article titled *Davison's foundation scoring big*, thousand-game NHLer Travis Zajac – who knew Todd from the early community club hockey days – said, "He was a special human being and it's a pleasure to be part of [his] event. No one that met Todd will forget him. Each year, more and more players want to be part of this. Guys that have played with him or knew him, all want to take part . . ."

In the same article, written by veteran TSN analyst Gary Lawless – who is currently working as the Vegas Golden Knights Insider – Toews, when reflecting on the meaning behind *Believe in the Goal*, got it right:

"As a hockey player we work hard for ourselves and for our team. Todd worked hard for other people and to change people's lives that have cancer. If we can take one lesson from that, it is to put that kind of effort into trying to help other people for a change."

Todd's efforts in founding *Believe in the Goal* were recognized when he was posthumously awarded the Never Alone Foundation *Difference Maker* award in 2007. *Believe in the Goal* events continued for five subsequent years, and grew to include a golf tournament and several various social events around Winnipeg. Countless people, businesses, and organizations contributed to its success, and when all was said and done the foundation had raised over three hundred thousand dollars.

The proceeds went to many great causes, all aimed at easing the cancer experience for children and adolescents suffering through the disease. Two special patient-care rooms were built at the Children's Hospital that included state-of-the-art gaming and entertainment systems, and specialized sleeper-chair furniture designed to allow parents and/or family members to more comfortably spend the nights with a patient. Mom, Dad, and Todd knew well the pains and perils of having family stay with you in a hospital room for hours and nights on end when there is no comfortable furniture involved. It was a little thing, but something that could help other families so much in their toughest times.

There was also, as mentioned, the "Believe Blanket" program – where *Believe in the Goal* NHLers visited Winnipeg hospitals and gave out special fleece blankets – and, best of all, the "NHL Experience Getaways," which sent youngsters to see their favorite NHL team or player in action and give them some special VIP treatment. Dane Hantscher, an eight-year-old leukemia patient, was sent to Vancouver to watch two Canucks games, including one against the San Jose Sharks, of which his favorite NHL player, Joe Thornton, was a member. Dane even got to meet "Jumbo Joe," which was no doubt one of those priceless life moments that will be cherished.

*Believe in the Goal* brought out the generous, dedicated, and philanthropic spirit of so many people. The majority were connected to Todd in some way, but there were also many who contributed their energy and resources without ever having met him. The *Believe in the Goal* board members, the participants, the volunteers, the donors, and the fans all came together in beautiful ways to contribute to a great cause. All in all, *Believe in the Goal* was a tremendous success that brought the hockey and cancer communities together, and contributed in fantastic ways to ease the suffering of those affected.

Part of Todd's vision was taking the event to the next level, which the foundation did after Todd's passing. Joel became our family's new leader for *Believe in the Goal*. He helped ensure the foundation operated smoothly and that the events were world-class. He also ensured that the *Believe in the Goal* golf tournaments were ridiculously fun (sometimes too fun). One year he even brought a dunk-tank onto the 16th hole at Rossmere Golf & Country Club! Joel did it big, and selflessly contributed to the foundation for its entire existence.

In addition to Auntie Donna, Glenn, Colleen and Ray – Todd's original teammates for *Believe in the Goal* – more friends and family joined the foundation, including Mom and Dad. Periodic meetings took place on Tache Avenue in St. Boniface, at one of Ray's offices. Around a big beautiful oval table sat the people connected to Todd in various intimate ways: Uncle Alan was the hilarious uncle who always made him laugh; Hammy, Decks, Katie Moe and Brendon Corbett were some of his closest friends with whom he had shared countless moments of laughter, joy, and love; and Hammy's parents, Kim Hampton and Kevin Hampton, had spent years with Todd through hockey and friendship. Kevin was also the owner of *Jersey Chair*, and made the first *Jersey Chair* ever of Todd's red Regina Pats jersey. Other talents joined the crew, including Al Klymochko, who was Ray's right-hand man for design, art production, and communications messaging, and Scott Kinnear, who was a franchise owner of Tim Hortons who wanted to help create reach in the community.

And so many other people volunteered and contributed in beautiful ways. From doing things like selling or taking tickets at the door to helping sell t-shirts and hats, there are too many people to name who helped make *Believe in the Goal* events great.

Within a few years of the inaugural game sparked by Todd's efforts, the 2009 game took place at the MTS Centre, now named the Canada Life Centre, which is the big house in Winnipeg where NHL games are played. Months prior to that game, Ray found a way to pull the right strings to get a giant *Believe in the Goal* banner advertising the Sizzling Summer Showdown hung on the Radisson Hotel in downtown Winnipeg. The banner was insanely big, and you couldn't drive by Portage and Main in Winnipeg without seeing it. People started to really hear about *Believe in the Goal* and its mission. Some of the most popular radio stations in Winnipeg were incredibly supportive and did a fabulous job of promoting the events. As mentioned, when the puck dropped at the MTS Centre months later, the entire lower bowl of the arena was sold out with over five thousand fans who showed up in the middle of August to create an amazing atmosphere and celebrate Todd's legacy and mission at the biggest and best arena in Manitoba. Everyone left that evening just a little more inspired than when they arrived. That is always what it was about.

The level of hockey talent on the ice at Winnipeg's big rink, decked out in *Believe in the Goal* uniforms, was a very cool sight to see.

From the time Todd dropped the puck for the ceremonial faceoff to kickoff the inaugural game in 2006 until the final play of the good-bye game in 2011, additional NHLers who wore the *Believe in the Goal* logo over their hearts included: Mike Keane, Colin Wilson, Ryan Reaves, Cody Eakin, Darren Helm, Dale Weise, Ryan White, Ryan Garbutt, Travis Hamonic, Justin Falk, and Fraser McClaren. For goalies, Rejean Beauchemin and Chet Pickard, both Winnipeggers who won gold medals playing for Team Canada at the World Juniors, played in several games, and NHLer Cory Schneider strapped on the pads one of the years.

Everyone involved in any way with *Believe in the Goal,* from volunteers through players, was so proud to see the games manifest.

Toews summed up the events in a beautiful way: "Todd left a great legacy and this is the way he would have pictured this."

*Design by Q-Power.*

*From left to right: Nigel Dawes, Jonathan Toews, and Travis Zajac,
decked out in Believe in the Goal uniforms. Design by Q-Power.*

# CHAPTER 29

# LIFE REVIEW

Prior to Dr. Bob's depressing lecture on near-death experiences two days before Todd died, I had not yet heard of the work of Dr. Raymond Moody, nor the experiences of Dannion Brinkley and the countless others who have testimonies of their personal NDE. Typically through some extreme trauma to their bodies – such as car accident; drowning; or, for example, during something like a brain hemorrhage – these people have peeked into the afterlife, if only for a few minutes, and then later returned back to their earthly bodies and everyday lives. Though many will scoff at these testimonies as being delusional in nature, the similar themes, experiences, and commonalities of these various experiences and perceptions are astounding. Along with all the previously mentioned characteristics of NDEs – the immersive white light; the feelings of unconditional love and peace pervading their being; the connection to God and Soul; the reunions with loved ones; and the feelings of being so much more than a body – they share another common theme: none of these people wanted to return to Earth! They wanted to stay where they were, wherever *that* was. Any truth to these accounts provides so much hope of what may await us when our physical vehicle shuts down.

## Like Lightning

Dannion Brinkley has one of the coolest NDE stories of all time. Dr. Moody, the "grandfather" of NDE research – who has conducted over twenty-thousand investigations into the experiences of NDEs – was especially intrigued with Dannion's testimonial because of the consistency it shared with his other research and because of the amount of detail Dannion recalls. Dannion's book, *Saved by the Light*, is an excellent account of his experience, and I highly encourage you to read it.

Dannion was a member of the United States military who had fought in several war zones. He admits that he was a bully in life, and had killed people in war. He described himself as not being calm or nice, and says that he liked dominating people and pushing them around. Dannion also said he liked liquor and women, which sounds like a lot of the fellas I know. Are you getting the picture of the rough-and-tough nature of this big man?

According to Dannion, he came home on September 17, 1975 to find his wife making dinner in the kitchen. At the time he was restoring a car he had and called a friend to get advice on how to proceed. He was on the phone in his bedroom when he heard a little thunder off in the distance; then, before he could end the phone call and hang up, he was struck by lightning *through the phone*! The force of the lightning raised him off the bed and slammed him back down. He felt like he was on fire, and the force was so hard that he thought, in the instant before everything went black, that it was caused by a bomb or powerful weapon. He was pronounced dead for twenty-eight minutes. After being revived he was fully paralyzed for six days and partially paralyzed for seven months; he would have to learn how to walk and feed himself again. What happened in those twenty-eight minutes changed his whole life.

Dannion recalls rising above his body in an out-of-body experience. He could see how each material thing around his body had an energy to it – an aura. He could see the exchange of energy between people, and between things and people. He could see the plants feeling some form of distress because he was in distress. He could see his lightning-fried body being loaded into the ambulance like a hunk of flesh, and was in the ambulance observing the actions of the paramedics as they worked to save him. But, during all of the foregoing, Dannion felt complete peace and love. Then, he heard one of the paramedics say, "He's Gone . . . "

Dannion describes a tunnel that began to form, and he heard chimes. Then he experienced "the most bright, brilliant, beautiful white light conceivable." This brilliant white light became a part of him, and he became a part of the light. Dannion then speaks of a "Blue-Gray" place where he became aware of a Being who was present. He said the Being put out rays of color, and Dannion was amazed by the Being's energy. The Being communicated with Dannion in a telepathic way; then, in the most intriguing and important part of the whole story, Dannion recounts his "Panoramic Life Review" – a holographic replay of his interactions with everyone from his life – all the moments of joy and love, but also all the pain, frustrations, humiliation, anger and anxiety that he had inflicted on thousands of people. He relived all that his life was.

Starting with childhood emotions and experiences, he became every person he had ever encountered, and experienced what the interaction was like from their perspective. He says this is not like watching a movie, but an interactive experience in which you are both in the moment again and watching it as a third-person witness. Observing himself from that point, he judged himself as if sitting in God's place.

Dannion's life review also surprised the hell out of him when he realized how much good he had done in his life as well! Every act of truth, love and generosity was recognized, and he felt the rewards of those deeds to the same extent others originally received that goodness from him. As bad of a person he thought he was in life, he was still a beautiful and whole radiant being at his core, and he was as deserving of love as any other. He came to understand that as bad as he was, he still did more good in the world. He felt that love and grace inside of himself like he never had before.

Dannion came to learn that this life on Earth truly is a powerful gift, and that we should be faithful regarding where we go from here. He believes his life purpose is to spread the word that no one really dies. This once rough and tough military man, who used to booze it up and get into bar fights – and who took one for the team, not once, but three times (he would have two more NDEs during heart and brain surgeries) – now lives by maxims such as:

"We are radiant, powerful beings";

"We are here because we chose to come"; and

"What we do here works to evolve other worlds and universes."

At the core of it, these NDEers all have one thing in common: a desire to share their extraordinary experiences with others in an effort to make the world a more loving, and peaceful place, and give us hope about what may await. Their consistent teaching is that the body dies but the Soul/Consciousness does not; in other words, we are not our body. NDEers want to share the message that we are so much more than what we can imagine, and have incarnated on Earth for purposes so much greater than we believe.

Several years after first hearing his story, I met Dannion in person. During a vacation in Florida, Mom and I drove from Naples to Fort Lauderdale to attend the New Life Expo, specifically to see him speak. As we entered the designated conference room and quickly turned into a row of chairs close to the back, a booming voice from the front of the room called out to us, "Don't sit back there…come right up front here!" It was Dannion's voice, and he was pointing to chairs that were literally right in front of him. Mom and I smiled as we bashfully walked through the crowded room and took our seats,

Dannion delivered a speech that started with principles of quantum physics and ended with his testimonial. At the end of his speech, he opened the floor for questions. Several hands immediately went up around me, so I sat back to further enjoy the show. He looked over the audience, deciding on which hand to call upon next. To my surprise, he stopped looking at the hands behind me, looked directly at me, pointed, and said, "You! You have a question for me. Uncross your arms and ask me a question!"

*"Uhhhhhhhh . . ."* was my internal dialogue as I scrambled to come up with a legitimate and worthy question so as to not make a fool of myself in a conference room full of people. Finally, I just blurted out the first thing that came to mind:

"Is there a spiritual war between Darkness and Light happening on Earth?"

I had always been intrigued by the concept of spiritual warfare taking place on Earth and in the surrounding invisible realms. You know – angels versus demons; good versus evil, all that good stuff. Dannion answered authoritatively: "Yes! But this war is not something external; it is happening inside of you, and inside of everyone individually."

His answer immediately reminded me of the Cherokee parable titled "Two Wolves." The parable, which I first read through foggy eyes one morning in Clear Lake, Manitoba, as it hung on the McCrimmon family cabin wall, after Kelly's son Mick and I had a big night out with lots of laughs and too many drinks, goes as follows:

An old Cherokee man is teaching his grandson about life. "A fight is going on inside me," he says to the boy.

"It is a terrible fight and it is between two wolves. One is evil – he is anger, envy, sorrow, regret, greed, arrogance, self-pity, guilt, resentment, inferiority, lies, false pride, superiority, and ego.

"The other," he continues, "is good – he is joy, peace, love, hope, serenity, humility, kindness, benevolence, empathy, generosity, truth, compassion, and faith.

The same fight is going on inside you – and inside every other person, too."

The grandson thinks about it for a minute and then asks his grandfather, "Which wolf will win?"

The old Cherokee replies simply, "The one you feed."

"So, with that said, which side are we on here?" Dannion asked as he walked directly in front of me. Keep in mind that I was sitting in a chair and Dannion is like six-foot-seven or something crazy like that. As he towered over me, he proceeded to kick my feet with his giant ones...first with his right foot on my left foot, and then with his left foot on my right foot. As he kicked my feet I felt a powerful transference of energy shoot up my body. I had never experienced an energy transfer from another person like that before. With that energy transference, I felt Dannion to be someone special, and nothing but earnest, authentic, and loving, and filled with a rare life-force that speaks of utmost faith for something real beyond this existence. To me, he was an example of someone who had seen the other side and had come back to tell the good news, and forewarn us that our actions – good or bad – will be felt again when we review our game-tape and re-experience all that we created during our lives.

# CHAPTER 30

# HIGHLIGHT-REEL LIFE

"The strongest metal goes through the hottest fire" was written atop the front cover of Todd's quote-book in black pen. Considering I couldn't find a source for this quote, it's ostensibly Todd's own spin on Richard M. Nixon's words: "The finest steel goes through the hottest fire." And despite the fact that they may have been derived from "Tricky Dick," they are nonetheless charged and powerful words that provide truth and meaning. Another quotation that appeared on that Media brand, three-hundred-page, three-subject notebook with an orange cover came from a more respectable United States president, Theodore Roosevelt. The quotation read:

> Far better is it to dare mighty things, to win glorious triumphs, even though checkered by failure . . . than to rank with those poor spirits who neither enjoy nor suffer much, because they live in a gray twilight that knows not victory nor defeat.

Without even opening its cover, the foregoing quotations, tapping into alchemy and triumph through mighty moves, already reveal the state of mind of a person who was looking at life through a more focused and refined lens than most.

When I first flipped through Todd's quote-book, I was stunned to read the concepts that he had been meditating and pondering on while he lived as a teenager with cancer. I presume having a life-threatening or terminal illness pushes most people to really question the nature of their reality and the meaning of their existence within that reality, and Todd was no exception. He was very clearly intentional and focused on living his best life as a person, and part of that included pondering the great philosophical and spiritual guidance and wisdom that we most often ignore.

Todd's quote-book was like a map of his mind and heart, and revealed that he was, in his private moments, tracking some of the most powerful spiritual principles known to humankind. It pointed to a young optimist who held himself to the highest standards of living and being. It pointed to his idealism; his goal-driven, competitive nature; and his powerful imagination. It pointed to a humble, earnest, independent seeker, not giving up on the meaning of life, or the battle within.

The quote-book's contents flirted with age-old concepts like good versus evil, right versus wrong, and truth versus falsehood. Other quotations touched on alchemy, angels, and avenues to the highest states of being and living in this world. The quotations delved into principles about goodness, vibration, God, and synchronicity. But, most importantly, the quote-book contained the simplest truths, and gave us directions and guiding principles for daily life.

On the inside white cover of this sacred and personal quote-book, written with a blue ballpoint pen in Todd's typical all-capital letter style, the following words stood alone atop the page:

"DO GOOD FOR THE SAKE OF JUST DOIN' GOOD."

There it was: Todd's clearest direction.

These words are simple to grasp but can be so challenging to put into action in daily life. If we always have the choice of doing good, why does it seem that goodness is so far from us? I think I have a solution, though: when we think about "doing good" in the world, we often associate that with helping strangers, volunteering, or involving ourselves with causes or charities. We think it is something we have to put effort in to "do." While I am certainly a proponent of all of those things, I think we need to rearrange this concept of "doing" good to "being" good. Aligned with this theory, Todd also inscribed the quote: "In life you don't have to do anything, it's all a question of what you are Being." In other words, we can focus on exuding goodness as an expression of who we are, rather than holding it up as some elusive thing we have to achieve through specific action. Just *be* good.

Be a good teammate.

Be a good friend.

Be a good brother.

Be a good sister.

Be a good son.

Be a good daughter.

Be a good partner.

Be a good coach.

Be a good dad.

Be a good mom.

Be a good person.

Be a good whatever!

This is the point. When we are *being* any of the foregoing things, we are doing good! We are all capable of bringing compassion and love into the world, in whatever relationship, dynamic, or situation we are in. And, we are all capable of doing good in the world, by being good in the world.

Then, written directly across the open notebook on the first sheet of paper was another quote from Conversations with God: "Motive is everything. Objectives determine outcomes. Life proceeds out of your intention. Your true intention is revealed in your actions, and your actions are determined by your true intention."

Let those words sink in: "Your actions are determined by your true intention."

When we set our true intention to be goodness in whatever role or relationship we are in, in whatever moment we are in, we make it so much easier to win! Let's start simplifying life and getting back to the basics.

When a young singer from St. Mary's High School sang "Ave Maria" at the St. Paul's High School Mother-Son mass in such a beautiful way that it brought tears to Mom's eyes, Todd said, "Go tell her how beautiful she sang." When Mom hesitated and didn't want to approach the girl, Todd said, "Come on, I'll take you up there." So Mom went up there and a beautiful compliment was given, which created a positive impact on the singer and a beautiful exchange that otherwise wouldn't have taken place. Todd knew the right thing to do, and he did it; he also inspired others to take action too.

He knew there was something about this game of life that required belief and action; right belief, and right action; positive belief and positive action. And he knew that goodness in the world had to start with him. He knew he had to "feed the good Wolf." It is through small acts of goodness that we send ripples of uplifting and positive vibrations out to the world and make it a better place.

Like the hockey player he was, Todd, no doubt, had many stellar life highlights of uplifting others and charging up an environment with his presence. By the end of his life, Todd wasn't looking for mediocre game highlights, though; he wanted righteousness! He wanted Sportscenter Top-10 moments on the daily! When he woke up each morning – when he got one more shift in the game of life – he didn't want to just score, he wanted top-corner, bardown snipes.

Many hockey fans flick on TSN, Sportsnet, or ESPN to watch the nightly highlights from games around the league. The reason these highlights are available, of course, is because these games were all filmed by various video cameras, from all different angles. While virtually everything is recorded, we usually only see the big plays and the big blunders. Regardless, the game is captured for all to see after it was played.

Imagine that your life on Earth was recorded by some sort of cosmic video camera – some technology that we cannot yet fathom. Now imagine that the recording capabilities went beyond capturing just audio and video to include the thoughts and feelings of all life. This technology could capture all of the energy and contextual information of any given situation, and play it back at any angle or intensity. Such a recording would make it possible to access, not just glimpses or limited memories from your life, but the entirety of your experience.

According to certain spiritual teachings, the Akashic Records contain all that has existed – not just for us as individuals but the Universe as a whole. The Akashic Records could be considered the alive and constantly evolving library of life. If one believes in learning from experience, the Akashic Records provide the ultimate game film. Just as we watch video to see how we executed when it really counted in a game situation, so do we review our lives to see how we did when we had our shot – now!

Our lives will consist of highlights and lowlights. Life highlights are moments of love, gratitude, peace, joy, and contentment; life lowlights are moments of hate, hostility, and shame. We all have great moments when we meet our potential as human beings in any given life circumstance, and we all have moments of shame, guilt, and regret that weigh us down and keep us living small. While we can't control what life throws at us, we can control how we will respond to whatever comes. When it's all over, did we create more highlights or lowlights? If everything comes back to you, what kind of life review do you want to experience?

If a total life review happens when we die – with the good and the bad to be shown back to you – will you be excited to experience it, or will you cover your eyes in shame? And, if you just experienced your life review to date – all the good, bad, beautiful and ugly – would you eagerly upload a holographic version of your life onto the galactic social network for all to see and share in your experiences on Earth? Or would you want to delete the file and move it into the Universal trash can, to be thrown away into some deep dark void?

Realizing the delicate nature and preciousness of life, I can't help but think about how my actions, however slight, affect this bizarre game we're playing out on this physical plane. Day by day, shift by shift, we create our way and write the stories through the moments we experience. We are looking to live our lives seeking top corner, bardown snipes; seeking right action and just thought in whatever situations might present themselves to shine bright, and post up some serious highlights.

If you are reading this, it is not too late: you can change the way you are living your life to ensure that you are creating love, rather than perpetuating hate. You can live to feed the good wolf, and starve the evil one. You can smile, live by a higher code, and do your best to align back to your best self. Then, when you die and enter the personal interactive theater, you can relive the highlights of your life with your head held high and a sparkle in your eye. Aim to live a highlight reel life.

# CHAPTER 31

# THE OTHER SIDE

Reminders of Todd's death would hit at the oddest times. Sometimes they were subtle, others they were like a blow. In the weeks after he died, I met some friends at Earls St. Vital – then one of our favorite Winnipeg lounges – to hang out and watch some Hockey Night in Canada. I wasn't overly social those days, but meeting up with a few friends to have a couple of beers and watch some hockey was a nice way to get back out into the world and take a step towards normalcy. As was customary with CBC's classic broadcast, "Coach's Corner" came on during the first intermission of the first game. As music played over the lounge, silent images of Don Cherry and Ron McLean were displayed on the screens of the dozen or so big-screen TVs that surrounded me, and the giant projector screen that I had my eyes on. As the segment continued, Don and Ron's faces appeared somber – an unusual look for that duo. Then, without warning, Don and Ron's screen cut to an image of Todd as a brief tribute was paid to one of hockey's fallen warriors. On what was supposed to be a respite from my feelings of loss and grief, I had instead come face to face with them, literally.

In that moment I was shown, again, that this whole death thing was not something I would be able to hide from. I had to face Todd's death head-on, just as I would one day have to face my own.

## The Mystery Awaits

Death is the ultimate mystery. Despite the strength of our faith, we, as individual human beings, do not know with detailed certainty what will happen to us when we die. When a loved one dies, the feeling of loss and heartbreak can be nothing short of devastating. It can feel as if the sorrow will last forever. It can feel as if the world will never be right again. It can seem that it will be an impossible task to transition to acceptance, or another state of mind or being. Beyond that, the conscious or subconscious fear of death often begins to sweep across the surrounding survivors as they attempt to process their loss, which leads to chaos. Family and friends of the deceased experience and perpetuate a heavy emotional environment filled with grief, anxiety, anger, sadness, and confusion. The uncertainty of what happens to our Soul and consciousness when our body expires creates confusion, anxiety, stress, and fear.

Again, according to so many who have brought messages to us, we shall not fear death, for we are not the body, but so much more. The spiritual person says we are a divine Soul operating through this body to experience this reality. The scientific person says we are consciousness that uses the body as an interface with this reality. Both of these perspectives acknowledge that we are the driver of the vehicle, not the vehicle itself. Just like John Lennon once said, "I'm not afraid of death because I don't believe in it. It's just getting out of one car, and into another." But, once again, without that first-hand experience – that personal knowing –the consistent message about the afterlife is still resisted. The primal fear of death seems to extend to and create doubt in even the most faithful of followers at times.

Some people attempt to ignore their inevitable death altogether and push any thoughts associated with it as far down as possible, hoping to never have to consciously face it. Others surrender to the lessons of a religion, a philosophy, a spiritual teacher, or some other figure who speaks of the afterlife, and cling to this message. Still others seek the truth for themselves, through introspection, experience, education and practices of whatever sort, for the purpose of connecting with our Higher Power.

But whatever you may do or believe, you cannot stop death from touching you sooner or later. We all must cross this bridge at some point. One day, we will see the other side. Until then, the mystery awaits.

## Dream World

Since Todd's death, I have had several dreams with him. By no means are they common, but every once in a while I will wake up with the memory of having experienced a whole new adventure with Todd. And though it didn't happen in this physical world, an exchange of energy – a communication of some type – still happened somewhere. To me, these are real and meaningful encounters in the astral realm that allow me to feel Todd's energy and presence in a way that is usually tied to a lesson.

The first dream I had with Todd took place in the bathroom at a house party. Kitchens and bathrooms always seem to draw a crowd at a really good house party – kitchens because they're usually where the fridge, keg and coolers are located; bathrooms for the obvious reason. Other people kept coming in and out of the bathroom, but they could not see Todd. To me, however, he was clear as day – decked out in full hockey gear, looking healthy and strong, smiling and shining like the old days. I was awestruck. He was incredibly happy and excited, and basically told me he was just fine!

In a subsequent dream with Todd, we went back to our roots and were playing hockey on the ODR. At first we were playing against each other one on one. Then, paradoxically, it was me and Todd versus Todd. We weren't playing full speed or going super-hard, but we were playing at a decent pace and were making good plays. At one point in the game he looked to pass to me, but he saw the passing lane wasn't available, so he held the puck. I was calling for it, thinking I was wide-open. I questioned why he didn't feed me the puck. He then stopped the game and gave me a little analogy:

He said, "I'll always try to pass to you and make the play, but sometimes the option isn't there because it isn't a good play."

In other words, he told me that he will pass to me only if it is the right play at the right time. The version of Todd on my team in that dream was the wise teacher, while the opponent Todd was just having fun on the outdoor ice. I wish I remembered more details, but to me it was about the message. It was about the way God is in our lives.

To use a hockey analogy, God is with us all the time, on our team, looking to set us up to score goals. He has the puck and wants to make a play to us, but sometimes that play would be a mistake, perhaps leading to a turnover and a goal against, putting us further behind, or a suicide pass in the neutral zone. You thought you were going to have a breakaway, but God knew you were going to get steamrolled with a shoulder to the jaw. Sometimes holding onto the puck, and passing to us at a different time, at a different angle, with a different look, in a different space, would be a much better play for our lives, leading to bardown snipes! It's from these seemingly small lessons that I gain significant takeaways for my life.

On a random funny note, one dream involved us being in a hotel pool area amongst a bunch of wild kids, kind of like the ones we used to be at during out-of-town hockey tournaments. Todd was explaining to me that sometimes you don't go in the hotel hot tub because some kid or kids pissed in there. The water can be hot and enticing, but sometimes it's just full of piss – a gross and dirty place that you don't want to be. I feel like this applies to real-life situations a lot more than we like to acknowledge. Lesson: stay away from the hot tubs filled with piss!

## Signs from the Other Side

Todd continues to show up in our lives in other mysterious ways as well. In the years following his death, "synchronicities" inspired and empowered me most when I was doubting meaning in this life. Carl Jung – the famous Swiss psychologist who came onto the academic scene in the early 1900s – extensively focused his work on *synchronicity*. Jung defined the concept in many ways, including, in its simplest and purest form, as "meaningful coincidences." I have been awestruck by synchronicities in my life, which have served as my guideposts and power boosts during uncertain times. From what I have encountered, these synchronicities typically appear as symbols and signs that come charged with connection, timing, and meaning. Beyond anything else in my life, synchronicities have inspired within me a sense of wonder about the truth of life and the Universe, and have guided me back to being hopeful that we are being divinely guided while we navigate ourselves through this world.

Todd was also strongly inspired and excited by the phenomenon of synchronicity. I learned long after he died – and only after seeing the contents of his quote-book – that synchronicity became something that drew Todd to start appreciating that something much more powerful than what we imagine is happening here.

Todd wrote the following words from Carolyn Myss in his quote-book:

"There are no such things as coincidences or accidents. Look for meaning in synchronistic encounters... Synchronistic encounters are meaningful, they are manifestations of an invisible power working with you and through you."

This invisible power may not be seen, but it is always all around us. And, if you are paying attention, you might just catch a glimpse of something or have an encounter that blows you away and leaves you beaming with curiosity and enthusiasm for the mysteries of life.

The days surrounding the anniversary of Todd's death – the end of November and first days of December – have, as one could expect, been very tough for our family. Despite our efforts to remember and focus on the good of Todd's life, these days are typically melancholy and filled with images of his tragic final hours. However, with the passing of time, these *death anniversary* days have become much more bearable, in part because of certain amazing synchronistic events that happened.

If there was ever a case for *signs from the other side* being real, the following represent some of the best evidence I've seen. Though it is easy to scoff at or downplay these moments as wishful thinking, I see these phenomena as winks from the Universe to remind us that something really cool is happening here on Earth. To me, these are the "signs from

God"; others might say they are messages from angels or guides. I don't know anything for certain; what I do know, however, is that synchronicities are like small gifts of energy sent to brighten our days and make us more faithful in believing that our lives are being guided and supported from a higher level and power. Synchronicities essentially serve as sacred reminders that more is going on here than we can comprehend, and we should be more faithful as we navigate this physical reality.

Certain signs are so blatant that they simply cannot be dismissed. One of the most wondrous was shown to Mom and Pa on November 30, 2016 – ten years from Todd's last functioning day on Earth. Though Todd technically died December 2, 2006, he had spent all of December 1st transitioning. He had also told Mom on November 30th that he thought that he was dying. That was his last full active and conscious day.

On that ten-year anniversary, Mom was driving around downtown Winnipeg with Pa as they ran errands. As they navigated Winnipeg's misplaced one-way streets and poorly-timed traffic lights, the stage for a series of events that would leave us in awe was being set.

Everything started when I called Mom's cell phone that afternoon to have a quick chat and see how she was doing. While she was obviously emotional and introspective, she was doing quite well and her spirits were high. It was shortly after two-thirty, so she had already made it through the first half of the day in a strong way, and now she was enjoying spending time with her dad. We ended the call with nothing of significance exchanged besides some sincere family love and support.

Within minutes of our conversation ending, something really special happened: "Live Like You Were Dying" by Tim McGraw – Todd's theme song – came on the radio. Considering that it had been released over twelve years earlier, it was certainly not a new hit song expected to be played on the radio that day. For Mom, it was a perfectly-timed and meaningful message that filled her heart with love and gratitude.

Just a couple of minutes after that song's closing notes, another, very different message validated the theory that Todd was saying a special "Hello" on that ten-year anniversary. As Mom continued driving on

Salter Street, on the side of a random building she saw, in foot-tall, spray-painted capital letters similar to the "graffiti-style" way of printing Todd had developed in junior high, were the following words:

"TODD WAS

HERE BOO!"

*Look closely at the building wall:*
*"TODD WAS HERE BOO!"*

Not only did Mom see Todd's name in big letters right after hearing "Live Like You Were Dying," but the word "BOO," a term commonly used to reference "ghosts" or the Spirit world. It was as if Todd, or God, or some mysterious graffiti-angel was ensuring she knew this was not a random occurrence! At the very least, as Mom was driving with her father and reminiscing about her youngest son long-passed, a big smile and waving hand came through those spray-painted letters to light up her heart!

Although that is an incredible occurrence, it is only one of many that continue to this day – in all kinds of forms at different times. Beyond symbols and signs, Todd's name, a fairly uncommon one, has been mentioned or seen at very interesting times. Another one of these incredibly powerful moments happened just the year before Mom's fateful drive, during the 2015 Manitoba Marathon.

Mom had run many full marathons and even more half marathons by 2015. But as she neared her sixtieth year, she made it her goal to earn at least one more full marathon medal. She was actually running the marathon that year to honor a promise made to Todd almost ten years earlier, to ease the heavy guilt he felt when he thought he was taking all of Mom's time, including her running time, as she cared for him. Of course, Mom didn't agree with Todd's assessment of the situation and knew there would be plenty of time to run and think about herself after Todd had been adequately cared for and was made comfortable. Though Mom waited almost a full decade before honoring the marathon promise to Todd – perhaps just to work up the internal strength before attempting the 26.2-mile race – she was determined to do so. While I had no doubt that Mom would accomplish this feat, I knew it would be challenging for her as a woman nearing sixty. But, as the start-gun was fired around seven a.m. at the University of Manitoba campus, Mom took off, her feet flying and with Todd in her heart.

I had been out late the night before with friends. Knowing that this marathon day was not one to selfishly waste away, I woke up, grabbed a coffee, and drove down Portage Avenue to catch Mom as she came out of Assiniboine Park and turned east towards downtown Winnipeg. She had sent me a GPS tracker link so I could monitor her progress and know precisely where she would be at any given moment. I waited to surprise her on the corner of Portage Avenue and Sergeant, next to some drummers. It was a charged place, and the marathoners ran by the drumming to power up a little bit as they ran along. After a few minutes I spotted Mom, and we had an emotional exchange as she came by.

After Mom continued on, I went over to Worky's place, which was only a couple blocks away to hang out for a bit and tell him of my plan to meet Mom one more time along the marathon course and give her a final push of support. Worky had never experienced a marathon, so he came along to check it out. We loaded up with some Bacon N' Eggers from A&W and monitored Mom's progress on the GPS, trying to figure out where to meet her next. I figured that she might need some energy in those last five miles or so, and we decided on a quiet residential location in St. Vital, close to where one of our friends lived. So there we were, Worky and I, just sitting on the curb of a residential Winnipeg street, hanging out eating A&W while all the exhausted marathoners were running by in the final stretch. It was quite a contrast of lifestyles at that moment.

After about thirty minutes, we stood up and prepared for Mom to come running by.

As she rounded the street corner we called out to her and cheered her on. Though she looked exhausted, her face lit up as she saw us, and ran over to give us both big hugs. She was powering on, and was so close to the finish line.

I started running beside her for a short time just to try to give her an extra boost of encouragement. I had been running for maybe fifty yards when, out of the corner of my eye, I saw a street sign, previously hidden by a tree, that blew me away. The name of the street – which I'd had no idea existed – was "Tod Dr."

"Mom, look!" I yelled, as I pointed over to the right. "It's Todd!"

Out of all the streets that we could have met her on, we were led to a street, totally unbeknownst to us, named "Tod Drive." In that moment of wonder and awe, Mom got the extra push of energy she needed to power through the final stretch of her last full Manitoba Marathon. She had crossed the finish line for Todd. He knew, and had been with her the whole way.

The most recent chilling and powerful of these blatant signs – as if the two above stories were not enough – appeared on Saturday, December 1, 2018 – twelve years, less a few hours, from Todd's death. I was living in San Diego, California, and Mom had come down to visit for a week. Mom usually spent the anniversary of Todd's death with her closest friends, having a day at her favorite spa; this year, however, she decided to break from tradition to spend some days with me and my wife, Samantha, in our new Southern Californian home.

We lived only a few miles from Torrey Pines State Park and the beautiful overlooks of the Pacific Ocean – a perfect setting for Mom to briefly escape the frigid temperatures of Winnipeg during an emotionally cold time. She was staying at Hotel Indigo, a quaint and quiet place near the ocean in south Del Mar. We made our way around hiking and sightseeing in that area, and played some rounds of golf at the world-famous Torrey Pines Golf Course. We caught some magnificent ocean and sunset views, which were taken in with reverence. In the first days of the visit, small signs had already appeared that hinted of Todd's energy and presence nearby. We observed these signs and appreciated them, but took them lightly.

On December 1st, for the first time during her visit, Mom walked a few blocks from her hotel to the Starbucks on 15th Street in Del Mar. She had previously been content to have the coffee provided by the hotel, but something spurred her that particular morning to make the kilometer-walk to Starbucks for an upgraded coffee experience. After getting her americano, she went out to the patio seating and chose a spot at a small table near the door. Within minutes the patio began to quickly fill up.

She noticed an adolescent male and several others who came to sit at the table closest to her, only a few feet away. The young man had a bald, white head, and was clearly a chemotherapy patient. He had similar physical characteristics to Todd, especially when he was going through his initial treatments. As she did not often see young chemo patients, this sight created an automatic connection to Todd for Mom to observe and ponder on an already significant day. At this point, it was an interesting sight, but just that.

The crew of people sitting around the young chemo patient were talking loudly, so Mom could easily hear their conversations. She heard the following question posed to the woman sitting next to the young one: "So, what did Wade buy you for your birthday?" Within only a few minutes of sitting on that patio and seeing the young chemo patient who reminded her of Todd, she heard my name, Wade – also an uncommon name – mentioned. After hearing that, Mom had become a little more intrigued with the events that were transpiring around her.

She continued to pay attention. She noticed that one of the ladies who was sitting at that nearby table seemed to be looking at her often, enough that Mom found it curious. People left and new ones came and the dynamic of the people nearby shifted, but the strange phenomena continued.

After hearing my name, the next unusual moment came when the lady who had been staring at Mom introduced herself and another woman as "Cheryl" and "Barb." Mom's first name is Barbara, and has gone by "Barb" her whole life. Mom was looking away when she heard those names said, so she couldn't identify which lady was which, but that was irrelevant. What was relevant, however, was that she'd heard her own name mentioned very shortly after seeing the young cancer patient who looked like Todd and hearing the name Wade. At that point, Mom could feel that there was something special brewing about during this whole Starbucks situation, but she was still just observing. She snapped a picture of the table to memorialize the moment, and texted it to me, telling me of the extraordinary connections that she had just witnessed, starting with the chemo patient sighting.

After spending some time pondering the occurrences, Mom accepted what she saw and heard at Starbucks as mysterious blessings on a special day, but was content with moving on. She got up and began walking away from the patio, making it only a few feet before she became intrigued with a nice water fountain and garden display. She stopped by the fountain and just observed and appreciated the views. Coins sparkled at the bottom of the water fountain, making it a magical wishing well for others who had come before. She did not make a wish at that moment, but if she had, it almost certainly would have involved Todd. Perhaps she would have wished for a sign that Todd was okay, despite the assurance she had already been given in past years.

Close to where Mom was standing near the fountain, another gathering of people was sparked when the woman who'd been staring at her and another woman were approached by an older man with a dog. Mom was right next to them as the man moved closer to introduce himself. In a moment that brought instant shock, followed by tears and chills, Mom heard clearly when the man reached out his hand to the women, and, at the exact same time that bells from the church above on the hill just began to ring, said, "Hi, I'm Todd."

If this was not a major spiritual sign, I don't know what would be considered one. It was certainly stranger than fiction, an event manifested beautifully in the material world with impeccable timing.

The Mother's Day letter Todd wrote twelve years earlier – the one referencing his discovery of the power of love – was written on the cover insert of a burnt CD titled "Mother's Day Mix". The CD included nineteen specially picked songs for Mom. It was a soundtrack from her dying son. "You'll be There" by George Strait – a powerful song about seeing your loved ones in Heaven, on "the other side" – was the last song of the tracklist. We played that song at Todd's funeral. Maybe, just maybe, ringing the church bells at that moment was Todd's way of playing music for Mom once again, from the other side.

Obviously there will be doubters of such things, or people who see no reason to be moved by such stories. They will see these occurrences as mere coincidence and will downplay any spiritual significance. These people may be atheists or other skeptics who simply don't want to challenge their established belief systems and worldview. Or, they're the purely scientific minds who see these types of occurrences only in terms of probability. And that is all perfectly fair. Everyone is entitled to their own interpretation of information and any subsequently formed opinions. For anyone not moved but such stories, all I can say is that I wish at some point in your lives you get to experience a moment in which you are so awestruck with *a sign* that you no longer want to deduce it to scientific proof, because it is what it is: a bright wink from the other side. For the believers, I only wish that you see these types of things appear in your life so you can derive inspiration from your own personal *spiritual winks*. It is these universal nods that can really empower someone to live a life filled with faith, awe and appreciation. Whatever one's belief system, they can be like a bright shooting star that crosses the sky at the very moment a wish is made or a prayer is said.

We fall asleep to the wonder of the world, and we take our lives for granted so often. Synchronicities are like messages sent from the other side to wake us up and light our paths in time of confusion or darkness. Synchronicities appear to show us or teach us something. In whatever form these synchronicities come, pay attention to and contemplate them. Consider them affirming signs that you are on the right path, and that bigger things are taking place behind the scenes. Soak them in at that moment. Appreciate that this life is so much more than we know. There is a bigger game being played here.

# CHAPTER 32

# IN A FLASH

As mentioned in the beginning of this book, Dad became a firefighter the year that Todd was born. We were always incredibly proud of him for this, and very emotionally tied to all things firefighting. On February 4, 2007, only two months after Todd's death, an intense fire took the lives of two City of Winnipeg firefighters – Harold Lessard and Tom Nichols. Despite the temperature being nearly forty degrees below outside, a "flashover" – essentially a fireball that spikes the temperature up thousands of degrees Celsius, within seconds – turned every firefighter's nightmare into a reality.

Winnipeg Fire Stations 1 and 2 were the stations called to that St. Boniface area fire. Lessard and Nichols, each with over thirty years of experience, were both captains of their respective platoon and stations. They were leaders of their squads who led from the frontline, and were of the first ones into the burning house. They were among the group of six firefighters who entered the blaze first in search of anyone else who needed help getting out. While upstairs, the flashover hit and trapped them on the second floor. It was a tragic and awful situation.

Dad – known around the Winnipeg firefighter community as "Bobby D" or "Little General" – worked at Winnipeg Fire Station No. 1 during those days. Lessard was captain of Platoon 3, Station 1, while Dad was then a branchman for Platoon 1, Station 1. Platoons 1 and 3 worked opposite day-night shifts. In other words, they worked out of the same hall, just on opposing shifts. The fatal fire occurred on a Sunday evening around eight p.m. Under "regular" circumstances, Dad would have been arriving at Station 1 that next Monday morning between seven and eight a.m., as Captain Lessard would have been leaving after his night shift. Foregoing the butterfly effect, Dad was twelve hours away from being at that deadly call; and, considering his position at the time, he would have been the very first one, or one of the first ones, to enter that house during the blaze.

Long ago I accepted the possibility that Dad may die in the line of duty. It easily could have been him who perished that night; or any other night; or any other day, in any other way. The family of a firefighter must just learn to live with that; however, the horror and tragedy of that specific event really hit home for me. I felt like I was twelve hours away from Dad dying; and, considering it had only been two months since I'd lost my brother, I don't know how I would have managed to cope if that happened. To say the least, I am incredibly grateful that Dad is still alive in this world.

Unlike people who lose loved ones in an unexpected tragedy, we were fortunate to have time to process and prepare for Todd's death. So many, including the families of Lessard and Nichols, don't get such an opportunity. For them, death came in an instant, with no warning at all, ending life as they knew it in a flash. It was frightening but reminded me of how lucky we were to have a chance to say goodbye.

On April 6, 2018, I drove from Bismarck, North Dakota – my wife's Samantha's hometown, where I was living and working as a lawyer shortly after I graduated from law school – to Winnipeg to attend Mom's surprise sixtieth birthday party. Mom's husband, Dave, arranged the party and wanted me to be a part of the festivities. It was to be one of those special life moments that I didn't want to miss.

The route of that six-hour drive was east to Fargo, then straight north through Grand Forks, and across the US-Canada border to Winnipeg. Although the snow can be completely melted by early April in the Midwest, blizzards can also enter the picture and wreak havoc on road conditions. In this case, that is exactly what happened. The highways that day were some of the worst I have driven on in my life, by far! Driving through Valley City – just west of Fargo – dozens of cars littered the snow-covered ditches like different colored sprinkles on vanilla ice cream. Blizzard conditions and severe scattered ice were the ingredients that led to this Midwestern mix of deadly roads conditions. White-knuckling the wheel and peering out the windshield through the blowing snow, I made my way home, sometimes traveling slower than the Zamboni during an intermission flood, trying to avoid the ditches, disaster or death.

Though I did not die that day, I easily could have. Any given occurrence when traveling on highways like that can lead to instant death. A heartbreaking number of people die on the highways every day – a fact that should never be forgotten as we zip along to our destinations. And, though not related to the bad-weather road conditions in North Dakota, just a few hundred miles north of where I drove, several others did die on the highway that day, in an unforeseen, tragic way.

It was unlikely that anyone who boarded the Humboldt Broncos team bus that day was contemplating their mortality. Said to be a tightly-knit team, they were no doubt charged up and focused on their big playoff game ahead that night. But fate had other plans, and a horrific accident between the team bus and a semi-truck at a Saskatchewan highway intersection took the lives of sixteen of the twenty-nine people involved. What should have been an exciting trip instead cut down these young men in their prime, as well as their adult leaders, and devastated so many others. Those Broncos weren't *supposed* to die that day; they were *supposed* to be playing a hockey game. But life doesn't always happen the way it is *supposed* to.

On the other side of the grief and sadness that accompanied this tragedy, #HumboldtStrong brought the hockey world together in an incredible way. That said, this tragic accident serves as a stark reminder of the real game of life we are playing and how suddenly it can end, for us or our teammates.

People close to someone else die every single day in both common and freakish ways. Without warning, [insert person's name here] no longer has the chance to [insert unfulfilled awesome bucket list item here] because they died "before their time." Despite this, we typically take our moments in life and our days on Earth for granted, often mindlessly living as if we were personally immune or protected from death. We live ignorantly, denying this reality and inevitability. In fact, we generally don't ponder death in any meaningful way until we have a personal brush with it or are forced to deal with the passing or terminal illness of a loved one. Only then do we take a step back and realize that this whole living and dying thing is not a joke.

Considering that death can come in a flash, why do we go about our days like it is so far away? Why do we hold back from ourselves and others? Why do we not send our loved ones off for their days as if we may never see them again? Why do we not appreciate the fragility of our lives, and what we have before us, until it is much too late – when the sudden-death goal has already been scored, and the game is over?

## Life in Sudden Death

Like many hockey players, my brother and I have played in intense games that went to sudden-death overtime, meaning victory or defeat could come at any given moment. And, because the stakes were so high, we did not allow our minds to be affected by thoughts of the past or future. We were there, fully present in all ways, reaching down to our depths and giving it everything we had! Whether those games were won or lost is beyond the point. Giving our full and best effort, so we could look back with no regrets, was the only thing that mattered.

The ultimate takeaway is that you never quite know when or how the game will end, but when it does it is over for good. You can't go back to change anything, so you need to put forth your best effort while you still can, playing for victory with all of your heart. We sometimes forget that our lives can end just as suddenly as a goal is scored in sudden death overtime. It is only when we realize this that the real game of life begins.

# CHAPTER 33

# YOU'RE STILL IN THE GAME

*Forrest Gump*, released in 1994, is one of the most heartwarming and legendary movies of all time. One of the most powerful scenes in the movie is when Forrest Gump's mother, "Mama," was dying, and Forrest rushed home to see her.

As he looked down at her on her deathbed, a confused and scared, Forrest asked, "Why are you dying, Mama?"

Mama replied, "It's my time. It's just my time."

Seeing Forrest's fear, she continued: "Aww, now, don't you be afraid, sweetheart...death is just a part of life...something we are all destined to do."

Todd had lived a short but powerful life and did not require extra time to fulfill his life's purpose. Year after year, big-time highlights happened, right until the end. He found a way to play big in the game of every day. He transformed the mundane moments into sacred celebrations of breath, love, laughter, and freedom to be in this form, however he was. In his last days, as he recognized life was quickly coming to a close, he amped up his game and lived truly worthy and righteous moments. And, when he had completed his mission – when it was time to graduate to this next level – he was ready to move on.

Todd grew into the belief that each one of our lives has a sacred plan – a reason why we came into this world. All the joy, excitement, and love . . . all the pain, suffering, and heartache . . . has been included on our personal blueprint for a reason. Tied in with this thought was that we incarnated here because we had something to offer; a gift to bring to the world by the presence of our Soul and its relationship with others and the world. Todd's sacred plan came with an early death – it was just his time.

## Death's Draft

A hockey player is scouted based on things like skating, shooting, passing, hockey intelligence and awareness, leadership abilities, teamwork, and attitude. The scouting report of a player incorporates various factors, and essentially forms a strength number for that player –similar to how players are rated in the EA Sports NHL video game, commonly known as "Chel." Strengths and weaknesses are weighed and balanced as every player is given a strength number. For example, in NHL 22, Connor McDavid has an overall strength rating of 95, while Sidney Crosby is rated 93, and Alexander Ovechkin and Auston Matthews are rated 92.

Think about the various things that you could be rated on and scouted for in your day-to-day life: your kindness to strangers, empathy, authenticity, intention, heart, added value, resiliency, and performance in unforeseen encounters. Just as hockey players are scouted, judged and rated for all they are in relation to a standard of perfection or optimization, so too could your life be scouted, judged, and rated for your human strength.

What if this life was a tryout for something much bigger than we can imagine? A "Soul Tryout," perhaps. Or maybe when we die, we enter a "draft" for the league beyond this world?

Imagine living your life on Earth as if you were preparing for this draft. This could be said to be similar to the supposed "judgment" that awaits us as foretold by near every religion. At the moment of your death, when your life is reviewed for all to see, including the *top executives, managers, scouts,* and *coaches* of these *teams,* who may choose you, and based on what moments from your performance? If you were to die today, who would want to have your heart and soul as part of their team, and why? Where does your true heart fit best, and where does your Soul deserve to rest?

I know these are heady, existential questions, but, when the final buzzer sounds in the sudden death overtime that is life and you can't go back to change anything, how did you live with the time you were given?

## No Regrets

According to a study discussed by Hockey Canada in 2003, a minor hockey player's chances of having a steady NHL career is approximately one in four thousand. These seem like extremely tough odds, until you compare that number to the likelihood of being born on Earth, as You! The odds that you were born on this planet, to your parents, with your individual genetic makeup has been approximated by some scientists as being one in *four hundred trillion.*

Based on those numbers, one has better odds of winning the lottery seven times over than being born to Earth. To illustrate this, consider the very same person winning the Powerball lottery jackpot, not once, or twice, but seven times over. In other words, this Earth team is the team that you want to make; and, if you're reading this, you made it! You made the League, baby!

Despite how astounding the odds are for us to just be born to this planet, most people seem far from being *truly* grateful for their life. Just as the hypothetical seven-time-lottery-winner no longer thinks it very special or exciting to win the lottery, so too it seems that we have lost our gratitude for life, here and now. But don't forget:

Eventually, you will be called off the ice.

Eventually, your contract will be up.

Eventually, you will play your last shift, and your game of life will end.

And when the sudden-death goal ends the game, it's too late to go back.

The Latin phrase *memento mori* – roughly translating to "remember that you will die" – is appropriate here. When we keep the end in mind, the now just means a little more! When we know we might be playing our last shift ever, we are going to give it everything we have while we have the chance.

Let the known fact that you will one day die motivate you to live a life that you can look back on with the feeling of total fulfillment, with no regrets. Let that thought be a beautiful wake-up call that, at least for this moment, you are still alive, and can give life everything you have while you are still here. You are still in the game!

When we play every shift like it's our last, we bless our past and our path. By living in such a way, we prepare ourselves to cross the bridge of death, today. And, when our time comes to move on – when our shift on Earth is over – we will be ready to skate hard to death.

With his head held high right until the end, and with a bursting heart of love too strong for his body, Todd got there first. He was the fastest. Like always, he was the first one there.

THE END

# ACKNOWLEDGMENTS

Writing this book was a mission I vowed to take a few years after Todd died. It is now before your eyes only because of the help and support I received from various people.

To Mom - Thank you for your unwavering encouragement and support since day one. Thank you for going over, in painstaking detail, the hardest moments of your life, with love and patience. You knew how much this meant to me, and you believed in me the whole way. Writing this book was my marathon, and I crossed the finish line because of you.

To Dad - Thank you for being our first coach, and for instilling passion to play the game with all of our hearts, striving to reach our potential. Thank you for all the help answering key questions and getting crucial bits and pieces of information I needed along the way for this book. *May the pain of Todd's passing be a distant feeling; may the joy and love that he brought to the world be with you every day.*

To Sam, my wife - Thank you for your love, support and patience as you saw me at the desk or on the couch, day after day, telling you that I was writing a book. You were my rock throughout all of this, and you gave me the energy to carry on until the very end. Most importantly, thank you for reminding me to live this life with laughter, in this moment, and to have fun every day, no matter what.

To Dana Micheli, my editor - Thank you for helping me refine and polish Todd's story to present it to the world in a smooth and powerful way. More than the long hours and late nights, I appreciate the love and energy that you put into this project, for me *and* Todd.

To Kipp Workman ("Worky") - Thank you for reading the earliest and longest version of this book, bit by bit, email after email, and providing me feedback and encouragement in the earliest days of tying the stories together. "You might really have something here" is a line that I will never forget. You gave me the spark I needed to stay at this until the end.

To Aaron Kolquist ("Doogie") - In 2014 in Grand Forks, North Dakota you were one of the first people to witness me writing this book, by hand. You encouraged me in those earliest days. Thank you for helping me edit the first draft, and helping me get things "dialed in." Your help was invaluable.

And thank you to all those who read early versions of this book and offered corrections, input or encouragement. Your feedback played a crucial role in creating this final version.

I love you all!

# ABOUT THE AUTHOR

Wade Davison is the author of *His Last Shift*, a book about his younger brother Todd's remarkable 20-year life – a story about living and playing with passion and purpose, and dying with no regrets. Born and raised in a hockey rink in Winnipeg, Manitoba, Canada, Wade is a lawyer, coach, speaker, and seeker of truth and meaning in this world. Currently living in San Diego, California with his wife Samantha and his dog Mari, Wade seeks to live a life of inspiration and love, knowing that our time on Earth is short and may end at any moment.

Stay in touch:
www.wadedavison.com
Instagram: @wade.davison

www.ingramcontent.com/pod-product-compliance
Lightning Source LLC
Chambersburg PA
CBHW071138130626
46553CB00004B/1428